MW01030685

A House of David in the Land of Jesus

Copyright © 2007 Robert Lewis Berman
All rights reserved.
ISBN: 1-4196-7394-7
ISBN-13: 978-1419673948
Library of Congress Control Number: 2007906136

A House of David in the Land of Jesus

Robert Lewis Berman

2007

A House of David in the Land of Jesus

Contents

Acknowledgements

The Title

Credit for the title goes first to Dr. Jennifer Stollman, historian, who in writing her thesis for her Ph.D. at Michigan State University entitled it "Building a House of Israel in the Land of Jesus." Her thesis was about Jews of the South. We first met when she came to Lexington as an assistant professor at the University of Mississippi, to discuss making a documentary about the Jewish community of Lexington. At that meeting with me was my wife Sondy, Henry Paris and Phil Cohen. Jennifer expressed her feeling that even though there have been books about Jews of the South, never has there been a detailed book, as this one, about the life of individual members of an entire Jewish community in a small southern town such as Lexington. After hearing some of the stories of the Lexington Jewish community, she encouraged me to either produce such a documentary or tell the story in writing. She felt such a compelling story needed to be told. She also volunteered to assist in such an undertaking. After the first rough draft of this book was written, I contacted her and asked if she would read it and check it for both content and accuracy. She agreed to do this.

Credit for the final title goes to Dr. Andrew Hacker, Ph.D., professor at Queens College in New York, relative, and noted book review columnist for the *New York Times*. When hearing of my proposed title he recommended that I use the word "David" instead of "Israel" and shorten the title to what it has now become—*A House of David in the Land of Jesus.*

The History

Credit for a considerable amount of the historical facts and stories of this book goes to Phil Cohen of Lexington. He and his family are discussed in a number of chapters. It must be stated that without his input, and knowledge of the past, passed down from one generation to the next, this book could not have been written as thoroughly as it was.

Credit also must go to all those members of both the Jewish and Christian communities of Lexington, both black and white, who contributed to this book. To name each of them in these credits would be redundant, since a section is devoted to each of them and what they related to me.

Credit also goes to my wife, Sondy, and the late Gus Herrman, who, one evening and well into the early morning hours, sat at a kitchen counter in our Jackson home and organized and drew a family tree on a long piece of butcher paper. The patriarch and beginning of this family tree was the first permanent Jewish resident of Lexington— my great-great-grandfather, Jacob Sontheimer.

Credit is due Lee Paris, who was the source of the early history of my great-great-grandfather, and his great-great-great-grandfather, Jacob Sontheimer. Lee inadvertently discovered this recorded history while a student in the School of Law at the University of Mississippi, when he was reading and researching early legal cases and court decisions in the State of Mississippi.

The Edits

There were three individuals who initially edited my book. The first was Sondy, with a BS degree in Education from Lesley College, Cambridge, MA. She was by far my most strict critic. She not only read, re-read, and critiqued each page, but also has continually read and critiqued them again every time I made any changes, deletions or additions. Her standards are so high; I felt that once I had passed her initial test, I was prepared to send the next version to the following two other critics:

> Phil Cohen, with a BA in Economics, Tulane University, New Orleans; leader of the Lexington Jewish Community and longtime member of Temple Beth El; local historian.

> Dr. Jennifer Stollman, with a BA in History and English, University of Michigan; and a Ph.D. in History at Michigan State; Chair of the History Department at Salem College, Winston-Salem, North Carolina; Former Assistant Professor of History and the Study of Southern Culture at the University of Mississippi.

A final edit was performed by a professional editor.

I am most grateful for each of their meticulous reviews and contributions.

Other Acknowledgements

Credit for certain pictures and partial biographical selections on the lives of some earlier Jewish Lexingtonians is given to Leo Z. Turitz and Evelyn Turitz, taken from their book *Jews in Early Mississippi*, published by the University Press of Mississippi in 1983. Three and a half pages of their book were dedicated to Lexington. Some of the information and pictures were used to either supplement or corroborate information contained in this book. Permission to use this material was granted by the publisher.

Credit for some of the other pictures in this book is due Mark Block, our son-in-law. In the early daybreak hours on a chilly fall morning in 2006, he drove with me to Lexington to take pictures of a number of selected sites for inclusion in this book.

Credit for the outstanding cover and graphics is given to Gary Davis, a close family friend and owner of PDW Design, a highly respected and successful graphic design company in Los Angeles.

Additional credit goes to Larry Eby, computer specialist and technical coordinator, in Delray Beach, FL for his expertise and assistance in coordinating the process from manuscript to book, between the publisher and me.

Credit for selected historical information about Lexington, Mississippi, is given to the Magnolia Garden Club, taken from their book *Lexington, Mississippi, Holmes County 1833–1976*, published by the Mississippi Press in 1976. Permission to use this material was given by the Magnolia Garden Club board by its president Ann Fant Davis, and by one of the main contributing editors, Juanita Powers Watson. Credit for other historical data is given to Lexington's two weekly newspapers, *The Lexington Advertiser* (no longer in print) and *The Holmes County Herald.*

Finally, I am most appreciative of our three daughters, Marjorie Berman Block, BA, University of Missouri; Deborah Berman Silver, BA, Washington University; and Sheryl Berman Spector, BSBA, University of Southern California, for their careful review of my manuscript.

About the Author

Robert Lewis Berman was born in Atlanta, Georgia, in 1931 to Fay and Joe Berman, a member of the Atlanta City Council. At the age of five, he moved with his family to Lexington, Mississippi, after his grandmother, Julia Lewis, was killed in an automobile accident. Julia was the wife of Morris Lewis, Sr.

At the age of ten, just prior to the beginning of World War II, he and his family returned to Atlanta, where his father was stationed at the Army Central Command.

When his father went overseas to the Pacific Theater, his mother Fay, sister Joan and Bob returned to Lexington, where he attended high school and was confirmed at Temple Beth El. He continued to reside there until he left to attend college at the University of Mississippi in Oxford.

At Ole Miss, he was president of Phi Eta Sigma, honorary scholastic society; a member of ODK, leadership society; Phi Epsilon Pi, Jewish social fraternity; Delta Sigma Pi, business fraternity; Co-Chair of Religious Emphasis Week; Vice President of the Student Body and President of the Campus Senate; and one of six members chosen for the Hall of Fame his senior year.

After graduating with a BBA degree, he served as a First Lieutenant in the United States Army 10th Infantry Division, as a platoon leader and company executive officer of a rifle company.

Upon his honorable discharge, he was accepted at the Harvard Business School where he received his MBA. Bob Berman claims the best part of his two years in Boston, Massachusetts was the fact that he met his future wife, Sondra (Sondy) Shindell. She was from New Haven, Connecticut and was attending Lesley College, and the New England Conservatory of Music in Boston. He said someone asked him if he wanted to meet a lovely young lady with beautiful eyes and a voice to match, and he accepted. Afterwards, one evening he said to her, "Let's go study." Due to his southern accent, she thought he said, "Let's go steady," and they have been together ever since, for the past fifty years.

They have three daughters, each of whom was raised in Jackson, Mississippi, had a bat mitzvah, and were confirmed at Beth Israel Congregation and married in that same synagogue. Marjie and her attorney husband, Mark Block, reside in Manhattan Beach, California, with their three sons, Jordan, Joshua and Jared. Debbie and her real estate developer husband, Larry Silver, reside in Boca Raton, Florida, with their son Spencer and daughter Madison. Sheri and her attorney husband, Steven Spector, reside in San Diego, California, with their daughter Megan and son Cole.

During his business career, Bob Berman was Vice President and Director of Corporate Development at the Lewis Grocer Company and Sunflower Food Stores, headquartered in Indianola, Mississippi. After nine years, he left there to enter the real estate business as a developer and realtor in Jackson, where he developed three shopping centers and the Prudential Office Building. During the interim, he took over his father's food brokerage business after his father's tragic death in a commercial airline crash. As President and CEO of that business, he expanded it from a few employees to eighty people, with offices in Jackson, Lafayette and New Orleans, Louisiana. He led his company, Southern Food Brokerage, through three mergers in Louisiana and later one in Little Rock, Arkansas, with the final merger being the only one where his company was not the surviving corporation. After five years on the board, he retired from the food brokerage, sales and marketing business. He continues to be a real estate developer.

Among his entrepreneurial ventures, he developed and owned two restaurants in Jackson. He is Past President of Beth Israel Congregation in Jackson, Past President of the 350-member Rotary Club of Jackson, and Past District Governor of Rotary International. He has served on the boards of Beth Israel Congregation, Rotary Club of Jackson, Jackson Chamber of Commerce, United Way, and Advisory Board of Horne CPA Group. He and his wife were Co-Presidents of the Murrah High PTSA.

Bob and Sondy continue to be members of both Beth Israel Congregation in Jackson and Temple Beth El in Lexington.

His first book, published in 1988 by Quail Ridge Press and entitled *More Than Survival*, was an apolitical, issue-oriented, nonfiction book about Mississippi and her people. *A House of David in the Land of Jesus* is his second nonfiction book.

*This book is dedicated to the God of Abraham, Isaac and Jacob,
of Sarah, Rebecca, Leah and Rachel;
The God of all humanity;
The Father of us all*

FOREWORD

By W. Charles Sallis

In *A House of David in the Land of Jesus,* Robert Lewis Berman gives a personal comprehensive account of the lives of an entire Jewish community in the small southern town of Lexington, Mississippi. Through recollections, research and taped interviews with Jewish and non-Jewish black and white citizens and former citizens of Lexington, he has compiled a heart-warming account of Lexington Jews. An inspiring story of personal courage, faith and civic virtue, it is a rich history worth preserving for future generations. Bob succeeds in providing this by writing in an intimate conversational style with compassion and insight.

A recurring theme throughout the book is aptly expressed by Bob in these words: "Ever since the first members of the Jewish faith settled in Lexington, Jews and Christians have respected and befriended one another and worked together for the betterment of their entire community." He goes on to say "...anti-Semitism was never manifested openly or surreptitiously, to the best of my knowledge, as a longtime resident with deep family roots in the community. By all historical accounts, anti-Semitism did not exist and was never a problem in Lexington...." Bob recounted an interview in which non-Jewish lawyer Don Barrett stated that "there never has been a Jewish community in Lexington, nor has there been a Christian community in Lexington. [Barrett] continued that there has, instead, always been one community in Lexington—all working together in concert for the betterment of the entire community and society as a whole." Bob commented: "That statement in itself summarizes nearly everything this book is about."

Lexington Jews were very active participants in business circles and community, social and civic organizations including, among others, the Masonic Order and Rotary International. Elected to local offices and on occasions, to district and regional offices, they more than lived up to the Rotary motto: "Service above self." Many were philanthropist and benefactors of eleemosynary endeavors.

Some of these extended beyond Lexington. Excellent examples of *tzedakah,* the Jewish tradition of giving, are proudly recounted by Bob. Gus and Cecil Herrman individually and independently gave unsolicited and unrestricted gifts totaling $10,000,000 to the Hebrew Union College in Cincinnati. Bob's and Sondy's daughters Debbie, Marjie and Sheri, from their respective homes in Florida and California, sent nine tractor trailers filled with supplies to the Mississippi Gulf Coast immediately following Hurricane Katrina.

Non-Jewish Dr. John Murrell McRae, a 1956 graduate of Harvard Medical School, recalled that, "As I look back, there was a large Jewish contingent in Lexington....I just never really thought much about the fact that they were Jewish." In like manner, Parham Williams, Jr., who was dean of the law schools at Ole Miss, Samford University and Chapman University in California, said, "I occasionally wondered whether any evidences of anti-Semitism—unkind words or acts—were ever directed toward Lexington's Jewish community. Perhaps there were, but I was not aware of them." Patti Povall Lewis, now a business woman in Oxford, remembered that "There were so many lovely families, both Jewish and Gentile, who cared about the community and worked together to make it a very special place to live."

I also remember Lexington as a very special place. I am a former Lexingtonian whose family lived there for only one year, 1949-1950, when my father, who was with the Farmers Home Administration, transferred there. I was in the ninth grade and knew or knew of many of the people Bob has profiled. This was a very happy and productive year in my life. I had excellent teachers at Lexington High School and I enjoyed my class work very much. I was a 125 pound "bench warmer" on the football team and played the baritone horn in the band. Before and after school, I delivered special delivery letters for the Post Office on my bicycle (I made 7 cents per letter for my efforts!) to Jewish and non-Jewish black and white citizens all over town. I got to know Lexington and her people well!

When my family moved to Greenville the next year, I met my future wife, Harrylyn, in the Hebrew Union Temple. Let me explain this happy occurrence. She was 15 and I was 16. Both of us were Methodists. At that time, the First Methodist Church was being rebuilt on the site of the old church and the Hebrew Union Congregation graciously offered their Methodist friends the opportunity to worship in their "House of David" on Sundays and Wednesday nights. Several years later, our Methodist congregation returned the favor when the Hebrew Union Temple was being renovated and their congregation worshiped in the new Methodist Church on Fridays and Saturdays. Harrylyn and I still remember one Sunday evening meeting of the Methodist Youth Fellowship in the Temple when Rabbi Harris Hirschberg taught our group the significance of symbolism in the Temple and showed us the Torah. This spirit of ecumenicalism was similar to that which I had experienced in Lexington. I never encountered anti-Semitism until I left the state as a young man in 1957 to serve in the Army at Fort Knox, Kentucky.

As an historian trained in American, southern, and Mississippi history, I have taught on the college level for forty years. In preparing for classes, I learned much about Jewish history. I have also researched the history of Jews in early Mississippi for several Mississippi Humanities Council projects, one resulting in a paper I read at the Mississippi Historical Society in 1993. I team-taught classes in multicultural American history for twenty years at Millsaps College and have participated in workshops on multicultural education at the Museum of the Southern Jewish Experience at the Henry S. Jacobs Camp for Living Judaism in Utica, Mississippi. I attribute my interest in multicultural history, in large part, to my early years in Lexington and Greenville.

Lexington is perhaps the smallest town in the United States with an active synagogue, but presently, there remain only twelve members from a peak membership of eighty-nine in the 1930s. Is Temple Beth El fated to become part of a pattern of diminishing Jewish presence in small southern towns? In the United States, including the South, small towns are losing both Jewish and non-Jewish populations to urban centers, and Lexington is no exception. Urban areas offer more opportunities for educated younger generations to pursue professional careers beyond family businesses. The mechanization of agriculture resulted in an enormous decrease of the number of farm workers needed. They had to search for other jobs. This decrease in the number of potential customers and the rise of retail chain stores contributed to the decline of small town businesses.

Bob Berman concludes his tribute with a well thought out and impassioned but feasible plan to keep the traditions of Temple Beth

El alive. Should Bob's dream become a reality, it will be a significant contribution to Mississippi, to the South and to the nation.

On the pulpit cover in Temple Beth El are these words of the prophet Micah: "Do justly. Love mercy. Walk humbly with thy God." Jewish citizens of Mississippi in general and Lexington in particular have, as William Faulkner put it, not merely survived but prevailed. This is the inspiring and uplifting story that Bob Berman is sharing with us.

W. Charles Sallis
Emeritus Professor of History
Millsaps College
Jackson, Mississippi
August 20, 2007

FOREWORD

By Robert N. Rosen

Southern Jewish history has come into its own in recent years. Eli N. Evans published his acclaimed history, *The Provincials: a Personal History of Jews in the South* in 1973. The Southern Jewish Historical Society was created in 1976. (The author's cousin Beryl Weiner of Atlanta was an early president.) Since then the field has blossomed with histories, memoirs, museums, collections, and organizations including the Goldring-Woldenberg Institute of Jewish Life in Jackson, Mississippi and Jewish Studies Programs all over the south, including in my hometown of Charleston, South Carolina at the College of Charleston. Histories of Jewish Southerners have proliferated as have histories of Jewish communities. Recently a major historical work edited by Marcie Cohen Ferris and Mark I. Greenberg, *Jewish Roots in Southern Soil, A New History* (Brandeis University Press, 2006) has provided an overview of Southern Jewish history. A number of brilliant memoirs have also been published, including Louis D. Rubin's *My Father's People: A Family of Southern Jews*, Stella Suberman's *The Jew Store: A Family Memoir*, and Edward Cohen's *The Peddler's Grandson: Growing up Jewish in Mississippi*.

As Eli Evans wrote in *The Lonely Days were Sundays*, "Southern Jewish history is alive and unfolding, and the search must continue not only for what events took place, but for what people felt, hoped and feared."

This book, *A House of David in the Land of Jesus*, is a classic in its own right. It is both a history of the Jewish community of a small Mississippi town, Lexington, and a memoir of the life of its author, Robert Lewis Berman.

The author, whose great-great-grandfather settled in Lexington in the 1840's, clearly and justifiably loves his hometown and takes enormous pride, as he should, in its accomplishments and its acceptance of its Jewish citizens as equals. He reflects the patriotism and love of country, state and town of Jews of his generation. He is proud that Southern Jews were proud. And he is not afraid to differ with other historians and commentators who see Jews in the South as conditioned to keep a low profile. "That simply wasn't the way it was with Joe Berman," the author's father, or in Lexington, Mississippi, he writes.

Mr. Berman, reflecting the views of many Jews who were raised in small southern towns, takes umbrage at negative statements made by Eli Evans, Alfred Uhry, author of *Driving Miss Daisy*, and Edward Cohen in *The Peddler's Grandson* to the effect that they felt different, ashamed, inferior, or alienated growing up in the South. "In all deference to Mr. Uhry, Mr. Evans, and to Mr. Cohen—none of them spoke for me, or any of my relatives and friends, or the Jews of Lexington". One need not choose sides in this debate. People and communities are different and the South is a big place.

The author describes the founding of Temple Beth El in 1905 and its history, the various waves of immigration, the families who made up the Jewish community, and the many businesses and civic activities they engaged in. He candidly and lovingly describes their successes and their failures. He provides numerous biographical sketches of his own family, including his father, a prominent member of the Atlanta City Council before coming to Lexington, as well as major businessmen, religious and civic leaders and philanthropists who hailed from Lexington. He discusses what event took place, but also what Jews in Lexington, Mississippi felt, hoped and feared.

Generations hence, historians will read his book to learn about and try to understand the rural Southern Jewish world of the late nineteenth and twentieth century, a world which is fast disappearing. It is a treasure trove of information ranging from Jewish customs and organizations, local families, immigration, social life, business and upward mobility, education, music, race relations, service in the armed forces, especially World War II, the civil rights movements and the role of Jewish women.

For all of us interested in American Jewish history, Robert Berman has performed a great mitzvah.

Robert N. Rosen
Author of *The Jewish Confederates*
Charleston, SC

Motivation for This Book

With all the hatred and strife that is rampant in this world today, globally and even politically within our own country, and a revival of virulent anti-Semitism that has spread from Islamic-populated countries to many parts of Europe and Russia, *A House of David in the Land of Jesus* tells a different, yet true story. It is all about goodness, kindness and the respect for the dignity of others that has existed for over one hundred and fifty years in a small Mississippi town known as Lexington, where Jews not only resided but excelled!

This story comes from a place where it would be least expected to happen—a town situated in a rural area in the heart of Mississippi. There, a relatively large number of members of the Jewish faith have lived and worshiped at their synagogue. Some continue there even today attending that same synagogue which is surrounded by a multitude of friendly churches; a true House of David in the Land of Jesus.

While the state of Mississippi has made great strides and taken positive steps in human and race relations, it does have a sordid history of bigotry and discrimination. Despite the progress the state has made to change for the better, there remain lingering doubts and continuing misconceptions about its people, their contributions to society and the way they treat their fellow humans. When such good things, as those described in this book, do happen within a state that has been—justly and unjustly—maligned for such a long period of time, in fairness, someone needs to tell that story. This is especially so since much of that goodness has been the result of a vibrant Jewish community that most would be surprised to learn ever resided in Mississippi, much less Lexington.

Anyone who takes the time to read this book from cover to cover will realize that this town, its people and its Jewish community have proven they are special. It is a picture of love, kindness and cooperation between the races and religions that does not exist everywhere. Readers will discover the following facts:

The Jews of Lexington have made up a larger percent of its population than Jews throughout the South and even the nation.[1] That didn't just happen. The welcome and hospitable environment made it a place where they chose to settle, multiply and thrive.

Citizens of Lexington, from all religions and races, continue to work together in harmony for the betterment of the overall community and society. Jews have been a large and recognized part of the leadership.

Throughout the years, Lexington has been a relatively peaceful town, unlike other parts of the state and nation. There has been little, if any, racial violence, and no demonstrations of anti-Semitism since Jews began to populate that little town well over a century and a half ago.

The Jews of Lexington have made significant contributions of value and enterprise, not just to the town itself, but also to the state and nation, as can be seen through the pages of this book. They have done this while ardently maintaining their own Jewish identity. Undoubtedly, there have also been other small Jewish communities in the South that were special, due to their "signature" accomplishments. Those types of achievements coming forth from the Lexington Jewish community made it likewise distinctive and deserving of recognition, individually and as a whole.

Temple Beth El's congregation has been determined to keep the synagogue's doors open for more than a hundred years, even though many other synagogues in rural towns of the South have closed as their Jewish populations either died or moved to more urban areas. Lexington is, without question, the smallest town in the state of Mississippi with an active synagogue. A Senior Archivist at Jacob Rader Marcus Center of the American Jewish Archives stated the following: "We can safely say that Lexington, Mississippi is one of

the smallest communities in the U.S. to have an active
synagogue in its midst."[2]

In his book *Jewish Life in Small-Town America,* published in 2005,
Lee Shai Weissbach's study focused on 490 urban places in the United
States that reported Jewish populations of at least 100 but fewer than
1,000 individuals in 1927. It stated: "The decision to define 'small
communities' as those with triple-digit populations was in part a
matter of convenience, but it relied also on the premise that in the
late nineteenth and early twentieth centuries, the classic era of small-
town Jewish life in America, settlements of fewer than 100 Jews were
unlikely to have attained the critical mass necessary to constitute
full-fledged communities." It continued: "The presumption that
at least 100 Jews were needed for the maintenance of an active
communal life is borne out, at least in part, by the fact that a triple-
digit population seemed to be a good predictor of the presence of
fundamental communal institutions in the decades before World
War II. For example, even though there were reported to be some
251 towns in the United States with at least fifty Jewish residents but
fewer than 100 in 1927, the comprehensive data collected about these
places indicate that only about half had established congregations.
Moreover, some of the congregations counted in these towns were
barely functioning in 1927 or had in fact disappeared."

The eighty-nine "Jewish souls" who made up Lexington's Jewish
community and its congregation, Temple Beth El, defied those
presumptions and were a clear exception to that premise.

It's past time that someone revealed to the rest of society this
particular Jewish community's unusual circumstances of goodness,
achievement and dedication to one's faith. This book does just that.
It is not a book about sensationalism, adventure, mystery, romance
or crime — the kind of book that attracts a large number of readers.
However, it is a book where one can find the teachings of Jesus (Do
unto others as you would have them do unto you) and of the Prophet
Micah (Do justly, love mercy and walk humbly with thy God). To
the best of my knowledge, never before has a book been researched
and written about such a microenvironment, wherein almost every
family of the Jewish faith and their relationship with their Christian
neighbors is so closely scrutinized and related.

Preface

It Is All About Keeping the Covenant

There have been many people in other parts of this nation, of all religious faiths, including Jews, who have expressed surprise to learn that there were members of the Jewish faith living in Mississippi— especially in a small community such as Lexington.

Therefore, this is a compelling story that should be told, about a small yet accomplished Jewish community in the little southern town of Lexington, Mississippi, whose members have made a difference. There have been a number of books written about Jews of the South, but none have ever covered, in depth, the individual families that represented one particular community, as this book does. It is a story that has never been told in its entirety about its members, their far-reaching effects on society, and their unwavering dedication to their faith of Judaism and its principles.

It has been said that everyone can't do great things, but each of us can do small things in a great way. While none of the Jewish community of Lexington has ever achieved national stardom or worldwide prominence or fame, during their lifetime almost every one of them brought something of value to their faith and their community, and a good many to their state and nation as well. Individually and as a whole, they have made a difference—and a good one at that. So has been the legacy of the Jewish community of Lexington, their outreach, good deeds, and contributions to the overall society. This book tells their story.

Citizens of the entire state of Mississippi are overwhelmingly of the Christian faith, with more churches per capita than any other state in this nation.[3] Mississippi is a veritable representative of what is known as the Bible belt. Yet Lexington's Jewish community, while being an active and important part of the overall community's life, has always proudly and openly maintained its Jewish identity. During its zenith when its population was at its peak, from the late 1800s through the 1930s up until World War II, as reform Jews, not many of its members read Hebrew. Irrespective of that, no one could ever justifiably question the deep and abiding dedication and devotion of each member of Lexington's Jewish community to their faith of Judaism. Very few intermarried. In that manner, it has survived over 150 years in the very heart of a large and respectful Christian community. The title of this book is taken from that circumstance — *A House of David in the Land of Jesus.*

A covenant was made over three thousand years ago at Mount Sinai when God gave Moses the Ten Commandments for the children of Israel. As God said unto them,

"This covenant made by you to keep my commandments and be a light unto the nations is made today not just with you and your elders, but also with all of your children for all the generations to come."

According to the *Midrash,* (an ancient rabbinical commentary on a Biblical text), when the children of Israel stood to receive the Torah, the Holy One said to them:

"I am giving you my Torah. It is my most prized possession. Before I give it to you, I ask that you present me guarantors—proof that you will guard it. Then I shall give it to you."

They said: "Our ancestors are our guarantors."

The Holy One said: "Your ancestors are not sufficient as guarantors. Bring me fitting guarantors, and I shall give you my Torah."

They said: "Ruler of the universe, our prophets are our guarantors."

God said to them: "The prophets are not sufficient guarantors. You have yet to present me with secure guarantors before I give you my Torah."

They said: "Here, our children shall be our guarantors."

The Holy One replied: "They are certainly good guarantors. For the sake of your children I will give my Torah to you."

The Lexington Jewish community has actually been all about "keeping the Covenant." L' dor va dor—"from generation to generation."

As of the publication of this book, there remain three active Jewish families living in Lexington and ninety-six Jewish graves in the Beth El cemetery. Jewish tradition says that while we do not know what there is after death, one thing we believe is certain, and that is as long as someone is remembered, there is eternal life. Therefore, it is my intent to tell about both those Jews still living in Lexington, as well as to breathe life back into as many of those ninety-six deceased Jewish souls as is possible, through the eyes of the reader. In this way, they will live on not only through those that remember them and cherish their memory, but also through the pages of this book and anyone who reads it.

While writing this book, I recalled the words of a great Islamic scholar and poetic philosopher, which I read many years ago during a human relations course at Harvard. The profundity of those words made a lasting impression on me. They were as follows:

"The moving finger writes, and having writ, moves on: nor all thy piety nor wit shall lure it back to cancel half a line. Nor all thy tears wash out a word of it."[4]

Over the past three years, I have done my best to accurately and meticulously research and write about the lives and accomplishments of the Jews of Lexington. My only regret would be if I inadvertently omitted anyone or any important part of one's life. If that be so, I assure my readers that it was entirely unintentional.

This book is written simplistically, in everyday conversational terms. It does not merely relate facts and figures; rather, it is a collection of heartwarming human interest stories about a Jewish community that most people never even knew existed.

Chapter 1

Town of Lexington, Mississippi
A Special Kind of Place
Description of the Town and Its History

Let there be no doubt that the town of Lexington, Mississippi, has been, and to a large extent continues to be, a very special place. Let there be no doubt that this one synagogue, Temple Beth El, and its surrounding array of churches have always demonstrated the highest example of tolerance, goodwill, understanding and respect for the faiths and beliefs of others.

John F. Kennedy, in his June 10th, 1963 commencement address at American University in Washington, D.C., signaled his approach to the Russians during the cold war by stating: "For in the final analysis, our most basic common link is that we all inhabit this small planet, we all breathe the same air, we all cherish our children's futures, and we are all mortal." He continued to say that rather than concentrate on our differences, we should instead focus on the good we all have in common. That has been and is the attitude of the citizens of this small community, with valuable lessons to be learned from its members of different races and religions.

While nothing on this planet is perfect, and perfection exists only in God's kingdom, if the world could emulate the fine spirit of friendship and cooperation that exists among the citizens of Lexington—Christian and Jew, black and white—then this globe would be a far safer and more peaceful place on which all could live.

Therefore, it may appear to be a contradiction for me to say that growing up in Lexington in the 1930s and 1940s was, to a large degree, like living in South Africa during the days of apartheid. There were the moderate to well-to-do whites, and the poor, mostly impoverished blacks. Segregation was the law of the land, both in Mississippi and throughout a large part of the United States, but especially in the South. Everything was segregated, including all public facilities, restaurants, schools, religious institutions, civic and country clubs, and elsewhere. There were signs in public buildings for restrooms, fountains, and many entrances that said "whites only." Whites occupied all the political offices and controlled the entire community. Few blacks were registered to vote. The infamous Mississippi poll tax (long since rescinded) saw to that, along with fear of intimidation. Most black residents farmed as sharecroppers, worked as servants, or did other menial and subservient tasks.

However, it also needs to be said that those societal standards of Lexington were, unfortunately, no different from other towns and cities throughout the South, and to a large extent in many parts of the nation. As a tribute to the white community of Lexington, there was a major difference between the social, political and economic climate of Lexington and that of South Africa. In those days, irrespective of total segregation, for the most part the whites of Lexington treated the blacks with as much respect as possible under such conditions, and with a certain degree of dignity, kindness and charity.

There was no Ku Klux Klan activity in Lexington. There were some prominent Lexington citizens who were members of the now defunct White Citizens Council, an organization dedicated to preserving segregation. However, instead of violence, those reactionaries resorted to social, political and economic means while attempting to accomplish an ill-fated and hopeless goal whose time has thankfully passed.

It is most significant and worthy to note that during those tense years, the Jewish community of Lexington for the most part remained neutral. They did not strive to preserve segregation, nor did they speak out against it. This position of neutrality actually served an important purpose as a moderating influence and mediating factor, which helped to promote calmness during that difficult period of transition from segregation to integration. The white community respected the Jewish community and their major contributions to the economic and social welfare of the town and county. The black community trusted members of the Jewish community, for it was the Jewish merchants who always treated them with dignity and respect, and helped them by extending credit and being considerably lenient in their collection terms.

As an example, following WWII, one leading Jewish merchant "went to bat" for a returning veteran and member of the white Christian community, by assisting him financially to establish his business. Today, that enterprise continues to operate successfully on the square. Without that help, such a success story would likely not have been possible. Later, that same Jewish businessman had the courage to "stand up" for a black school teacher to have his job restored, when he was fired without legitimate cause.

These and other facts can be verified by statements from both the white and black Christian communities in a later section of this book pertaining to their respective relationships with the Jewish community of Lexington.

As a tribute to the black community of Lexington, in spite of the high percentage of blacks (today 67.3 percent),[5] there was no black rioting like in Soweto, South Africa and other parts of the United States, such as in Harlem, Detroit, Chicago, and Watts in Los Angeles.

To the credit of Lexington's good citizens, both black and white, and their positive approach to tolerance and the peaceful resolution of racial problems, the town has been spared racial and religious violence that has in the past plagued some other communities in Mississippi and its neighboring states. There have been no racially motivated murders; church, synagogue or home burnings or bombings; rioting by any group, or anything of the kind in Lexington. Compared with most other towns and cities in the South and nation, Lexington has been, relatively speaking, a racially and ecumenically peaceful community.

Segregation of the races in those days was a fact, but it must be reemphasized that violence on the part of both the white and black communities in Lexington for the most part did not exist. There were examples of demonstrations on each side, but they were peaceful. For instance, members of the white community did protest against Hazel Brannon Smith, the white owner and editor of the *Lexington Advertiser*, the county's weekly newspaper. They objected to her frequent and courageous defense of the black community at a time when few others would publicly stand up for them in their plight and quest for equality. This white coalition formed another weekly newspaper to compete with hers known as the *Holmes County Herald*. The two papers competed against one another for nearly twenty years before the *Lexington Advertiser* finally closed its press. Her husband was even fired from his position as administrator of the Holmes County Hospital. In the early 1960s during voter registration drives, as blacks lined up to register at the Court House, there were taunts from a minority of what some would refer to as "rednecks." However, that was the extent of their protest.

At the other end of the spectrum, the blacks demonstrated against the white merchants by way of three separate boycotts in 1967, 1973 and 1978. During those boycotts, the Ku Klux Klan showed up, but they were from Alabama, not from Mississippi, and they were not welcomed by either the whites or the blacks. It needs to be reiterated, so there will be no misunderstanding, that these protests and demonstrations on the part of the whites and blacks, while hurtful, were unequivocally and consistently non-violent.

During the 1978 boycott, the president of the local chapter of the NAACP, Robert Smith, a retired black schoolteacher who resided in Lexington, took the side of the white merchants. For that action, a small contingent of blacks threatened to shoot him. Phil Cohen of Temple Beth El, apprehensive about the situation, called the FBI. When an agent from the Justice Department, who was black, came to Lexington to investigate, he commented that Lexington was different. He said that unlike other communities with racial problems, the whites and blacks at least spoke to one another. Without that communication, it would have been much more difficult to compromise and resolve any problems.

The racial climate changed dramatically in Lexington, as it did throughout the South and nation, with the passage of civil rights legislation. Now, with the exception of the mayor, Robin McCrory, the city government of Lexington and Holmes County is controlled by the blacks, including four of five aldermen, tax assessor, tax collector, chancery clerk, circuit clerk, sheriff, and chief of police. In Holmes County there are four black supervisors and one white. There is a white district attorney representing Holmes and two other counties. Just as significantly, the first black state legislator since the days of Reconstruction was elected from the Lexington community. All public facilities are integrated. There does remain an element of segregation throughout Lexington's schools, with the great majority of whites enrolled in private school, and mostly blacks in public school. However, it must be noted that Central Holmes Christian Academy (initially an all-white private school) has been integrated for a number of years, with over 10 percent of the student body being non-white. This situation is similar to a number of other areas of the state and nation, especially where there is a sizable majority of blacks in the school system. Nevertheless, the mostly all-black public schools in Lexington are a far cry from what they used to be, when they were located in the so-called "school house bottom" area of the town. Their facilities are now virtually on par with the predominately white private school system. Regardless, over 90 percent of all the school children in the state of Mississippi continue to attend public schools, especially in areas where there is a white majority or at least a more balanced racial mix of students.

Surprisingly, for many years there was a major private and well-respected black school, grades kindergarten through 8th, located in Lexington, supported by the Church of God in Christ (a Pentecostal Christian denomination). It was named Saints Academy, and was formerly known as Saints Industrial College. Saints Academy closed in 2006. Its future remains uncertain.

While religious institutions and the country club remain segregated in the Lexington community, today many civic organizations are also integrated. The Holmes County Chamber of Commerce's board of directors is about 50 percent black, and a black member served as president a few years ago. Blacks serve on the boards of the Lexington Main Street Association and the Holmes County Arts Council. The Lexington Rotary Club is scheduled to take in its first black member this year. The great majority of the whites and blacks in Lexington show mutual respect for one another, and live and work together in a peaceful environment.

With reference to the Jewish community, as you read the pages of this book, you will note that historically, even with a relatively sizable Jewish community in Lexington,[6] there has not been any public evidence of anti-Semitism from the very beginning of this community in the early to mid 1800s. You will recognize what a good and special place the Lexington community has been ecumenically and continues to be today.

Description of the Town and Its History

Driving into Lexington on State Highway 17, a thirteen-mile stretch just off I-55, you can see miles of green pine forest and rolling hills covered with grass above a mixture of topsoil and clay. Occasionally, along the sides of the road, one can see an unusual looking vine know as kudzu. It has broad green leaves and is planted to prevent erosion of the hillsides. However it has a propensity to climb and encapsulate most every object with which it comes in contact that doesn't move, including fences and trees. It actually gives the appearance of a jungle. Across the lush countryside, cattle can also be seen grazing behind barbed wire fences.

There is enough open land to build more than one entire metropolitan city, but there is no skilled labor force of any size available to attract industry that would support such residential and commercial development. Sondy's parents, Stanley and Rhea Shindell, now deceased, were from New Haven, Connecticut. Years ago, when they came to visit Lexington, they were amazed at the vast acreage of unused land they saw along both sides of the highway as we drove to Lexington from Jackson. In their New England environment, both commercial and residential buildings are almost wall-to-wall. Actually, Lexington is situated many miles from the hustle and bustle of everyday city life. However, many Lexingtonians like it that way; it's a calm, peaceful environment, as is most of the area surrounding this small southern town. Due primarily to greater economic opportunities in the urban areas of Mississippi and elsewhere, Lexington's total population has dramatically declined since the 1930s and 1940s when the Jewish population there was at its peak.[7] In 1930, the town's total population was 2,590; in 1940 (just prior to World War II), the population had grown to 2,930. In the year 2000, the population had decreased to 2,025, and in 2005, it had declined to 1,941.

Lexington is situated in the heart of Mississippi, just 65 miles northwest of Jackson, the state's capital. It is built around a square, with a large courthouse and a clock tower located in the square's center. Lexington's rolling hills are situated just a few miles away from where the Mississippi hill country overlooks its vast, fertile delta region.

In its earliest days, Lexington was established as a trading post, and by 1830 had grown to be a small village.

Lexington's streets were originally cotton patches and the surrounding hills were covered with cane. In the 1820s, the great-grandfather of a family known as the Waltons moved with his family and slaves to what is now Holmes County. They cleared the land on which the courthouse now stands. After a government survey, this spot was chosen as the county seat of Holmes County.[8]

Mississippi became a state in 1817. At that time, the central and northern parts of the state were controlled by the Choctaw and Chickasaw Indian tribes.[9]

The Choctaws signed the treaty of Doak's Stand in 1820 and the treaty of Dancing Rabbit Creek in 1830, and ceded the land that presently comprises the counties of Hinds, Madison, Yazoo and Holmes.[10]

In 1833, a bill was passed by the Mississippi legislature to establish a new county from part of Yazoo County, and Holmes County was created. The act establishing the county called for a county seat within three miles of the geographical center of the county. Lexington was chosen, and a new town was born.[11]

The sixty-acre minimum requirement for the new county seat was met, and Lexington officially became a town on June 7, 1833. The new town of Lexington was incorporated on February 26, 1836. The 1923 minutes of the Presbyterian Church stated that one of its congregants saw a wild duck alight on a pond in the early days of the trade area of Lexington. Later, that pond was filled and replaced by the county's first courthouse, which was built of logs and included several dwellings. This first courthouse was built in the center of the square around which the new town was planned. A second courthouse was built of brick. It was designed by William Nichols, the architect for the old capitol and the governor's mansion. This courthouse burned in 1893.[12]

Basancon's Annual Register of the State of Mississippi for 1838 contains the following report:[13]

"Lexington, near the geographical center, is the county (Holmes) seat, and has a population of two hundred and ninety-four whites; males...one hundred and seventy-eight, females...one hundred and sixteen, and slaves one hundred and twenty, making in all four hundred and fourteen.[14] The public buildings in Lexington are a court house and Presbyterian Church. There are eight stores, four groceries and one apothecary shop. By 1838 the town also had a newspaper office, several lawyer's offices, two doctors, a bank and the office of a stage line. A post office was established in 1833."

The name Lexington was chosen to honor Lexington,

Massachusetts, where the first shot was fired in the American Revolution.[15]

The Magnolia Garden Club's recorded history stated that Lexington became a banking and trade center for the surrounding settlements. Settlers came from a number of states, namely North Carolina, South Carolina, Virginia, Alabama, Georgia, Tennessee and Kentucky. A few immigrants reached the raw new town coming from Ireland, Sweden, Hungary and Germany. This caused Lexington to grow and prosper, until the period of the Civil War and the Reconstruction days that followed. According to W.W. Lunsford, "from 1860 to 1875 was almost a blank in the history of the city...five years of war and ten years of carpetbag rule proved a great drawback."

Then Lexington began to grow again. In 1902, the Lexington *Progress-Advertiser* newspaper reported that "Lexington's prosperity is emphasized by the successful operations of its three banks: the Bank of Holmes County, the Bank of Lexington and the Bank of Commerce." It also stated that the spiritual interest of Lexington was well represented at an early time, including a Catholic, an Episcopal, a Presbyterian, a Methodist and a Baptist Church, with resident ministers in each. "Our Israelitish fellow citizens have also made arrangements to have a monthly visitation from a distinguished rabbi. Our Colored people, too, have three or four churches of different denominations in town."[16]

Lexington became an active economic center in the early 1900s. It had four banks and four hotels, and the railroad trains made four stops a day at Lexington's depot.[17]

Lexington celebrated its sesquicentennial in 1986 (1836-1986). Most of the factual information in this history was taken from *Holmes County Herald* Sesquicentennial Edition of August 28, 1986.

Excerpts from the *Lexington Adverstiser* from 1927 to 1956 give some highlights of and insights to the early days of Lexington and the changing city. Below are excerpts which pertain in particular to the Jewish community:[18]

January 13, 1927—New officers named by the Merchants & Farmers Bank...

All officers and directors were reelected to serve during the present year, including: Morris Lewis, president.

February 3, 1927—Lexington boys' band working hard for a trip with Rotarians. An article in this issue told of the Lexington boys' band trying to raise funds to pay their expenses to attend a Rotary convention in Memphis.

Members of the band and instruments they played were listed as follows...Celian H. Lewis, cornet...Eugene S. Herrman, tenor saxophone; Herman F. Flowers, Morris Lewis, Jr., melody saxophone; Herbert A. Hyman,...Cecil Herrman, Abe M. Applebaum, Manuel A. Applebaum, clarinet.

[Note: Almost 30 percent of the band consisted of Jewish members.

About the same percent of Jews were members of the high school football team, which was one of only two that ever went undefeated, according to attorney Don Barrett of Lexington.]

February 3, 1927—Hyman and Herrman buy out Sontheimer.

One of the largest deals in this county was closed Friday, when Jesse Hyman and Sam Herrman bought the store building, stock of goods, accounts, notes, farming land and good will of R. & B. Sontheimer.

The amount involved in the transaction was more than one hundred thousand dollars. [It should be said here that R. & B. Sontheimer was the largest retail merchant Lexington ever had, based upon the value of the dollar in that day compared to that of today. Their annual volume at that time is purported to have been $300,000.]

December 1, 1927—Lexington cemetery being developed as spot of real beauty.

Extensive improvements now underway will, when completed, result in the development of the historic old Odd Fellows Cemetery in this city into one of the most beautiful burial spots in the state located in the rolling grass-covered hills just outside the city limits, with trees that have developed to full maturity, and with stones marking the final resting places of Holmes County dead for almost a hundred years, the setting of nature is perfect...the entire front is being beautified and modernized and the front to the Jewish cemetery, which is adjoining, is being beautified in uniformity, so that the two may appear as one. An entrance gate of pressed brick pillars equipped with a 12-foot steel gate will be placed at the entrance of each, and the entire front equipped with a 5-foot chain length fence

September 20, 1934—Lexington Junior Chamber of Commerce organized in '34.

A meeting of the...Businessmen of Lexington numbering around 45 was held at the courthouse auditorium for the purpose of organizing a Junior Chamber of Commerce...short talks relative to the undertakings of the new organization were made by Leroy Paris...Eugene Herrman, younger business leaders. The committee named the following committee to visit other active organizations and acquaint themselves with their aims and purposes and also to draft by-laws and a constitution for the local junior chamber of commerce. They were: Leroy Paris, Eugene Herrman...Besides Leroy Paris and Eugene Herrman, were Nathan Schur, Herman Flowers, Julius (Pinky) Flowers, Ephraim Cohen.

Courthouse Olden Days

Courthouse Present

Chapter 2

Temple Beth El (House of God)
A House of David in the Land of Jesus
Celebrating Its 100th Anniversary
1905-2005
Beth El Cemetery

At one time, there were eighty-nine members of Temple Beth El in the small southern town of Lexington. This statistic was corroborated in a 1986 sesquicentennial article in the *Holmes County Herald* weekly newspaper celebrating Lexington's 150th birthday. According to Eli Evans in his book *The Provincials*, Jews across the South represented 1 percent of the population. Those eighty-nine "Jewish souls" of Lexington made up almost 3.5 percent of the town's population. That was quite significant, especially in a small southern town of Mississippi.

Before Temple Beth El was built, Lexington had so many churches that it was like living entirely in the land of Jesus, especially since there was no local synagogue. Two of Lexington's largest churches actually continue to display a Star of David at their entrances. The Baptist Church has a large Mogen David on its front entrance, and the Methodist Church has Stars of David on three sides of its steeple. After all, according to Christianity, Jesus descended from the house of David. While the churches would have been pleased to have local Jews join their congregations, those symbols were not necessarily for the purpose of proselytizing; more so, they were seen as offering a hand of welcome and friendship. Members of a number of prominent Jewish families were actually married in the local Methodist Church by a rabbi, including Morris and Julia Lewis before Temple Beth El was constructed, and Leroy and Irma Paris after Temple Beth El was open, since the Temple was not large enough to accommodate the large overflow crowd of well-wishers in attendance. This demonstrated the wonderful spirit of ecumenicalism and friendship that existed, and continues to this date, among the different faiths within the town of Lexington.

Before Temple Beth El existed, in the late 1800s there were a dozen Jewish families that had established homes in Lexington, comprising approximately thirty individual members of the Jewish faith. They first worshiped in the home of Henry Rosenthal, and later in what was then the Lexington Opera House, where the Lexington City Hall now sits. Henry Rosenthal, son-in-law of Jacob Sontheimer, Lexington's first permanent Jewish resident, conducted the services there.

As Lexington's Jewish population continued to grow, just after the turn of the century, Morris Lewis, Sr., and his brother-in-law, Sam Herrman, discussed the possibility and need for a permanent house of worship where members of the Jewish faith could join together in prayer. They first bought two acres of land from Stuart Watson, adjacent to the Odd Fellows Cemetery, to be used as a burial place for members of the Jewish faith. The land for the cemetery was purchased in 1904. Over a half century later, in 1957, the town of Lexington needed to add another road into the cemetery, so they traded for a ten-foot strip of land on the south side of Beth El's cemetery to construct an additional entry into Odd Fellows Cemetery. The terms of the trade for this entry, agreed to by the congregation of Temple Beth El, were that the town would maintain the Beth El cemetery grounds on a perpetual basis for a small sum of money paid annually. The cemetery is well maintained and landscaped by the city of Lexington, and is one of the most peaceful places in the entire state. Located on a seldom traveled country road, its tranquility is matched by the beauty of its setting. Only the sound of a visitor, an occasional car passing by, or an airplane flying high overhead disturbs the quiet solitude of the entire area. It is truly a cemetery where the words "rest in peace" have a veritable meaning.

There happened to be a small subdivision on Spring Street, downhill about a mile west of the square, across the street from Sam and Flora Herrman's home. The property was known in 1903 as the Lewis-Barrett subdivision, and was owned by Morris Lewis and W.O. Barrett. The lot where the Temple now stands was purchased by Morris Lewis and his brother-in-law, Sam Herrman. They donated the land, and that site was selected for a synagogue.

To raise funds for the building of Temple Beth El, Miss Lena Levy organized a group to perform a play at the Lexington Opera House. Most of the cast were members of the Baptist Church. They raised $164.00 at this big event. Today, considering inflation, that equates to more than $8,000.

With additional funds coming from the members of Lexington's Jewish community, a "House of David" was then built in the middle of the land of Jesus—where it still stands today, over one hundred years later.

Temple Beth El was chartered by the Union of American Hebrew Congregations in 1904 as a reform Jewish congregation. It opened in 1905 and celebrated its 100th birthday in December 2005. The Temple's construction was completed in November 1905. The first High Holy Day services were conducted by Henry A. Rosenthal.

After Temple Beth El opened, the land of Jesus continued to exist and grow. However, now there was finally a house of worship in Lexington for members of the Jewish faith. For what eventually became eighty-nine individual members of Temple Beth El in Lexington, there was a place to congregate within—their own house of David.

Organizing members of the congregation were:[19]
Mr. Sol Auerbach
Mr. and Mrs. L. Dobroski
Mr. Abram Flowers
Mr. and Mrs. Isaac Flower
Mr. and Mrs. S.J. Fisher
Mr. and Mrs. Abraham Herrman
Mr. and Mrs. Sam Herrman
Mr. and Mrs. Isadore Herrman
Mr. Isadore Levy
Mr. and Mrs. Morris Lewis
Mr. and Mrs. Myer A. Lewis
Mr. and Mrs. Henry A. Rosenthal
Mr. Joe Rosenthal

Henry Rosenthal, the congregation's first president, was followed in succession by Sam Herrman and Morris Lewis.

The building was constructed of wooden frame and painted white. Until recently, there were no markings on the outside of the building to differentiate it from a "little ole country church"—except that it naturally bore no Cross. However, the interior gracefully displays all the settings and markings of what anyone would expect to see in a synagogue and sanctuary, including the bima and ark, where the Torah is stored.

With the construction of the Temple in 1905, the members initially had radiantly beautiful stained glass windows installed along both sides, in memory of various early Jewish families and congregational members. When the rays of the sun shine brilliantly through these multicolored stained glass windows, it evokes a feeling of spirituality, as if to manifest God's very presence within the Temple itself.

The stained glass doors entering the sanctuary from the lobby were installed in 1926. The doors to the ark and the Ten Commandments above the ark were installed in 1949.

Stained glass windows were dedicated as follows:

West wall

In loving remembrance of
Carrie Sontheimer Rosenthal
Wife of H.A. Rosenthal

In loving memory of our father
Jacob Sontheimer

In memory of my wife
Sarah Sontheimer Auerbach

In memory of our mother
Mary Sontheimer

East wall

In sacred memory of my mother
Anna Easter Levy
Lena Levy

In memory of my sister
Jeannette Sontheimer
Bettie S. Fisher

In memory of Viola Lichtenstein Lewis
Wife of Myer A. Lewis
Died April 30, 1905

In memory of our two infant children
Morris and Julia Lewis

Stained glass doors at the entrance to the sanctuary

In loving memory of   In loving memory of
Philip Cohen   David Miller

Stained glass doors to the ark

In memory of Samuel J. Cohen   In memory of Rosa Schur Cohen

A Tablet containing the Ten Commandments above the ark
In loving memory of
Aaron Jacobson

Each of these deceased will be described in the pages that follow.

It wasn't until recently, in 2004, that the congregation finally installed a Star of David—in stained glass, above the Temple's double door entrance—in memory of Herbert and Henrietta Hyman, past president of the Temple and past president of the Temple Sisterhood, respectively. As devout and dedicated as the Jewish community of Lexington was, it took a long time for its congregation to match the Stars of David that were on the churches of its Christian neighbors. Apparently they felt it was their devotion to the faith of Judaism, more than any outward symbols, which really counted.

For many years after the Temple was in use, it had no bathroom. During breaks in the long High Holy Day services on Rosh Hashanah and Yom Kippur, the congregants stood in long lines across the street at Sam and Flora Herrman's home, in order to use their bathroom facilities.

As one walks up the five concrete steps to the double door entrance, you look around at the neatly trimmed landscaping. Upon entering the building, you pass through the double screen doors; in the days before air conditioning, these were used to keep insects out. One then moves into a wood-floored lobby. On either side of the lobby are two classrooms where many Jewish students, including myself, were instructed in the faith of our forefathers: Abraham, Isaac and Jacob; Sarah, Rebecca, Leah and Rachel; Moses, Saul, David and Solomon; the prophets, and other many notables in the Old Testament. These two classrooms, one of which now contains a bathroom, have double doors that open into the sanctuary for use when capacity crowds attend services and other life cycle events.

From the entrance lobby, passing through two more swinging doors with stained glass insets, one looks down a green-carpeted center aisle toward the raised and carpeted platform known as the bima. In the front center of the bima is a wooden pulpit. At the rear of the pulpit is a beautiful wooden ark with stained glass windows, in which a large Torah is located. It contains the five books of Moses in the Old Testament—Genesis, Exodus, Leviticus, Numbers and Deuteronomy, all hand-inscribed on parchment. This Torah, still in use, was purchased by Morris Lewis, Sr., in New York City around 1924. Two golden Menorahs are mounted on tall golden stands, one on each side of the bima, with a Star of David under the seven lights on each Menorah. The Menorah is a seven-branched candelabrum lit by olive oil in the Tabernacle (the portable sanctuary used by the Jewish people) and later its successor, the Temple in Jerusalem. The Menorah is one of the oldest symbols of the Jewish people. It is said to symbolize the burning bush as seen by Moses on Mount Sinai (Exodus 25).[20] The Menorah is also a symbol closely associated with the Jewish holiday of Chanukah. An American flag adorns the right corner of the sanctuary, just off the bima.

Set back on each side of the ark are three heavy, majestic arm chairs for the rabbi, temple president, and guest. Facing the pulpit, to the left, is the raised choir area and an organ, separated from the seats in the sanctuary by a low spindled wooden railing. On the wall to the rear of the choir area is a large brass memorial plaque, with lights beside each name.

To the left and right of the center aisle are wooden benches with green cushions, with outside aisles on each side.

A white silken cover drapes the pulpit, adorned with a golden Star of David. Encircling the Mogen David, inscribed in gold letters, are the words from the Prophet Micah—"Do justly, love mercy, walk humbly with thy God."

On one wall of the outer entrance lobby is a bronze plaque with a raised bust of the late Joseph Emile Berman, lay rabbi of Temple Beth El from the time he returned from his service in World War II, from 1946 to 1967. On the plaque under his bust are inscribed the words of a prayer he wrote for Beth El's Sisterhood, which reads:

> Be with us, o God as we go forth from this meeting. Kindle in us a passion for doing only that which is just and honorable. Our powers, our achievements, our good fortune, our happiness, all come from thee. May we never cease to be grateful unto Thee. Teach us to walk in thy footsteps; to be generous, helpful and good, so that our hearts may reflect thine endless bounty. May we be thy messengers of blessing, aiding the poor, helping the helpless, healing the sick at heart. Draw us neigh unto thee, that we may love thee and rejoice in thy service. Amen
>
> *Joseph Emile Berman*

Described in the next chapter is the Jewish community of Lexington, both past and present, and how they continue to keep the Covenant and Temple Beth El alive.

Temple Beth El

Entrance Doors to Sanctuary

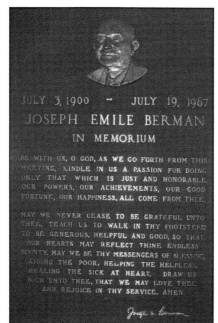

JULY 3, 1900   —   JULY 19, 1967
JOSEPH EMILE BERMAN
IN MEMORIUM

BE WITH US, O GOD, AS WE GO FORTH FROM THIS
MEETING. KINDLE IN US A PASSION FOR DOING
ONLY THAT WHICH IS JUST AND HONORABLE.
OUR POWERS, OUR ACHIEVEMENTS, OUR GOOD
FORTUNE, OUR HAPPINESS, ALL COME FROM THEE.

MAY WE NEVER CEASE TO BE GRATEFUL UNTO
THEE. TEACH US TO WALK IN THY FOOTSTEPS;
TO BE GENEROUS, HELPFUL AND GOOD, SO THAT
OUR HEARTS MAY REFLECT THINE ENDLESS
BOUNTY. MAY WE BE THY MESSENGERS OF BLESSING,
AIDING THE POOR, HELPING THE HELPLESS,
HEALING THE SICK AT HEART. DRAW US
NIGH UNTO THEE, THAT WE MAY LOVE THEE
AND REJOICE IN THY SERVICE. AMEN

Lobby Plaque

Inside Sanctuary

Stained Glass Windows

ARK (top)   TORAH inside ARK (bottom)

Beth EL Cemetery

Chapter 3

Lexington's Jewish Community—
Past and Present
General Comments About Its Origin
Early Beginnings to Present

After both Temples in Jerusalem were destroyed in 580 B.C.E. (Before the Common Era) by the Babylonians and again in 70 C.E. by the Romans, Jews have since been scattered around the world in what is known as the Diaspora (dispersion). Nevertheless, Judaism has been able to survive throughout the centuries despite the many tyrants and nations that have tried to destroy it; from Pharaoh and the Egyptians, to the Spanish Inquisition, to the Czar and Russian Pogroms, to Hitler's Nazi Germany. One reason for its survival is that Jews are not attached to any particular central religious dogma or location. They, in effect, have been able to carry their Torah (the first five books of Moses in the Old Testament) with them, either literally or in their hearts, wherever they landed. Once the state of Israel was reestablished in 1948 as the God-given homeland of the Jewish people, many Jews have resettled there, especially those who have been persecuted and/or have not been allowed to practice their religion openly and freely elsewhere. Yet Jews in the United States continue to outnumber Jews in Israel[21] because of the very freedoms and liberties, including that of religion, upon which this magnificent country was founded. That foundation of freedom, equality and respect for the rights of all its citizens is surely one of the reasons why the United States of America has been so blessed by the Almighty as the greatest nation on earth.

Before my great-great-grandfather, Jacob Sontheimer, settled in Lexington in the 1840s, numerous Jewish peddlers came through that community peddling their wares. However, it was the peddler Jacob Sontheimer who was the first permanent Jewish resident of Lexington, Mississippi. Jacob and his family came to America from

Bavaria, in Germany. They immigrated through New Orleans, moving up into Mississippi through Natchez, and later north to Lexington.

Jacob married Mary Auerbach. They had six daughters, five of whom married and remained in Lexington to form the nucleus of the first Jews in the population of that town. Abraham Herrman, from Georgia, married Celia Sontheimer; Henry Rosenthal married Carrie Sontheimer; Simon Fisher married Bettie Sontheimer; Sol Auerbach married Sarah Sontheimer; Isadore Hyman married Rosa Sontheimer. After Rosa passed away, Isadore married Rosa's niece, Claudia Herrman Hyman, my great-aunt. The sixth daughter was Jeannette Sontheimer, who also grew up in Lexington, but passed away at a relatively young age.

All of these families remained in Lexington and prospered. Jews were well accepted by the Christian community, and two members of the Levy family were elected to the city board of aldermen in the late 1880s.

Abraham Herrman, my great-grandfather, was born in Bavaria and migrated to Lexington from Davisborough, Georgia. Lexington is where he met and married Celia Sontheimer, my great-grandmother. They had three daughters and four sons. It was there that one of their daughters, Julia, my grandmother, met and married my grandfather, Morris Lewis, Sr. He had emigrated from Poland as a young boy with his younger brother, Myer, in 1886.

Initially, religious observations in Lexington were usually confined to each family in their own home. By the late 1890s, Henry Rosenthal began conducting services for all Lexington Jews in his home. Since his home was next door to that of his brother-in-law, Isadore Hyman, both homes were used for large religious affairs and social gatherings. Later, as the number of Jewish families in Lexington continued to grow, the High Holy Day services of Rosh Hashanah and Yom Kippur were moved to what was then the Lexington Opera House, where they continued to be held until Temple Beth El was opened in 1905.

With the first president of Temple Beth El, Henry A. Rosenthal, was Simon Fisher, the first secretary and treasurer of the Temple. Simon served in that capacity from 1905 to 1925, when he became ill. Ephraim Cohen was asked to serve as a temporary secretary and treasurer, and served in that "temporary" capacity for the next fifty years.

When Ephraim Cohen's son, Phil, returned in 1975, Ephraim handed the books to him. Unelected, but greatly appreciated, Phil Cohen continues to currently serve in that capacity.

Before Temple Beth El Cemetery was established in 1904, Jacob Sontheimer and some thirteen other members of the Lexington Jewish community were buried in the Lexington Odd Fellows Cemetery, adjacent to what was later founded as Beth El Cemetery.

Carrie Sontheimer Rosenthal was the first member of the Jewish faith to be buried in the new Beth El Cemetery. Ninety-six members of the Jewish faith who once lived in Lexington are now buried in the local cemetery.

Henry Rosenthal initially conducted services. Then a shuttle railroad was constructed to connect the two main roads traversing Mississippi for the Illinois Central railroad, which passed through Lexington. Once completed, that railroad was used by Rabbi Abraham Brill to travel to Lexington to conduct services. In 1902, the Lexington Jewish community hired Rabbi Brill from Greenville to conduct services once a month. He was the first rabbi to serve Temple Beth El, and helped organize the congregation. He would take a train from Greenville to Greenwood, where he would change to another train to travel to Tchula, a small town just a few miles west of Lexington. From there he would change trains once again to go to Lexington, the county seat. This was an exceedingly dedicated rabbi. As one can imagine, this was quite an ordeal. He would spend the night, and once a month was all he could physically afford to do—and about all the congregation could financially afford.

Shortly after World War I began, in 1918, a patriotic rally was held on the town square in Lexington to encourage and recruit soldiers for the United States armed forces. Among those giving patriotic speeches was Rabbi Brill. His words were inspiring and delighted the large crowd. It gave the Jewish community a great sense of pride. Immediately following his stirring and motivational speech, several members of Temple Beth El volunteered for military service, including Nathan Kern, Phil Cohen, and his brother Ephraim—who was rejected because he was only fifteen years old at the time.

Years later, during World War II, eighteen members of Temple Beth El served their country in the military.

Following Rabbi Brill, Temple Beth El was served by Rabbi Sol Kory of Vicksburg, who presided over the marriage of my mother,

Fay Lewis, daughter of Morris and Julia Lewis, to my father, Joe Berman, originally of Atlanta, Georgia.

The story is told of Rabbi Kory, who would drive a very old car from Vicksburg to Lexington, a trip of about ninety miles. He always wore this very tattered frock coat. One December, during Chanukah, the members of Temple Beth El raised some money to present to Rabbi Kory so he could afford to buy a new coat. Fifty dollars was raised for that purpose and given to Rabbi Kory, with many hints about his then being able to enhance his wardrobe by getting a new coat. When he returned in January the following year, he was still wearing the same old tattered coat. When asked why he had not bought himself a new one, or what he had done with the money given to him, he replied that he was very thankful to get the fifty dollars, and had been able to buy many poor families food so that they could enjoy their Christmas.

The next year, when funds were raised to give Rabbi Kory another gift, Abraham Flowers, who owned and operated a department store on the Lexington square, was asked to purchase a frock coat for Rabbi Kory. There was then no turning back for the rabbi, and he wore the new coat on nearly all occasions thereafter.

Rabbi Kory was followed by two more rabbis from Vicksburg: Rabbi Stanley Brav, who confirmed my cousin Henry Paris and me together in 1947, and then Rabbi Samuel Shillman.

In 1954, Rabbi Perry Nussbaum, religious leader of Beth Israel Congregation in Jackson, Mississippi, took over the pulpit and services for the Lexington congregation. It was during his term of office that the 50th anniversary celebration of Temple Beth El was held. He was later followed by Rabbi Allan Schwartzman of Vicksburg, and then by Rabbi Eric Gurvis, Rabbi Steven Engle, Rabbi Jim Egolf, and currently Rabbi Valerie Cohen, all of Beth Israel Congregation in Jackson.

Temple Beth El has held monthly services since its inception, with time off during the summer months during vacation time. For many years, the High Holy Day services of Rosh Hashanah and Yom Kippur were conducted by student rabbis from the Hebrew Union College—Jewish Institute of Religion in Cincinnati. One of these student rabbis was Dr. James Wax, later renowned chief rabbi for Temple Israel in Memphis, Tennessee. On many such occasions, one of the High Holy Day dinners was customarily held in the home of Morris and Julia Lewis, at their southern mansion home of Faymorcele. It was during that time that two young Jewish men of the Lexington congregation, Cecil and his younger brother Gus Herrman, sons of Morris and Jessie Herrman and next-door neighbors, met and established a long-term friendship with Dr. Wax. This close relationship, which had its beginnings during such a High Holy Day period, would result in an amazing story of major consequences to the Hebrew Union College. This story is related in detail in the chapter about Cecil and Gus Herrman.

In the late 1940s, with the congregation shrinking due to attrition of its members after World War II, and expenses rising, Joseph E. Berman, son-in-law of Morris Lewis, Sr., volunteered to become the lay rabbi for Temple Beth El and conduct High Holy Day services, thereby saving that expense. Joe Berman, a man of deep faith and oratory skills, continued to conduct these services until his untimely and tragic death in a commercial airline crash in 1967. The High Holy Day services were then conducted by me for a number of years thereafter. After I became treasurer of Beth Israel Congregation in Jackson and involved with the Temple administration there, my cousin Henry Paris, of Indianola, Mississippi, took over the position. He has been conducting Rosh Hashanah and Yom Kippur services ever since.

The first Sunday school was organized in 1901. Miss Lena Levy and Miss Julia Cohen (Flowers) were Temple Beth El's first Sunday school teachers. They were followed by Mrs. Agathene Applebaum (who taught me), Ephraim Cohen, Herman Flowers, Joe Berman and Phil Cohen.

Since 1905, in addition to religious services, Temple Beth El has hosted weddings, funerals, confirmations, bar mitzvahs, and bat mitzvahs. The largest confirmation class in the history of Temple Beth El was in 1929, with some thirteen confirmants. The first person to have a bar mitzvah at Temple Beth El was Samuel Cohen, son of Phil and Sally Cohen, which was conducted in 1994 and attended by an overflow crowd.

A silver anniversary was held in 1955, with several original members in attendance. At this and all other events where the general public has been invited, friends in the community and members filled the Temple's seating of over 150 people to capacity.

The contributions of the Jewish community to the overall community of Lexington, Holmes County, the state of Mississippi, and the nation have been so numerous that it would be difficult to name them all. Among them, serving as presidents of the Lexington Rotary club, Lions club, country club and school board have been Morris Lewis, Sr., Ephraim Cohen, Joe Berman, Herbert Hyman, Herman Flowers, Edward Schur, Phil Cohen and Eugene Herrman, who also served on the board of aldermen for some twenty years in the 1960s and 1970s. The entire Jewish community of Mississippi and surrounding states, the Hebrew Union College, the University of Mississippi, the state of Mississippi, and the nation have all been advantageously affected by and have significantly benefited from the actions of various members of the Lexington Jewish community.

These are the beginnings of Judaism in Lexington. In the next section of this book, entitled "Pillars of the Jewish Community," a number of these contributions are described in detail.

To reiterate, the Lexington Jewish community at one time numbered eighty-nine "Jewish souls", according to Ephraim Cohen, deceased father of Lexington resident Phil Cohen. Temple Beth El was a place of worship for each of them. Most were merchants, but there were also food brokers, bankers, wholesale grocers, retail grocers, tailors, salesmen, farmers and a plantation owner, as well as a lawyer, insurance agent, cattle trader, oil man, theater owner, scrap metal dealer, manufacturer, baker and butcher.

World War II was primarily responsible for the attrition of most of the Jews in the Lexington community. The great majority of Jewish men departed to serve in the armed forces during the war. Afterwards, many of them and their families never returned. Yet some did. Today there remain three Jewish family units, plus other continuing members of Temple Beth El living outside of Lexington, with a total Temple membership of sixteen families comprising twenty-five individuals.

So why did the Jewish population of Lexington shrink from eighty-nine at its pinnacle in the 1930s, to the few that now remain? As older members passed away, their ranks were not replaced by younger Jews bringing in new blood. This was mostly due to a lack of economic opportunities. Most members of the Jewish faith today are college educated. Hence, whether they grew up in Lexington or elsewhere, they were overqualified for nearly all jobs that were available in the community. Additionally, an urban environment was more appealing, offering far more cultural and entertainment activities. For some of the same reasons, between 1940 and 1960, Holmes County's population decreased from approximately 43,000 in 1940 to 25,000 in 1960. Today, its population is approximately 22,000. The main reason for the county's population decline was the advent of mechanized farming. Mechanical cotton pickers and tractors replaced a large number of farm workers. This loss of population had a devastating effect on the Jewish merchants, who depended upon many of the farming community for their business. Most eventually closed their doors. Today only one department store remains in Lexington, and it continues to be owned and operated by a Jewish family as Cohen's Department Store.

There was also another factor for the decline that served to discourage farm workers from remaining in the county and new workers from locating there. For instance, a number of influential farmers discouraged factories from locating in the town and county to preclude competition in the marketplace for the labor force that remained. It wasn't until 1954 that Henson-Kickernick, a lingerie plant, became Lexington's first factory. All of these are reasons why the Jewish population of Lexington today is only a small fraction of what it used to be.[22]

It should be noted that a number of non-member Jews and guests living in the general vicinity also attend services at Beth El. Along with members of its current sixteen-family congregation, this has helped to keep Temple Beth El's doors open. Attendance at monthly services usually amounts to eight to twelve members. Services today are led by the rabbi of Beth Israel Congregation in Jackson. When Rabbi Valerie Cohen cannot attend monthly services at Temple Beth El, the itinerant rabbi of the Institute of Southern Jewish Life, headquartered in Jackson, takes her place.

However, on the High Holy Days of Rosh Hashanah and Yom Kippur, twenty-five to thirty Jews normally attend. These services continue to be led today by Henry Paris, a former Lexington resident and continuing member from nearby Indianola.

Thus Temple Beth El, with its distinguished history, continues to actively live on through the support of a small contingent of dedicated members who still reside in Lexington, and those throughout the local and surrounding area and elsewhere.

Frequently in Judaism, our forefathers are referred to as Abraham, Isaac and Jacob. Individual stories that follow will mention these names, along with other biblical names such as Solomon, Joseph, Aaron, Samuel, Ephraim, Sarah, Ruth, and Esther, and all in the context of how they relate to the dedicated Jewish community of Lexington, Mississippi.

Pillars of the Jewish Community

Chapter 4

Jacob Sontheimer
and Mary Auerbach Sontheimer
Lexington's First Permanent Jewish Resident

Jacob Sontheimer, my great-great-grandfather, was Lexington's first permanent Jewish resident, and marked the beginning of Lexington's Jewish community.

Jacob was born in Germany in 1819 and immigrated with his family to the United States when he was a very young man. They originally settled in New Orleans, where some of his family continues to live and thrive, as does the Sontheimer Funeral Home. Part of the family later moved north to Natchez, Mississippi.

Jacob began earning a living as a peddler, the same way many Jewish immigrant men got started. He was traveling in the central Mississippi area, which had just been opened by the treaty of Dancing Rabbit Creek. The settlement was only a few years old at that time. During his travels, around 1849, he ran across a man who became one of his clients. He would visit the man about once a month and sell wares to him.

His customer was named Hugh Johnson. Mr. Johnson lived alone in a very isolated area of the territory, near what is now the small community of Ebenezer, a few miles southwest of Lexington. Hugh Johnson was roughly eighty years old at the time, and lived on a prime farmland plantation of about 4,000 acres. Mr. Johnson was a very lonely person. After several months, he became accustomed to Jacob coming by. He liked Jacob's company and the stories Jacob would tell and share with him during his monthly visits.

One day Mr. Johnson asked Jacob to come in and visit with him for awhile. As they were visiting, Mr. Johnson told Jacob that he surely did not want him to leave. He said, "In fact, if you will stay here and take care of me and my plantation until I die, then I'll leave you my entire plantation at the time of my death." Well, that was quite an offer to a poor, young Jewish peddler. So Jacob took him up on the offer and stayed with him for a number of years. During those years, Hugh Johnson became indebted to Jacob Sontheimer, not just for his devoted friendship and care, but also for helping to run his plantation, for disposing of the crops grown on it, and for the wares and supplies Jacob sold to him for his plantation needs.

Hugh Johnson died on August 8, 1856. Prior to his death, he had appointed his brother, Jesse Johnson, and his trusted friend Jacob Sontheimer as his co-executors. He also signed a will, in which he stayed true to his word by leaving the entire plantation, including his slaves, to Jacob. Based on that bequest, Jacob cancelled the sizable financial debt owed to him by Hugh Johnson. The probate judge approved the will and upheld the bequest.

But the sister of Hugh Johnson, Margaret Matthews, on behalf of their family, some of whom were from Vicksburg, filed a suit against Jacob Sontheimer in the Mississippi Court of Appeals to set aside the probate. They were most upset by the circumstances and didn't take kindly to it at all. They sued Jacob for undue influence in the writing of the will, in order to get the plantation back. They used the old, timeworn anti-Semitic approach, insinuating and accusing Jacob of wrongdoing, and saying that Jacob had wrongly influenced Hugh Johnson by supplying him with alcoholic beverages and feigned friendship. So, in his defense, Jacob called upon neighbors in the area as witnesses, and they said, "Oh, no; that was Mr. Johnson's and Jacob's deal." They stated that Jacob had fed and clothed Mr. Johnson, bathed him and changed his bedpan, told him stories about the old country from whence he came, and taken good care of him and his plantation—including managing and furnishing the plantation, without compensation, for several years—and that had been their agreement, which the neighbors testified was bona fide.

The appellate judge was quite confused. After hearing the sister, he thought well, maybe Jacob had, to some degree, used undue influence by perhaps getting Mr. Johnson drunk and had made him will his plantation to Jacob. Then he listened to Mr. Johnson's neighbors, who insisted that Jacob had truly and faithfully done what Mr. Johnson had asked him to do, and that Jacob deserved the plantation. After hearing arguments from both sides, the high court of errors and appeals of Mississippi reversed the judgment, set aside the verdict of the probate court, and remanded the case for a new trial.

At the new trial, the judge in his infinite wisdom tried to be fair to all parties involved. He left the plantation intact to Jacob, as Mr. Johnson had apparently promised to do and had specified in his will, out of gratitude to Jacob for his faithful care and to repay the valid and sizable financial debt he owed to Jacob. However, the judge said, since there was some doubt in the case, irrespective of the likelihood of Jacob's right to the property, he was taking the slaves and leaving them to the family of Hugh Johnson.

Once the case was settled, Jacob was left with approximately 4,000 acres of prime farmland. But this was the "land of cotton, old times there are not forgotten" in the days long before mechanical cotton pickers. With only a few slaves who had remained with him because he had treated them kindly, Jacob realized he could not till the soil and plant, grow and harvest cotton, cane, corn, beans or any other crop without a lot of laborers to help. So Jacob sold about 2,800 of the 4,000. That left him with the 1,200 acres of land that has ever since been known as "the Sontheimer place." In this way, he could continue to be considered in the land of gentry and a major property owner in his part of the world. The Sontheimer place lies just a few miles outside of Lexington.

The sale of the large acreage gave Jacob enough money to venture into the nearby newly incorporated town and county seat of Lexington, established as such in 1836. It was there that he opened the first brick store on the square of Lexington, in the mid 1850s. His action played a major role in establishing commerce in that area of the state. To a large extent, Jacob Sontheimer breathed commercial life into the town of Lexington and started it on its way through history.

The Sontheimer mercantile store was located on the northwest side of the square. After years of operation it became one of the largest retail businesses in the entire state, with an annual volume of over $300,000. In today's figures, adjusted for inflation, this would equal well over $3 million, according to Professor Andrew Hacker of Queens College and a *New York Times* book critic.

Jacob's brother, Solomon Sontheimer, was born in 1825. He came to Lexington from New Orleans to work with Jacob in managing his large business venture. Solomon married the future Fannie Sontheimer, who also had immigrated to the United States from Herkheim, Germany. They had three daughters in Lexington; Emma

Sontheimer, born in 1855; Necie Sontheimer, born in 1859; and Lily Sontheimer, born in 1867.

Jacob met and married Mary Auerbach, my great-great-grandmother, born in 1821, to whom a memorial stained glass window in Temple Beth El is dedicated. While Mary is not a typical Jewish name today, it was the name of Jesus' mother, who, along with Jesus and his father, Joseph, was a devout member of the Jewish faith. Mary must have been a Jewish name in the days before Christianity evolved.

As mentioned in the previous chapter, Jacob and Mary were blessed with six daughters; Celia, Rosa, Bettie, Carrie, Sarah and Jeanette.

Rosa and Bettie eventually took over the Sontheimer mercantile store on the square in Lexington, and renamed it R & B Sontheimer (for Rosa and Bettie). Bettie was the main storekeeper and continued to develop one of the largest department store businesses in the entire state.

The story of Jacob and Mary Sontheimer, my great-great-grandparents, and their family is, in essence, the beginning of the Lexington Jewish community, the beginning of any significant commerce in the town of Lexington, as well as the beginning of our family's Mississippi roots and its genesis.

Jacob died in 1886 at the age of 67. Mary died in 1895 at the age of 74.

Jacob and Mary Sontheimer Lexington Home

Chapter 5

Bettie Sontheimer Fisher and Simon Fisher Yesterday's "Sam Walton" of the Opposite Gender

When Bettie Sontheimer Fisher, born in 1861, and her sister Rosa Sontheimer Hyman took over the reins of the Sontheimer store, they were determined from the very beginning to do more than simply continue to expand the successful business their father, Jacob, had started. Bettie, who had studied in New York, especially knew that she had the capability and business acumen to develop a mercantile giant, and that is exactly what she did. At the peak of its operation, R & B Sontheimer was grossing the $300,000.00 annually mentioned earlier. That was an enormous amount of business for any operation in a town the size of 2,000 people at that time, even if located in the middle of a trading center.

The store carried a large variety of items; from food to clothing, to farm equipment and supplies, including feed and seed; to salt meat and housewares. Sam Walton would have been amazed at the way Bettie and Rosa conducted their business. In that day and time, it could have been compared to one of Wal-Mart's first stores—perhaps with an even greater assortment of merchandise similar to the new Wal-Mart Superstores.

The Sontheimer store was located on the square where Thurmond Appliances is today. They had the lot behind there all the way to the corner, and they used to keep wagons loaded with merchandise from the trains—thirty or forty of them, covered with tarpaulins at night to protect the merchandise—and in those days few people ever stole anything! Unfortunately, that's not the way it is in today's society.

There is a story about the R & B Sontheimer store and "the missing saddle." One day, Rosa and Bettie noticed that a saddle was missing from their inventory. No one in the store knew where it had gone. Being the olden days, when crime was not as prevalent as it is today, each of them thought it must have been sold to someone in the community. However, there was no record of any such sale. Saddles were an expensive item, even in those days. Then Miss Bettie, as she was known, had a brilliant idea. She said, "Let's just bill all of our customers for the saddle." When each of them came in and stated they had never purchased a saddle, the employees apologized and said there must have been a mistake on the invoice. When the person who had actually bought the saddle paid for it, they knew to whom they made the sale. It worked!

Another tale about the Sontheimer store involved Celian Lewis and Herbert Hyman. They were close in age and grew up in Lexington as closely as any two brothers could. When they were youngsters, they worked in the R & B Sontheimer store on the weekends to earn money to go to movies at the local theatre, called the "picture show" in those days. They didn't need to earn money for candy or food, as they ate as much as they could from the candy barrels, cracker barrels, pickle barrels, cheese and oil sausages sold by the store. The word was that these two young Lexingtonians ate so much during their working hours that almost every Saturday night they would have old-fashioned bellyaches from their gluttony.

Simon Fisher, born in 1859, was Bettie's husband who outlived her. He was content to let Bettie run the store and be the "front man." He would sit on a chair in front of the store during business hours and greet all the customers, just as the Wal-Mart greeters do today. Had they lived in our day, they might have given Wal-Mart a run for their money.

Morris Lewis, Sr., another Lexingtonian who built a food empire that began in Lexington, always felt that Bettie Sontheimer Fisher, his wife's aunt, need not order truckloads and carloads of flour directly from the manufacturer, as was her custom. He believed his local warehouse could give her the advantage of much quicker service in supplying her store, and she would not need to buy in such large quantities. Nevertheless, realizing that was her prerogative, and the fact that she was such an outstanding and successful businesswoman, he never pursued the matter.

Bettie died in 1926. Simon died in 1932.

In 1927, Jesse Hyman (son of Isadore and Rosa Sontheimer Hyman and half brother to Herbert Hyman) and Sam Herrman (brother-in-law to Morris Lewis) bought the R & B Sontheimer store, including the building and farmland, in one of the largest deals the county had ever known.

Bettie Sontheimer Fisher

1922 Excerpt of letter from Bettie Sontheimer
Fisher letter to Jessie and Morris Herrman

Chapter 6

Isadore Hyman and Rosa Sontheimer Hyman, and Claudia Herrman Hyman
Plantation Owner

Isadore Hyman, born in 1861, came to this country in the late 1860s. He was brought to America by an aunt and initially settled in the delta town of Greenwood, Mississippi about thirty-eight miles from Lexington. Upon marrying Rosa Sontheimer, born in 1850, one of the six daughters of Jacob and Mary Sontheimer, he joined the R & B Sontheimer company.

Isadore managed the 1,200 acres of the plantation on the Sontheimer place, utilizing tenant farmers, called sharecroppers, as laborers. They did the work on the farmland, and for their efforts they were "furnished" shelter, food and clothing, and shared the harvest with the landowner, in this case Isadore Hyman. All of this took place while Bettie Sontheimer Fisher and Isadore's wife Rosa ran the large Sontheimer "furnishings"and general mercantile store in Lexington.

The story goes that when one of the sharecropper women who worked on Isadore's land bore an illegitimate child and did not want the baby, he assumed its care. He established a small private orphanage, where a woman took care of all the unwanted children born out of wedlock on the 1,200 acres he supervised. He provided them food, shelter and clothing until they were able to go and make a living for themselves.

The Sontheimer place has passed through a number of owners since those days in the 1800s and early 1900s. Before the present owner, another person had offered to buy the plantation. He inquired whether Williams Creek, which flowed through the middle of the property, ever flooded. He was assured that it didn't. Shortly after he became the new owner of the Sontheimer place, there came a deluge. The creek rose over its banks and flooded a large portion of the property, doing considerable damage to livestock and fences.

Afterwards, he mentioned to one of his workers on the site that he had been told the creek never flooded. The reply he received was: "Well, boss, *sontheime* it do and *sontheime* it don't; *sontheime* we make a crop and *sontheime* we don't." It has been stated that the present owner purchased the property for its sheer beauty.

Isadore was married three times. He had a son, Ike (1883-1955) by his first wife. He and his second wife Rosa had a son, Jesse Hyman. After Rosa died, Isadore took as his bride Claudia Herrman, niece of Rosa and sister to Julia Herrman Lewis, Daisy Herrman Jacobson, Morris Herrman, Sam Herrman, Isadore Herrman and Jake Herrman. Isadore and Claudia had one son, Herbert A. Hyman.

Rosa died in 1911. Isadore died in 1921. Claudia was born in 1879 and died in 1957.

Isadore Hyman (top)   Claudia Herrman Hyman (bottom)

.

Chapter 7

Herbert A. Hyman
and Henrietta Baum Hyman
A Man of Honor

Herbert was related to almost every Jewish family in Lexington. His father, Isadore Hyman, had a sister named Ester who married Isaac Flower. The Flower and Flowers families were related to the Cohens. Herbert's mother was a Herrman and was related to the Lewis family.

Herbert Hyman was born in 1914 and grew up in Lexington. After his father died in 1921, Herbert and his mother, Claudia, moved into Faymorcele, the large antebellum home of Morris and Julia Lewis, Claudia's sister. Those were the days when Jewish families lovingly shared their homes with close relatives.

Herbert and Celian Lewis (son of Morris and Julia) were close to the same age and grew up together as if they were blood brothers. They went through elementary, junior high and high school together. Both were members of the Lexington High School band. They each were stars on the high school's football team, and played on one of only two undefeated teams that Lexington ever produced. Both were confirmed in Lexington's Temple Beth El.

Each of them went to Tulane University and were roommates while at college. When Celian began work with the Lewis Grocer Co. started by his father, Morris Lewis, Sr., Herbert did likewise. After spending two years at Tulane, both Herbert and Celian left school and moved to Indianola, to begin working at Lewis Grocer's newly acquired warehouse in that Mississippi delta town.

When World War II came about, Herbert received his commission as an officer and shipped out to the Azores, a group of islands in the Atlantic Ocean, between the United States and Europe. These islands were where he served during that global conflict.

At the war's end, he came home and married Henrietta Baum

of Oklahoma City. She was born in 1920. They had two daughters, Barbara and Regina, both of whom grew up in the Lexington Jewish community and were confirmed in Temple Beth El.

Herbert was an entrepreneur. After the war, he took up farming as a career, carrying on the traditional farming interest of his father, Isadore. He also, along with his mother, had a large number of rental homes for black residents in the Lexington area.

Later he looked at several other opportunities and then settled on what was known as "Black Creek Charcoal." He sold his SuperValu stock (formerly Lewis Grocer stock, prior to the merger with SuperValu) and borrowed additional funds to open a large plant in Lexington to manufacture charcoal for outside barbecuing. That was a popular way of family cooking, especially in the South and with more leisure time after the war.

He built it into a sizable business, selling his charcoal all over the United States. However, to compete with the more well-known brands, such as Dizzy Dean charcoal, and to achieve his large volume, he sold his new brand of charcoal products at such low prices that it became difficult to turn a profit. Then more hard times came about. With all the vast timberlands in the southern United States, where in most rural areas land was more plentiful than people, large paper companies such as International Paper, Georgia Pacific, and others were locating their paper mills and plants around the South, in the heart of the resources for their paper products — timber.

As the U.S. economy grew, these large paper companies had such demand for their products that the timber supply was stretched. Herbert found it very difficult to compete with the paper companies for timber as a resource for his charcoal, having to pay more for his raw material. To be more competitive than major brands and sell in volume, he had to keep his prices somewhat lower than his major competition. After years of struggle, the end result of what had started as a new venture with great potential was that the business shut down.

To get his charcoal business started and set up his charcoal plant, Herbert borrowed from many of his relatives in the Lexington area. When the business folded, he had no source of sustainable income, aside from his farming and rental interests, with which to pay back those loans. His farming interest had suffered because he had put so much emphasis on the charcoal plant.

Distraught as he was over these conditions, Herbert was not one to give up. During World War II, while serving in the Azores, he had heard many times on the radio the inspiring voice of Winston Churchill, who had said, "Never surrender, never give up, never ever give up"—and neither did Herbert.

Herbert could have done it the easy way by simply taking bankruptcy—and repaid his loans and interest due in only partial amounts, if any. But his pride, determination and ethical values would not let him take bankruptcy, which was anathema to his heritage and family tradition. He would never give up, never ever give up.

He went back into farming and, with whatever meager funds he had to work with, he went into the commercial and farmland real estate business. He got his real estate brokerage license and began selling farmland. One of his first real estate successes came when he heard of a large, prime piece of rich delta farmland that could be purchased at a price both reasonable and below its true value. Herbert, Celian and others purchased this land, and Herbert made a $40,000 commission from the purchasers as a finder's fee. Afterwards, he became enormously successful in the real estate business and, shortly thereafter, he repaid every penny he had borrowed, plus interest due. This was in light of his relatives' offer to forgive the debt he owed them, and showed the high standard of integrity that lived in the soul of Herbert Hyman.

So, after a tough break in the charcoal business—conquered by Herbert's tenacity, courage and success in real estate and his farming interest—he overcame adversity and was living a secure and comfortable life with his wife, Henrietta, with frequent visits from their daughters and participation in community life, including Rotary. That's when something happened that shocked the entire community of Lexington.

One warm Sunday afternoon in the month of January 1991, Herbert was just outside his carport cooking a roast on his barbecue grill (no doubt with Black Creek Charcoal). A young Caucasian couple stopped their car, came up to Herbert, and asked if they could fish in his pond, situated about 200 yards behind his home. Herbert was most congenial and consented.

About the time this couple was leaving, a young African-American walked up to Herbert. The couple heard Herbert say, "James, where is your car?" Then the couple drove off and heard no more. It was later discovered that James and his mother rented from Herbert one of his rental property homes.

This is apparently what transpired after the couple departed. James (who was known to his friends in the community as "Fruit Loop") did not need a car, since he planned to steal Herbert's car. But that's not all he had in mind.

He pulled a handgun and ordered Herbert to get into the car. James then drove to Herbert's office, a mile down the road toward the Lexington square. Once they got to the office, while Herbert was unlocking the door, a sheriff's car passed by. The attacker waved at the sheriff, who waved back and then, initially suspecting no foul play, drove on.

Once inside Herbert's real estate office, James ordered Herbert to sign a blank check and give it to him. Herbert did, but he tore it out from the back of the checkbook and signed it with a signature that was different from the way he usually signed his name.

Then James ordered Herbert back into the car, and proceeded to drive to a wooded area just behind the Lexington hospital. At that point, Herbert—apparently realizing he had nothing to lose—put up a fight, and was shot three times. There he lay, at the edge of the woods, with no one to help or come to his rescue. The shooter got into Herbert's car and attempted to drive off, but the wheels of the car had sunk into the soft ground which was wet from a recent rain. He then walked off, leaving the car, and Herbert was left alone to die.

I received a call early the next morning from Herbert's wife, Henrietta, who said Herbert was missing. The search had continued throughout most of the previous night, until after her call to me, when Herbert's body was found. Had the car been spotted during the search, Herbert's life might have been spared, but that is sheer supposition, and fate was not to intervene.

James was arrested the next day, when he attempted to cash the check Herbert had signed, under duress, in his office. He had entered a liquor store near the scene of the crime. The liquor store owner, having heard that Herbert was missing, was suspicious and refused to cash it. After the murderer left the liquor store, the owner promptly called the police. As James crossed the street to cash the check at a local Piggly Wiggly supermarket, the police picked him up.

For that premeditated and cold-blooded murder and robbery, James—the defendant, suspect and murderer—plea bargained. Due to the fact that Lexington has a large African-American populace, it was felt that the prosecution would not be able to secure a unanimous guilty verdict, especially needed for the death penalty, which led to the acceptance of the plea. He was sentenced to twenty years in prison. A number of times he came up for parole, for good behavior, but was denied each time. He was about twenty years old when he entered prison, and is now out—likely waiting for the chance to strike again. Anyone believing that this person could be rehabilitated should have second thoughts after reading my interview with the sheriff of Holmes County, in the latter part of this book.

It must be said that while alive, Herbert was a visionary, especially for Temple Beth El. He recommended to Phil Cohen that the temple buy the empty house next door to it and own it for future use. As the temple treasurer, Phil said there were not enough funds in the till to buy the building. Herbert, however, being a real estate broker, knew how the temple could benefit from such a purchase, above even simply owning the land. He advised Phil to go ahead and purchase the property for the temple, saying he would tear down the house and sell the fixtures and bricks, and it would pay for itself. Phil proceeded to make the real estate transaction. After all was said and done, the temple owned the lot next door and netted $12,000 in addition. Because of Herbert's wisdom, the lot was used for the first time as a parking area for the overflow crowd in attendance at the Centennial Celebration on December 3, 2005.

Herbert died in 1991 as a direct result of the robbery and subsequent shooting. Henrietta, an active choir member and leader of Temple Beth El Sisterhood, died in 1999.

Herbert A. Hyman (top)   Henrietta Baum Hyman (bottom)

Chapter 8

Henry Aaron Rosenthal
and Carrie Sontheimer Rosenthal
First President of Temple Beth El
Merchant and Builder

Henry Aaron Rosenthal, born in March 1852, married Carrie Sontheimer, born 1855, a daughter of Jacob and Mary Sontheimer. He and his younger brother, Joseph, born in 1866, joined together and began the firm of Rosenthal Brothers in Lexington.

H.A. Rosenthal built a large home two blocks north of the town square in Lexington, on the corner of Cedar and Carrolton Streets. His brother-in-law, Isadore Hyman, married to Rosa Sontheimer, built a home adjacent to and south of the Rosenthal home. In the 1890s, members of their families began to hold services at the Rosenthal home, which were conducted by H.A. Rosenthal. This was before Temple Beth El was dedicated in 1905.

In 1905, the firm of Rosenthal Bros. bought the block on the southeast section of the town square in Lexington. They contracted a construction company to put up a building for $10,000 that would accommodate four businesses. The Rosenthals operated one of these as a variety store, sold one to a Mr. Stigler, and rented the other two. In 1908, one of the two rental stores became vacant and Henry Rosenthal convinced Samuel Cohen to rent it.

When Temple Beth El was completed, H.A. Rosenthal conducted services until a rabbi became available. As mentioned earlier, the first rabbi to serve Temple Beth El on a regular basis was Rabbi Abraham Brill from Greenville. It was said that Mr. Rosenthal always occupied the front pew so that he might participate in the service. Most believed it was because, weighing over 300 pounds, he could not fit between the pews.

Also, such a seat would serve to keep him awake during the rabbi's sermons. There is a story that one day after services, another member of the congregation came up to the rabbi and told him how much he had enjoyed the sermon that evening. The rabbi was most gracious and thanked him. However, the rabbi said to the congregant, "I'm pleased that you found my sermon interesting tonight. However, I must ask you, why is it that halfway through most of my sermons, I notice that you have fallen asleep?" The congregant looked at the rabbi and said, "Rabbi, do you think I would go to sleep if I didn't trust you?!"

Henry and Carrie Rosenthal had one son, Jacob, who grew up in Lexington. He went to medical school at the University of Virginia, and chose to remain there to practice medicine.

Carrie Sontheimer Rosenthal died in 1904. Henry Rosenthal passed away in 1921, at the age of sixty-nine. His brother-in-law, Isadore Hyman, died two nights later.

H.A. Rosenthal's brother, Joseph (1866-1923), worked with H.A. in his businesses. Rosa Dreyfus Rosenthal (1863-1935) was a sister to H.A. Rosenthal.

Dr. Jacob "Jake" Rosenthal returned to Lexington briefly to settle his father's estate. The three store buildings were sold to Samuel J. Cohen, who had been renting one for some sixteen years. Dr. Rosenthal and his wife, Annette, had one son, Jack, who continues to reside in Virginia. Dr. Rosenthal died in 1959, and both he and Annette are buried in Beth El Cemetery.

Henry A. Rosenthal

Chapter 9

Abraham Herrman
and Celia Sontheimer Herrman
From Bavaria to Davisborough, Georgia,
and on to Lexington, Mississippi

Abraham Herrman, my great-grandfather, was born in Bavaria, Germany, in 1833. He lived across the river from his first cousin Isaac. Abraham lived on the German side of the river and Isaac lived on the Alsace-Lorraine side in France, which their respective passports reflected. In 1850, when Abraham was seventeen, he and Isaac came to America together to live with relatives in Davisborough, Georgia. Abraham became a peddler and traveled through Mississippi selling his wares. It was there, when he was in the Lexington area, that he met his future wife, Celia Sontheimer, born in 1847. They married and settled in Davisborough, where they had three daughters, Julia, Claudia and Daisy; and four sons, Morris, Isadore, Sam and Jake.

When Abraham noticed what a good life the Jewish people had in Lexington, how prosperous they were becoming, and how well accepted they had been in the overall community, he and his family packed up and all moved to Lexington.

It was there that Julia met and married Morris Lewis, Sr., of Lexington. Sam married Flora Levy of Vicksburg, Morris married Jessie Waterman of Dumas, Arkansas, and Isadore married Mildred Reichburg (former home unknown). Jake died at an early age. Daisy married Aaron Jacobson and Claudia married Isadore Hyman, after his second wife, Rosa Sontheimer, died. All settled with their spouses in Lexington, as did the entire Herrman family.

Abraham continued to peddle his wares. In his later years, Abraham resided with Julia and Morris Lewis. He died in 1924, having lived to the ripe old age of ninety-one. Celia predeceased him in 1912, at the age of sixty-five.

Abraham Herrman

Chapter 10

Morris Lewis, Sr., and Julia Herrman Lewis
A Horatio Alger Story of Success

Morris Lewis, Sr., was born on July 29, 1873, in a small Polish village to Jacob and Emily "Emma" Goldstein Lewis. Jacob's father was Avrum Hirsh Lewis. His mother was Sarah Lewis. Morris and Myer's parents knew that their two sons were exceedingly bright youngsters, especially when it came to mathematics. Yet in their hearts, they believed that their sons' potential would be wasted if they remained in Poland, due to centuries of anti-Semitism and pogroms that were rampant in their country. They also had heard from relatives and others living in America the glowing reports of the great opportunities that existed in "the land of plenty."

So, in 1886, when Morris was thirteen and Myer was ten, their parents arranged for them to board a steamship bound for New York, and sent them with their blessings to live with relatives in the country of promise. Morris had the responsibility of looking after his younger brother during the long and tedious voyage to America.

Imagine the feelings of joy and wonder, and some degree of apprehension, that filled these two young immigrant boys as they sailed into New York harbor, past the Statue of Liberty on their way to Ellis Island. If "Miss Liberty" could have spoken, she surely would have smiled and said, "Welcome, my dears, to the Land of the Free and the Home of the Brave." At that point in their lives, neither Morris nor Myer could envision the heights of success they would each reach in their eventual home state of Mississippi and throughout the entire mid-South.

Morris Lewis' first job was in New York as an office boy for a wholesale establishment. He received his only formal education in night school during his first four years in the new land. He learned the English language as a shoeshine boy in New York City. Later, in 1890, at the age of seventeen, he was sent to live with other relatives in the Mississippi delta town with the biblical name of Sidon. With his acumen for numbers, it was soon realized that he could be of immense help by clerking and keeping the books for the mercantile store owned by his Mississippi relatives. For this work he was paid $25.00 per month. Myer was sent to live with relatives in Houston, Texas.

Morris was a hard worker. Since there was very little to spend his money on in Sidon, he managed to save several years of earnings, which eventually totaled five hundred dollars. That's when he began to have visions of bigger and better things to come.

In 1895, when the citizens of Lexington had only recently started recovering from the ravages of the times and the Civil War, Morris selected that city, the county seat, as the best site in which to locate and open a business. He left Sidon and moved to Lexington with the $500.00 he had managed to save. Once there, he met and became friends with Sam Herrman, his future brother-in-law, who had recently moved to that Mississippi hill town from Davisborough, Georgia.

The two formed a partnership and pooled their funds to buy a small stock of goods and began what eventually grew into the Lewis Grocer Company, a wholesale food distributor, and later Sunflower Food Stores, a regional supermarket chain. That business was one of the South's largest privately owned wholesale and retail food concerns. In 1965, Lewis merged with SuperValu, a New York Stock Exchange company. Today it is one of the largest wholesale and retail food distributors in America.

It was in Lexington where Morris met and married Sam's sister, Julia Herrman, born in 1873 in Davisborough, Georgia. She and Sam were from one of Mississippi's pioneer families. The year was 1899. Julia was a relative of the Sontheimers and Rosenthals. As there was no synagogue in Lexington at that time, the marriage was performed by Rabbi Abraham Brill in the Methodist Church. This demonstrated the close relationship between the Jewish and Christian communities. It also showed the need for a Jewish place of worship in Lexington, a synagogue.

As mentioned in Chapter 3, in 1904, Morris Lewis, Sr., and his brother-in-law, Sam Herrman, purchased land on Spring Street, a few blocks off the square east of town, for a temple. They donated it to the newly formed official congregation, to be known thereafter as Temple Beth El. The synagogue was dedicated in November 1905.

The year before, the two of them also purchased the land for Beth El Cemetery and donated it to the temple.

By 1900, the business had grown to where Morris Lewis felt the need to incorporate as the Lewis-Herrman Company. In 1905, he founded the Merchants and Farmers Bank and Trust Company.

It was 1912 when Morris Lewis, Sr., began expanding his business and using traveling men for contacts and salesmen. In those days, the company provided horses and buggies for its sales force, as the business plan was for continued expansion. It also made its deliveries in mule-driven wagons. Lewis modernized in 1916 with its first purchase of an automobile, a Model T Ford, valued at $350, about the same price of a healthy mule.

In 1915, the Lewis-Herrman Company merged with the Barrett Grocer Company, owned by William Oliver Barrett, a good friend of Morris Lewis. It was renamed the Barrett-Lewis Grocer Company. A few years later, in 1916, the Barrett-Lewis Company merged with the Gwin Company to become the Gwin-Lewis Grocer Co., and Morris Lewis became president. In 1922, the company was renamed the Lewis Grocer Company, with its headquarters in Lexington.

During the early days of the Lewis wholesale operation, Morris Lewis made the only business decision he lived to regret. The company held the franchise rights to both Coca-Cola and a private-label soda pop. When Coca-Cola pressured Lewis to drop the competing brand, as a conflict, he instead dropped the Coke franchise. In today's dollars, it literally cost the company many millions in lost sales and profits.

The company continued to expand when, in 1924, it bought a company in the nearby town of Durant, Mississippi, and opened a warehouse there.

In 1927, Leroy Paris, Morris Lewis' "adopted son" became vice president and general manager of the Durant operation. However, he made his permanent residence in Lexington which was only thirteen miles from Durant.

Then came another expansion. The Mississippi Delta offered a big opportunity in food, supplies, fertilizer and cotton poison for boll weevils, without which the important cotton crops would have been devastated. This included taking advantage of the custom of "furnishing," where plantation owners in the fertile region would "furnish" food and clothing each year to their tenant farmers. In turn, the tenant farmers would pay back the landowners after the harvest, out of their share of the earnings from what they produced.

Morris Lewis held a $5,000 mortgage on a building in Indianola. When the mortgagee disappeared and abandoned his debt, Lewis took over the building and opened an operation in the heart of the Mississippi Delta. This was in 1934, during the middle of the Depression years, but the company expanded boldly again with another wholesale warehouse operation.

Two years later, Morris Lewis, Jr., was named president of the company and Celian Lewis, his brother, was named executive vice president. These two brothers continued to operate it until World War II when they departed for military service.

That's when Morris Lewis, Sr., took up part-time residence in Indianola, sixty miles from Lexington, while Morris Herrman, another brother-in-law, managed the Lexington operation.

After World War II when Morris, Jr., and Celian returned, the Lewis Grocer Company expanded into the retail food business known as Sunflower Food Stores. It grew into a regional supermarket chain of corporate and franchised stores, with the first store opening in Philadelphia, Mississippi, in 1948.

To support the fast-growing supermarket chain and its other wholesale customers, the company opened a new multimillion-dollar state-of-the-art warehouse in Indianola in 1957.

The company eventually had twenty-seven corporate stores and fifty-eight franchised stores, totaling eighty-five Sunflower Food Stores. Following the Lewis merger with SuperValu in 1965, years later most of the retail stores in the former Lewis organization began to operate under the name of SuperValu.

Morris and Julia Lewis had three children; Fay Emily Lewis, Morris Lewis, Jr., and Celian Herrman Lewis. Their beautiful antebellum home, which they moved into in 1919, was a showplace for all to behold. It was named Faymorcele, after their three children. The home, with its stately white columns, continues to sit majestically on a large hill, approached from a long, winding driveway lined with large cedars and oaks. As beautiful as Faymorcele and its grounds were when it was purchased in the early 1900s, it is unfortunate that the present owner, until recently, had let it slide into a state of disrepair.

Morris Lewis, Sr., was known in Lexington and its area of Mississippi as the most active, progressive and successful man in that portion of the state. It was evident from the first that he was destined for big things. His vision went beyond the mere selling of goods to those who happened to come to Lexington to buy and sell cotton. He first went after more cotton, and hence more customers. The city was getting only five thousand bales of cotton yearly. He made connections with leading cotton firms of this country and Europe, by which he was able to get the maximum price for cotton. It was not long before Lexington was recognized as one of the best cotton markets in the state. Cotton receipts quickly grew to be in excess of twenty thousand bales.

In quick succession, he organized a compress, an oil mill and an ice factory, which put life into the city. He also organized the electric light plant and the building of the waterworks and sewer system for the city of Lexington, by negotiating for the sale of bonds and buying himself what other investors were not eager to purchase.

After organizing the Merchants and Farmers Bank and Trust Company during the Depression when this bank as well as most all others suffered, he reorganized the bank as the Holmes County Bank & Trust Company. It was the largest bank in Holmes County. During the Depression, Morris Lewis, Sr., helped many a business in financial trouble by not foreclosing, risking his own funds to spare depositors from bankruptcy. When hard times hit Mississippi in the early 1930s, Morris Lewis, Sr., risked everything he had to help his customers through the very difficult times. He mortgaged his company, his bank stock, and even his family mansion to protect depositors in his bank and to assist his customers. Because several of the customers were owners of large farm commissaries, many of these accounts went uncollected during the Depression. Eventually, the Lewis family lost the grocery company to mortgage foreclosures. Growth of the business had halted and the Lewis family had temporarily lost control of the company.

He told his children, "If things don't work out for the best, I may not have much in material wealth to leave you, but I will leave you with the greatest wealth one can own, and that is a good name."

When better times came, slowly the Lewis family was ready to rebuild with the limited resources that remained. The family repurchased control of the company and planned their expansion.

That's when they took over the old Gilmer warehouse in Indianola and began to expand the business throughout the entire Delta region.

Although Morris Lewis, Sr., was well-known for his ability to organize, finance and operate successfully, he was equally well-known for his contributions to society and the development of his community, and for charitable deeds to people from every walk of life and of every race and creed. He never knew of any need for charity that he did not give generously of his time, money and advice. It was an established fact that when someone was in trouble and needed assistance—black or white—all that was necessary was to let Morris Lewis, Sr., know of the need. He would promptly furnish the impetus that secured the help needed, including not only financial aid, but friendly counsel and advice. He also provided employment and assistance to help the ones that were in need. There are countless people who came under his guidance that have proven worthy of the trouble and time he gave; and many, without his financial help, would not have attained their useful place in society.

Virtually alone, he established the first community hospital in Holmes County and served as its first chairman of the board. He helped organize the Lexington Country Club and was responsible for raising the funds to build its clubhouse. He was responsible for organizing the first Lexington High School band and for buying the uniforms. He was president of Temple Beth El and president of his Rotary club, being one of its founders in 1925.

Considering all this, he never lost touch with the common man, receiving advice and ideas from any person in his organization. He always gave credit where credit was due.

Last, but far from least, was his interest in his religion, as demonstrated by he and his former partner and brother-in-law, Sam Herrman's, donation of the land where now stands Temple Beth El, "The House of David in the Land of Jesus," now over one hundred years old. Largely through Morris Lewis' support, as its third president, and always his financial contributions and influence, Temple Beth El has taken its place among the other honored religious groups of the city of Lexington and Holmes County.

Morris and Myer's father, Jacob, remarried after the death of their mother, Emma. He moved to New York with his second wife, Rosa, who was from Germany, and two of their children who had been born in Europe. They eventually had six daughters and one son. A photo is shown in this book, taken at a Seder in Brooklyn, New York, on April 8, 1925. In it is Jacob, leading the service, his wife Rosa, their daughters, son and extended family. Others at the Seder were Morris and Julia Lewis and Myer Lewis, who were visiting for Passover that year. They appear in the picture. This was Jacob's last Seder as he died in May of that same year.

In 1957, Morris Lewis, Sr., died at the age of eighty-four as a result of his second major automobile accident. The first had killed his beloved wife, Julia, many years before, in 1935. He never remarried. At the time of his death, he was continuing to serve as chairman of the board of the Lewis Grocer Company and Sunflower Food Stores.

Morris Lewis, Sr. (top)   Julia Herrman Lewis (bottom)

Faymorcele

Chapter 11

Morris Lewis, Jr., and Freda Lantor Lewis
The Saga of Two Sons
A Tribute to the Spirit of Free Enterprise
A Brilliant Business Mind

Just as Morris Lewis, Sr., and his brother, Myer Lewis, became highly successful, each in his own way, Morris Lewis, Jr., and his younger brother, Celian, did likewise.

Morris Lewis, Jr., born in 1910, grew up in Lexington and graduated from the Lexington schools. He was a member of the high school band and football team. During half time he would grab his saxophone and play in the band until it was time to start the game again. He was also confirmed in Temple Beth El.

A few years after graduating from Wharton Business School at the University of Pennsylvania, Morris succeeded his father, Morris Lewis, Sr., as president and chief executive officer of the Lewis Grocer Company. He became a leader in Indianola, state and national affairs. During World War II he served as a major in the Pacific in charge of the Post Exchange in Hawaii.

Upon returning home to Mississippi, he became president of the National Wholesale Grocers Association, chairman of the state Delta Council and the Mississippi Economic Council (the state's chamber of commerce), a member of the school board, a board member of his synagogue, a member of the board of trustees of Millsaps College and the Hebrew Union College, and a member of the food advisory committee to the Federal Cost of Living Council during the Nixon administration. He was a director of the Supermarket Institute, now known as the National Food Marketing Institute. He also chaired the statewide committee for the reorganization of public education in the 1950s, which spearheaded the state's massive public school reorganization and construction program of that era. He was president of his Rotary club. He and his wife, Freda Lantor Lewis, were magnanimous contributors to schools and libraries, following in the footsteps of his father in civic affairs, charitable contributions and business.

Morris also became chairman of the board of SuperValu, Inc., after its merger with the Lewis Grocer Company and Sunflower Food Stores. Because of his love for Mississippi, and the fact that Indianola had a 7,000-foot runway leftover from jet training during World War II, each week he flew in a private company jet to SuperValu headquarters in Hopkins, Minnesota, a suburb of Minneapolis. His devoted Freda would be by his side in Minneapolis, and together they would fly home to Mississippi each weekend. That's when SuperValu's profits began to rise, resulting in greater recognition on Wall Street.

Morris Lewis, Jr., also received the Herbert Hoover award in 1973, presented to only twenty-three persons at the time, since being authorized by former President Hoover. It was awarded to Morris for "outstanding achievement in the humanistic approach to distinguished service." The honor was given in recognition of his achievement in the area of food distribution, a matter that greatly interested Hoover.

Morris and Freda had two children. Morris Lewis, III, resides in Atlanta with his wife, Harriett, and Julia resides in Houston, Texas. Morris, Jr., died at the age of eighty-four in 1994. Freda had predeceased him one year earlier, in 1993.

Morris Lewis, Jr.

Chapter 12

Celian Herrman Lewis
and Norma Thompson Lewis
The Saga of Two Sons
A Tribute to the Spirit of Free Enterprise
Respected Business Executive

Like his brother, Morris, and his sister, Fay Lewis Berman, Celian also was born in Lexington. The year was 1914. He grew up there, attending all grades of school. In high school he was lead trumpet in the Lexington band. Celian achieved high school fame, along with sixteen other members of the high school football team, which was the first—and only one of two—that ever went undefeated. He was a star lineman on that special team. He was confirmed at Temple Beth El, and later attended Tulane University in New Orleans. During the Depression, with his parent's permission, he left Tulane after two years of study to join Morris in the newly opened Lewis Grocer Company warehouse in Indianola, Mississippi.

Afterwards, at the beginning of World War II, Celian Herrman Lewis volunteered and joined the United States Army. He served as a major in the Pacific Theater, as the commanding supply officer in New Guinea. Later he was transferred to American headquarters in Sydney, Australia, where he was the Director of Food Distribution to the army throughout the South Pacific.

Once the war was over, he returned to Indianola to help manage the business. Some years later, upon Morris Lewis, Jr.'s, promotion to chairman of SuperValu, Celian succeeded his brother as president of the Lewis Grocer Company and Sunflower Food Stores. He was also a member of the board of directors of SuperValu. The company experienced some of its best and most profitable years under his astute guidance and leadership.

After the horrific Hurricane Camille devastated the Mississippi Gulf Coast in 1969, Celian was appointed by the governor to oversee all shipments and distribution of food and related products to victims of the storm. Due to his business expertise and past success, had Celian not been ninety years of age when Hurricane Katrina came ashore in 2005, he most likely would have been called upon once again by state and federal officials to take over distribution of food and supplies to the damaged area. FEMA could well have used a man of Celian Lewis' capabilities and expertise in their relief efforts, and so could have the people of Mississippi.

Celian and his lovely wife, Norma Thompson Lewis, whom he met in Australia during WWII, reside in Destin, Florida. Celian continues to demonstrate much concern for the needy in their community. Weekly, he furnishes and, with his driver, delivers food to those in need in the Florida Panhandle. Celian also has been president of his city's chamber of commerce and Rotary Club.

Celian is a good storyteller with a great sense of humor, and has an appropriate and tasteful anecdote for most every occasion. He has always been well liked and highly respected in his communities of Lexington, Indianola and Destin, and among his peers within the military and the world of commerce.

Celian and Norma have three children; Karen in Atlanta, Richard, who owns the famous Bones restaurant in Atlanta, and Bill, who resides in Nashville and is in the real estate business. Celian continues to be a member of Temple Beth El, and annually gives generous financial support to that congregation.

A Capsule Summary of Morris Lewis, Sr., and Sons

Morris Lewis, Sr., and his two sons, Morris Lewis, Jr., and Celian Herrman Lewis, made as significant a contribution to free enterprise, the entrepreneurial spirit and philanthropy as any businessmen in the history of Mississippi.

Celian Herrman Lewis

1928 Lexington Boys Band

LEXINGTON HIGH SCHOOL UNDEFEATED FOOTBALL TEAM 1932

Front row: Cellan Lewis, Tackle, Fincher Word, Halfback, Herbert Hyman, Guard (Alternate Captain), Ben Beall III, Center, Lowery Steele, End; Second Row: L. R. (Jelly) Thompson, Coach, J. T. Buck, Guard, R. P. Ellis, Halfback, Bill Gulledge, Guard, Clower Johnson, Halfback, Marvin Shanks, Tackle, Sidney Henley, End; Third Row: Philip McRae, Tackle, Hiriam Wilks, halfback, William Moses, Tackle, Herman Flowers, Quarterback, Harold Hammett, End (Captain), Raiford Herbert, Halfback and William Hester, Fullback. (Not in picture V. K. Smith, Assistant Coach)

Elementary: A.-Cecil Herrman, B.-Herbert Hyman, C. -Celian Lewis

High School Grads: A.-Herbert Hyman, B. -Cecil Herrman C. -Celian Lewis

Peabody Roof after WWll: L to R Herbert Hyman, Celian Lewis, Cecil Herrman

Chapter 13

Myer A. Lewis and Viola Lichenstein Lewis, and Eva Hart Lewis
A Visionary in Banking

Myer A. Lewis was born in Poland to Jacob and Emma Lewis on December 10, 1876. Myer Lewis came over to the United States on the ship with his older brother, Morris Lewis, as young boys intrepidly traveling alone from their former home in Poland.

After landing in New York, Myer was later sent to live with relatives in Houston, Texas. As the years passed and Morris found such success in the Lexington community, Myer joined him for a brief few years, where he traveled as a key salesman for the Lewis Grocer Company, organized earlier by his brother.

It was during that time period in Lexington when Myer met and married his first wife, Viola Lichenstein Lewis. As were his brother, Morris, and sister-in-law, Julia Lewis, Myer and Viola were among the organizers and founders of Temple Beth El, where they were members.

Unfortunately, Viola died at an early age in 1905, the same year Temple Beth El opened. A beautiful stained glass window in the temple was dedicated by Myer in her memory.

Afterwards, Myer moved to Jackson, Mississippi, and became a self-educated architect and engineer. It was there that he met and married Eva Hart of Jackson. They had three children; M.A. Lewis, Jr., Elaine, and John Hart. Their entire family was highly respected as citizens of both the Jewish and overall Jackson community.

Myer was one of the three founders of Deposit Guaranty Bank in Jackson and a major stockholder of that financial institution. The bank later became known as Am South, and recently merged with Regions Bank, under which name it will eventually operate.

Myer passed away at the age of seventy-six on July 26, 1956, and left behind a fine legacy as a loving father, a man of great integrity, and banking success.

1925 NY Seder, Head of table, Jacob Lewis. Standing 2nd from right Morris Lewis, Sr. 3rd from right Myer A. Lewis, far right seated Julia Herrman Lewis

Chapter 14

Joseph Emile Berman and Fay Lewis Berman
A Man for the Ages

In his earlier life as an attorney in Atlanta, Georgia, they called him "Honest Joe." As a member of the Atlanta City Council and Chairman of the Aviation Committee, he literally brought aviation to Atlanta.

Joe Berman's life began in the small Georgia town of Camilla, south of Atlanta, where he was born in 1900. He was the son of Israel and Sarah Berman. Joe would eventually be one of nine children, with three brothers and five sisters; Abe, Ike, Max, Fannie, Freda, Rae, Ada and Sophie.

Some sixty-six years later, while residing in Lexington, Joe Berman was writing his second novel, entitled *Return To The Beginning*, which he was never able to complete. A year later, he met a tragic death as a passenger on a commercial airliner, Piedmont Airlines. It collided with a private plane on takeoff over Hendersonville, North Carolina, on July 19, 1967, at 12:03 p.m. At that time, Joe was a healthy, vibrant and most gregarious individual of sixty-seven years of age. He made a lasting impression in the minds of all who ever knew him.

That particular flight was a trip he had earned to celebrate a banner year of production as a food broker representing the Stokely Van Camp Company, a line of quality canned fruits and vegetables. He was on his way from Lexington to the Greenbrier Resort in White Sulphur Springs, West Virginia, for the celebration and to receive an award. Both his journey and his life were, suddenly and without warning, cut far too short.

But this Lexingtonian, Joe Berman, was far more than a food broker. Here's the fascinating story of his beginning and his life as an attorney, politician, food broker, army colonel, author, humanitarian and vivacious human being. *Return To The Beginning*, the title to his unfinished novel, refers to where he began and ended his life's remarkable career, in Atlanta, Georgia. It is ironically sad and coincidental that Atlanta was where the last flight of his life connected.

As Joe Berman departed Jackson, Mississippi early on the morning of July 19, 1967, he was in excellent spirits. The night before, he had visited with his son, daughter-in-law and three grandchildren; Bob, Sondy, Marjie, Debbie and Sheri. Later that evening, he stayed with his brother, Dr. Max Berman, and his wife, Flo. As he boarded the Delta flight to Atlanta, where he would take the fatal Piedmont flight, he was truly relaxed and calm, looking forward to the celebration and awards banquet he was to attend. He had previously flown hundreds of thousands of air miles with no problems whatsoever, as he had related to a nervous friend during a somewhat rough flight earlier that year. Little did he dream that the title of the novel he was writing would truly reflect the beginning and end of what had been a wholesome and adventurous life and career.

The unfinished book was about his trip to the Holy Land in 1964. After his return from that trip, he had presented many lectures and slide presentations of his experiences in the land of his forefathers and his own parents. That's how he came to entitle it *Return To The Beginning.* I have kept the original copy of his unfinished manuscript since the tragic day of his death. It begins with such a vivid description of his beginning and how his parents met and eventually settled in Camilla, Georgia, that I felt it interesting enough to share with the readers of this book. In another way, it tells a colorful history of his heritage; one that fate never allowed him to personally relate. Here is an excerpt from his story taken from the first few pages of his unfinished nonfiction work:

Return To The Beginning

By Joseph Emile Berman

"The desire for a journey to the Holy Land began at my mother's knee. My parents had lived in many countries, before they finally came to residence in Camilla, Georgia. Eventually there were twelve children, six boys and six girls. Three died in infancy. My mother and father both would tell us wondrous tales of their eventful past. So, naturally, a spirit of adventure developed within me. I resolved someday I would endeavor to travel over the same roads to the same countries and see the same wondrous sights that their eyes had beheld.

The beginning for my mother, Sarah Dora Lubin and my father, Israel Berman, arose when they both joined, as immigrants in Poland, a colony that was organized by my father's uncle. At that time, Queen Victoria ruled over England. They were to establish a colony in South Africa under the rule of England. My mother was then only fifteen years old and my father was seventeen years old. For a while, the colony in South Africa flourished with subsistence and material and aid received from the British government. It was a Jewish settlement. Some people began to try to proselyte or convert this Jewish colony to the Christian faith. Resistance developed against helping the colonists as a Jewish colony. Dissension developed and my great-uncle was accused of betraying his fellow-Jews. He was so depressed and humiliated that he committed suicide. Immediately the colony began to break up. Although my mother and father had not known each other until they both joined his colonial expedition, they had begun to be attracted to each other and had fallen in love. My father suggested to my mother that they go to Nicosia, Cyprus, and there get married. So, they sailed with some of the other colonists to Cyprus and there they were married. Other colonists went to other countries after the failure of the expedition. After living awhile in Cyprus, my father and mother moved to Egypt. They lived awhile in Alexandria, and for some time in Cairo, Egypt. My father worked as a brick-mason, going back to the tasks at which his ancestors had slaved centuries ago. He was still ambitious and also loved to travel. So, they went from Egypt to Turkey. My mother told many interesting stories of how she had become a close friend of one of the sultan's wives. She would visit her often in the harem and there they would knit, embroider and crochet beautiful things. My mother brought this talent with her to Camilla where she also made many beautiful things for our home.

My parents left Turkey and moved to Paris. They were joined there by my mother's brother, Uncle Ben Lubin. They lived in a small hotel in Paris that had several floors with stairways leading to the upper floors. Unfortunately, my uncle who was a young man tried to slide down the banisters one day and fell and injured his back so severely that he was partly hunch-backed the rest of his life. After a few years, my parents moved to England, where my father opened a furniture store in London.

Although my father was fairly successful in the furniture business in London, again the spirit of adventure arose in him and he developed a desire to immigrate to America, the land of opportunity, where the streets were "paved with gold."

He made final arrangements (in about 1891) and left the furniture store to be operated by my mother and their three children with whom they had been blessed; two girls and a boy. Two children had previously died in infancy.

My father reached America and bought some merchandise and a pack and began to peddle in the South, in the states of Tennessee, Alabama and Georgia.

My mother ran the store in London patiently and successfully. Finally, after three years, she felt that my father had surely by this time been able to establish himself so that she could take the three children and join him in America. She sold the furniture store, took passage on a ship as steerage passengers. After a long, tiresome voyage, they finally reached Ellis Island, New York, where they were processed as immigrants. They had an immigrant service aid at Ellis Island, which finally located my father at Camilla, Georgia and advised him that his wife and three children had arrived in America. My father had not established a permanent residence at this time. When he received the news of the arrival of his family, he decided that he would make his home in Camilla, and there open a business. He sent for his wife and three children and they joined him in Camilla, where seven other children, including myself, were born. One other child died in infancy (totaling three in all), so this left nine children, five girls and four boys.

I was born in 1900 and travel was not easy in my youthful years. There were only a few automobiles at that time. They were not too fast. Thirty miles an hour was considered top speed, so most travel was done then by horse and buggy or horseback. It was impossible to travel thirty or forty miles for Sunday school by horse and buggy. Therefore, in my younger years, I did not have the privilege of attending a Sunday school of my faith.

My father was a very devout Jew. Camilla was a small, southern town and there was no synagogue or temple where Jews could worship. In my high school years, we had a Studebaker car and we would sometimes go to the synagogue at Thomasville, Georgia, which was the orthodox house of worship and at other times we would go to Albany, Georgia, where there was a Jewish temple or a reform house of worship.

I can still vision my father praying in the morning and at night with his tallish (prayer shawl). This is a shawl-like garment made of silk or wool with black or blue stripes at the end and with fringes at each of the four corners. The Talmud explains that blue resembles the sea and the sky; the sky resembles the throne of glory. Thus, looking at the blue in the fringe is a reminder of God, and fulfilling the commandments in Numbers, 15th chapter, 37th verse.

As a matter of fact, I attended the youth groups of the different Protestant churches more than I was able to attend one of my own faith. Although I was and am faithful to the tenets of my religion, I have been broadminded and tolerant all my life and learned early the principles in the second chapter of Malachi, verse 10, as follows:

> "Have we not all one faith;
> Hath not one God created us;
> Why do we deal treacherously
> Every man against his brother...?"

Religious prejudice has always been like anathema to me, so I have always numbered my friends and close companions from among all faiths. I also am a firm believer in religious tolerance.

All of my family grew up as reform Jews and are members of a Jewish temple."

So began Joseph Emile Berman in the first few pages of his book *Return To The Beginning*, a book which, because of a tragic event, he was never able to complete.

While alone in London with her three children one evening, Joe's mother, Sarah, was on the second floor of their home, which was over their furniture store. It was a very warm and humid night, with no air conditioning or even electric fans in those days. Therefore, the windows were all raised to the top, providing easy entrance for anyone wanting to burglarize the home. While rocking one of her children to sleep, she was shocked to notice a man's boot protruding from under the bed. Keeping her "Berman cool" and using her kepalah ("head" in Yiddish), she began singing a lullaby in Yiddish. However, the words of the lullaby were not about "rock a bye baby," but instead a plea for help. The stranger under the bed did not know Yiddish, so he was unaware of her sense of peril and her call for someone to come save them. She began to sing quietly until her voice and lullaby of distress rang out through the open window. Passersby heard her cry for help and came immediately to her rescue, dragging the potential assailant and burglar out from under the bed, down the public stairway and on to the local jail.

Joe graduated from the University of Georgia Law School in 1921, as a key member of the debate team. He then moved to Atlanta to begin his practice of law. Recognizing his potential, he was asked to join and become a partner in the prestigious law firm of Walter Sims, former mayor of Atlanta.

Early in his legal career in Atlanta, his college roommate and fraternity brother, Leroy Paris, had invited Joe to be in his wedding in Lexington, Mississippi, when Leroy married Irma Herrman. At that wedding, Joe met his future bride, Fay Emily Lewis, born in Lexington in 1909, the daughter of Morris Lewis, Sr. Shortly after, on July 16, 1929, they were married at Faymorcele, the beautiful antebellum mansion of Morris and Julia Lewis, in Lexington. The wedding took place on the expansive veranda, with hundreds of guests seated on the large front lawn, which was shaded by huge oak trees interlaced with tall cedars and magnolias. Fay and Joe then settled in Atlanta.

Joe made friends easily. One of his mottos was "always leave them laughing when you say goodbye." Another was "you can catch more flies with honey than with vinegar." He always believed in treating people, regardless of their status in life, with dignity—for he knew well that when you take away another person's dignity, they have nothing left. Holding true to that feeling, he never made fun of others, publicly or privately, at their expense.

In Eli Evans' book *The Lonely Days Were Sundays,* he described the shock that went throughout the Jewish community of Georgia and the South when a well-to-do German-Jewish assimilated man, Leo Frank, was hanged in 1915 by an anti-Semitic mob. This shameful event occurred after Leo Frank had been pardoned by the governor for a charge of the murder of a young girl, which he did not commit. Eli Evans wrote that after the incident "southern Jews just learned to keep a low profile and hope for the best. The Ku Klux Klan was always there. The bigotry was there and it didn't take much to set it off." He continued that southern Jews, in that time, were "conditioned by an instinctive wariness in a land where cross burnings were frequent reminders that they were hated too." Eli Evans also referred to that trepidation on the part of Jews of the South in his book *The Provincials*, when he wrote about the now-permanent exhibit in Atlanta, housed in the Breman Jewish Heritage Museum of the Selig Center. The exhibit, opened in 1994, is entitled *Creating Community: The Jews of Atlanta from 1865 to the Present*. While writing of his admiration of today's Jews of Atlanta, he also wrote the following: "Jews in the south were conditioned to keeping a low profile, especially in Atlanta, which had experienced the Leo Frank lynching in 1915 and the Temple bombing in 1958."

That simply wasn't the way it was with Joe Berman in his earlier days in Atlanta or afterwards, or the way it was in Lexington, Mississippi, where the relatively large Jewish community—individually and as a whole—were well accepted, respected and appreciated. This held true from the very beginning of its existence in the early 1800s through the current time period.

In Evans' meticulous study and writings of Southern Jewry, he definitely missed the history of Joe Berman of Atlanta, which has been displayed in the Atlanta Breman Museum, as well as his later life in Lexington. He also overlooked the remarkable history of the Jewish community of Lexington, Mississippi.

Just over a decade after the Leo Frank incident in his native Georgia, before Joe Berman became a Lexingtonian, his intrepid spirit didn't let that tragic event put any fear into him. At the urging of his law partner, former Atlanta mayor Walter Sims, he ran for a seat on the Atlanta City Council in the fourth ward. Walter Sims had served two terms as mayor of Atlanta and as a state senator. This was during the third and fourth decades of the twentieth century. It was during that time that Gutzon Borglum was carving statues on Stone Mountain. It was the beginning of air travel on commercial planes, a historic event that would some day play a major part in both the life and death of Joe Berman. The fourth ward of Atlanta at that time had a population of about 25,000. Many of Joe's friends asked him not to run, as they were afraid it would create a religious issue. Joe Berman felt he had the right to run, so he went ahead with his plans.

His first speech was at a schoolhouse on North Avenue. His opponent, a Mr. Hollingsworth, got up and said, "The only issue in this race is a Jew running against a Protestant." Joe stood up and replied, "I don't care what religion people follow, but I promise that I will abide by the wishes of the majority." About four o'clock on the eve of the election, his opponent congratulated him. Flushed with victory, Joe decided to go home and wait for the announcement. It came about eight o'clock that evening. He had been beaten by 144 votes. He had been bitterly fought by the Ku Klux Klan under Dr. Samuel Green, the grand dragon and imperial wizard. Joe later found out that the city clerk, Walter Taylor (who was later indicted for graft and corruption), had issued about 200 certificates for people who didn't even live in the ward, so they could vote for Joe's opponent. Those same votes were held out until between the hours of six and seven p.m., the last hour of voting. They had lulled Joe Berman into a false sense of security.

Joe decided that he would be ready the next time. Two years later he ran again, and this time he was prepared. He found 200 people who were positively going to vote for him and asked them to wait until about 5:30 p.m., and he would send a car to pick them up. He hired about ten automobiles and had them ready. When the zero hour came, they rounded up these friends of Joe's and brought them to the polls to vote. There were three in the race: Mr. Hollingsworth, the victor in the first election; Fred Stinchcomb, a lawyer; and Joe Berman.

Mr. Hollingsworth and Joe tied and Stinchcomb came in a poor third. They had a run-off two weeks later. For that, Joe got 300 friends lined up, and Stinchcomb threw his support to Joe as a fellow lawyer. Joe actually won by a single vote. His opponent did not contest the election. Dr. Samuel Green, the imperial wizard of the Klan who had been fighting Joe all along, called Joe over to his office and advised him that they were not going to fight him any more. After that, Joe was reelected twice more without opposition. During his fourth term, he resigned to move to Lexington, at the request of relatives in Mississippi. The move was due to the death of Fay's mother and severe injuries to her father as a result of an automobile accident.

Throughout Joe's service on the city council of Atlanta, he was known for his integrity and proactive stance in promoting many new projects to aid his constituents and the city. During his six years on the city council there were numerous headlines and articles in the

Atlanta Constitution and *Atlanta Journal* publicizing those efforts. Among them were the following:

"Berman proposes that city make its own electricity"

"City hall sale urged by Berman—Councilman Berman will recommend disposal of not less than $750,000 out right sale of the present city hall for not less than $750,000 and utilization of proceeds to the following purposes, will be advocated on the floor of city council May 6 by councilman Joe Berman: he announced yesterday:

1. One-half the fund to construction and equipment of a central police and fire department in one building.
2. One-fourth for furnishing and equipping the new city hall now nearing completion.
3. Remaining one-fourth for employment of additional Atlanta policemen and firemen and better equipping the two departments."

"Berman plans fight for clean food law"

"Berman urges gas rate delay"

"Leading food men support Berman's health bill plan"

"New state-wide sales tax and local tax rate increase advocated by Joseph Berman—abolition of ad valorem tax part of plan to be proposed to governor by councilman"

"New ward slash proposal made—councilman Berman's proposal to be offered to council Monday—to reduce wards and council"

"Cut in gas rate is now in order, Berman asserts"

"Berman to seek phone rate cut"

And many others too numerous to include in this book.

However, Joe Berman's highest achievement during his too few years on the city council was his chairmanship of the Atlanta airport committee. Joe Berman was the primary force that literally brought aviation to Atlanta. In the late 1920s, after he took office, the city airport was the old Candler racetrack, which the city was buying from Asa Candler, founder of Coca-Cola, for $100,000. Joe's city airport committee appointed Jack Gray as airport manager. They got an offer of a discount from Mr. Candler, paid for the airport, and started to develop it. American and Eastern Airlines were operating out of wooden shacks. Joe and his committee, and representatives from the junior chamber of commerce, went to Mr. Walter Candler and asked for a $50,000 donation to build an administration building, which would be named for Candler as a memorial. Joe remembered how Mr. Candler reached down for his briefcase, opened it and said, "The answer is no. We have enough dirt in our portfolio." As they went out the door, Joe turned back and said, "Mr. Candler, tomorrow morning we are changing the name of the airport from Candler Field to Atlanta Municipal Airport." Through his committee they raised the money, and on July 9, 1933, they had a big air show to celebrate. Joe, as chairman of the committee that had made Atlanta a major airport hub, dedicated the new building in a speech from the round tower on the top. Among the famous pilots participating in that air show was Captain Claire L. Chennault, later General Chennault, of the famous "Flying Tigers" during World War II. Coincidentally, Joe's wife Fay was expecting their second child on that same day. He asked her to please wait until after the air show. She cooperated, and their little girl, Joan Fay (named after both Joe and Fay), was born later that night. For his remarkable efforts as the leader of Atlanta's aviation history, Joe received the following letter from Clark Howell, editor and general manager of the *Atlanta Constitution*, dated November 3, 1931. It stated:

> Hon. Joseph E. Berman
> Attorney-at-law
> Atlanta
>
> Dear Joe:
>
> Thanks for yours of the 30th ultimo with enclosure of booklet of ordinances governing aviation in Atlanta.
>
> I will, between now and next Sunday, take up the matter

along the line of your suggestion, handling the subject not only in a local article, but with editorial comment.

I do not know what Atlanta would have done without you as chairman of the aviation committee of council. You have rendered the city splendid service in the development of its aviation field and have done more for it than has been done by another man, or set of men.

Some of these days you should have a monument there, as testifying to the excellent public service you have rendered.

Sincerely your friend,

Clark Howell

Editor
The Atlanta Constitution

For many years that followed, Joe Berman's name was on a plaque at an entrance to the Atlanta airport. When Delta Airlines expanded its Atlanta hub, it needed more space, and today that plaque rests in the Atlanta Archives.

Joe Berman was such a popular man of the people that, by 1933, he was being urged by some and encouraged by his own law firm to make a run for mayor of Atlanta.

Then one of a number of tragedies occurred in his life that changed it forever. In 1934, Fay's parents, Morris Lewis, Sr., and Julia Lewis, along with her aunt, Claudia Hyman, and brother, Celian Lewis, were driving on a return trip from Memphis. As they neared Grenada, Mississippi, a car driven by an intoxicated individual was speeding, and swerved into them in a head-on collision. It was reported that shortly before, the inebriated occupants of the other car had been bragging, along the way, about how fast their car would go. Morris ended up lying on the road with crushed chest, along with his mortally injured wife. Claudia and Celian were also seriously hurt. Morris was not expected to live, but it was Julia who died a few days later.

The family was devastated. Morris, Jr., and Celian asked Fay to return to the family home of Faymorcele in Lexington, and live there with Morris, Sr., and Claudia, in order to look after them in a manner that only a daughter and niece could do. In other words, they wanted her to move from Atlanta back to Lexington.

Joe was one of the most loving persons who ever lived. So, for the woman he loved, he gave up a brilliant legal and political career and future to move with his wife and two children to Lexington, in 1935. Their son, Bob, then known as Bobby, was nearly five years old at the time; their daughter, Joan Fay, was just over two years old.

A new life began for Joe Berman in Lexington. Since there was a paucity of legal business in a town of only 2,500 people just coming out of the Depression, he decided to venture into the food brokerage business. In that way, he could sell his products to his father-in-law's business (the Lewis Grocer Company), and any other distributors he could find that would buy them, among which was Stokely Van Camp.

As expected, Joe rapidly became an active member of the Lexington Jewish and overall communities. He was president of the chamber of commerce, country club, and member of Rotary and other civic organizations.

Fay, born in 1909, was confirmed at Temple Beth El, and graduated from Lexington High. She was a world traveler in her earlier life, after graduating from Washington Seminary, a girl's school in Washington D.C. She was a socialite, and later an avid and expert bridge player and gourmet cook. She kept an immaculate home, and always looked elegant and dressed fashionably. Fay was in every sense a true southern lady, and was devoted to her family, her Judaism and her country. She dedicated herself to taking care of her children, husband and father. She also spent many hours visiting the sick and doing charitable work in the Lexington community, as had her mother, Julia Lewis. When I matriculated to Ole Miss (the University of Mississippi), she displayed her dexterity and skill, along with her love of family, by crocheting two brightly colored woolen blankets for me. One side was crimson; the other side dark royal blue. Those are the colors of the Ole Miss Rebels, originally taken from the crimson of Harvard and the royal blue of Yale. Both blankets were lined with brilliant red silk. They remain in my home today.

In his heart, Joe missed the hustle and bustle of Atlanta and the opportunities it and the state of Georgia had afforded him—especially considering the outstanding reputation he had already established in that city and state, and the bright future that had lain ahead. Then another situation occurred that would once again change his world and that of his family: the prelude to World War II.

Joe knew the repercussions of a world taken over by Nazi Germany and the Third Reich of Hitler. He had always said, "My country, right or wrong, but my country." He knew his country was right in its fight to defend freedom. He was a true patriot, and volunteered for military service in early 1941, several months before the bombing of Pearl Harbor.

At the end of World War I he had been a lieutenant in the infantry, and was now a captain in the reserve. He was immediately assigned to the Judge Advocates Generals department at the Army Central Command[23] in Atlanta, so the family returned to Georgia.

In 1944, as a lieutenant colonel, he requested reassignment to overseas duty and served in both Okinawa and later Korea as a military judge, administering war criminal tribunals of Japanese war criminals. While on Okinawa, during the plans for the invasion of Japan, a fellow officer came to Joe and said, "Colonel, I know that you have a family and I don't, so let me take your place in the invasion." Joe gratefully refused. Then came Hiroshima and Nagasaki, and the atom bombs, and the war was over. During the war he served as an inspiration to the men under his command, as described by the following letter written to his wife, Fay, while he was on his way home from the Pacific Theater.

Dear Mrs. Berman,

Joe Berman, whom most of us admiringly and respectfully call judge has departed from our military realm and it is as though we have lost the only ray of sunshine in this cloudy and dismal atmosphere which gave us a sense of warmth and comfort.

I have been so fortunate as to have lived closely with the judge through most of our campaign from the early days in Hawaii through Okinawa and into the initial phase of the occupation of Korea, and I am keenly aware that he has contributed much to the officers and men with whom he served. Of all the persons I have known there is not one that is as greatly thought of and appreciated by his fellow officers and men than the judge. It has been more than his keen intelligence and superior manner of performance in office that has merited this admiration; it has been his great concern for the welfare of all of us, the men about him, his family and friends at home that has endeared him to our hearts.

In addition to his busy regular duties he has found time to bring joy and laughter and good council to so many of us who needed such.

I have always been one to judge a man by his loyalty to his family and in every instance it has been a great satisfaction to witness the concern and pride which the judge has shown toward his loved ones. Your pictures were his shrine and your letters his daily sustenance; in all his talk and thoughts of you I feel that I have lived almost as closely to you as I have him. Far from home and living in conditions which bring out the best and the worst in a man, I know that you would be so proud of his every performance.

I take the privilege of writing these few lines to you because in a world that has been torn asunder by greed and hate it is a wonderful thing to meet and know a man like your husband. I may never see him again, but long after I have returned to my own dear wife I will be telling her about the judge; his friendship and companionship has been one of the nicest things that ever happened to me.

Upon his return to the ones whom he loves so dearly all of us will miss him so very much but will be happy in knowing that a great guy has at last come home to his very own."

Sincerely,

Robert J. Patrick
Lt. Col., infantry

For his meritorious service during World War II, Joe Berman was awarded the Bronze Star and the Oak Leaf Cluster.

When Colonel Berman returned home to Lexington as a full

colonel, he was one of—if not the—highest-ranking military officers of the Jewish faith in the state of Mississippi. He was elected president of the Mississippi Reserve Officers Association and served on the national council. He picked up where he had left off in both business and civic affairs, serving as president of the Lexington Rotary Club. When Joe assumed the office of club president, they had a tradition (as many Rotary clubs do) of saying the pledge of allegiance to the flag at the beginning of each meeting, after which followed a prayer of the day. However, Joe took note that there was no American flag in the room which they could face and pledge. Therefore, he went out and purchased a large American flag and flag pole, and gave it to his club. That same flag continues to be displayed today at club meetings and affairs.

He was also lay rabbi at Temple Beth El, in particular presiding over the High Holy Days of Rosh Hashanah and Yom Kippur for many years. He was so beloved that a bronze plaque, with his picture and a prayer he wrote engraved on it, adorns the lobby of Temple Beth El.

After the war, Joe led a full life in Lexington. He wrote a book about the experiences of a young attorney in a growing southern city. He entitled that fictional novel *With Apologies To No One*. He quipped, "Once I took out fifty pages of law and added ten pages of sex, I got the book published." His first book signing was at Lenox Square in Atlanta, his former home city, where he was greeted by many old friends and relatives.

In 1964, he fulfilled his longtime desire to travel the paths of his parents in the Holy Land. As a known Jew, he traveled extensively throughout the Middle East, in Israel, Egypt, Jordan and Lebanon, even though it was unsafe for a Jew to travel through those Arab nations. After returning from that trip, he began an illustrated lecture tour and visited various churches, synagogues and civic clubs, relating his experiences in the Middle East and what he had discovered about religious history—both Judaic and Christian—and the attitudes of the people themselves. During those lectures, he was so well received that a lady came up to him after one and said, "Joe Berman, you are a true Christian," to which Joe replied, "Thank you, Mrs. Jones, and I want you to know you truly have a beautiful Jewish heart."

An anecdote: Joe was always interested in having something

unique. Thus he and Fay decided to own a mynah bird, which they named Sabu. The bird distinguished itself by speaking the "Queen's English" as clearly as any human being. A lady by the name of Mrs. Andrew Smith was running for the office of sheriff, to replace her husband, as Mississippi law did not permit a sheriff to succeed himself. One day, she drove up the long winding concrete driveway leading to Faymorcele to solicit the vote of the Bermans. What she didn't know was that Joe and Fay were not at home at the time of her visit. However, as she pulled up to the screened porch on the east side of the house next to the covered driveway entrance, she didn't see anyone sitting there. Undetected by her, Sabu happened to be in his cage on the porch. As Mrs. Smith parked her car and opened the door, the following conversation occurred:

Sabu: What's your name?

Mrs. Smith: I'm Mrs. Andrew Smith and I'm running for the office of sheriff, to replace my husband.

Sabu: Want a beer?

Mrs. Smith: No, thank you, I don't drink. I just wanted to talk with you about my desire to replace my husband for sheriff of Holmes County.

Sabu: Scotch and soda, please?!

Mrs. Smith: No, thank you; as I said, I don't drink. But I would like to talk with you about my plans to succeed my husband for the office of sheriff.

Sabu: Are you a talking bird?

Mrs. Smith: No, of course not. I don't know what you are talking about.

Sabu: I'm a talking bird.

That's when Mrs. Smith looked more closely and saw Sabu sitting there in his cage, just looking her over. She nearly fell back into her car with astonishment and laughter.

This story was told all over the county, and Mrs. Smith did succeed her husband in that position of law enforcement. She gave Sabu at least some of the credit for her popular victory.

However, Joe's active and interesting life was not destined to continue. It was doomed to end far too early at the age of sixty-seven through the ultimate tragedy in his life's story. This was not due to any problem with his health, but to a multiplicity of pilot and tower errors, when the commercial airliner on which he was a passenger collided—only three minutes after takeoff—with a private plane that was off-course. It was a clear day and, had the pilots of either plane been alert, it may never have happened. The planes crashed over Hendersonville, North Carolina, falling just short of a children's summer camp. On that same flight happened to be the newly appointed Secretary of the Navy and his wife, along with many Stokely brokers and members of the Stokely Van Camp organization.

That summer of 1967, I was teaching a night class in human relations at the University Center, then located on the Belhaven College campus. I was preparing for the evening's session when I got the call. Incidentally, in the class that I was teaching was a very bright and capable pupil by the name of Sister Dorothea Mary Sondgeroth. I was using the Harvard Business School case study method of instruction. Most any student of human relations is aware of the saying that "when Peter talks about Paul, I learn more about Peter than I do about Paul." That held true about Sister Dorothea, as I feel quite certain I learned more from her than she ever learned from me. Today, many years later, Sister Dorothea is the president of St. Dominic Health Services and was recently honored as a member of the Jackson Hall of Fame. I am also pleased to say that we are fellow Rotarians in the Rotary Club of Jackson, and she is scheduled to become its next president.

Before I could complete my lesson plan, shortly after noon I received a call from my father's youngest brother, my uncle, Dr. Maxwell D. Berman. Max was one of the last of a breed of old-fashioned doctors who would make house calls, regardless of the time of day or night, and no one had a kinder bedside manner than he. Max truly loved his patients as much as they loved him. My dad used to say, "Where there is life, there is hope," and my Uncle Max, wherever there was the slightest possibility of a patient's recovery, would give them that hope—never false hope, but the kind of hope that can raise one's spirits and mentally be an important part of one's recovery. "Hope is one of the most powerful emotions known to humankind. There is no medicine like hope; no incentive so great, and no tonics so powerful as the expectation of something better tomorrow."[24]

However, there was no hope in my uncle's voice when he broke the news to me about the airliner crash. Usually he spoke in a calming southern drawl, but this time it was flat and toneless. Upon hearing his words, I ran to the bedroom to tell my wife, Sondy, who was in bed with a patch over her eye, recovering from an injury from a tree branch. I recall telling her, "Dad's just been killed in a plane crash," then I sat down on the bed and began sobbing. Our daughter, Sheri, was in her crib and didn't know the difference, but our other two daughters, Marjie and Debbie, ages eight and four at the time, had never seen me cry and hysterically joined in. My wife, who has always been a calming influence in our lives, helped our daughters and me get control of our emotions. I hurriedly packed and flew to New York to pick up my mother, Fay, and sister, Brenda. The plan had been for Joe to meet them there after his sales meeting in Greenbrier. Upon leaving our home, I noticed that in my shock, I had left the phone receiver dangling when I left the kitchen to break the awful news. The only personal item of my father's I have from that terrible tragedy is his battered Rolex watch, which ominously stopped at 12:03 p.m., the exact time of the fatal event. Even today, almost forty years later, I have not been able to part with it.

In 2004, many years after that tragic mid-air collision, the City of Hendersonville laid a monument at the crash site. There was a memorial service for all who died on that sad day of July 19, 1967.

Shortly after the turn of the century in the early 2000's, our daughter, Debbie Berman Silver, who recalled her grandfather with love, went to the site of the crash. She used her cell phone to call her two sisters, Marjie Berman Block and Sheri Berman Spector, since the three were there when I received the fateful call notifying us of what had happened. Together, at the same time of 12:03 p.m. on the same date of July 19, many years later, via telephone they plaintively chanted in unison the Kaddish, the traditional Jewish prayer for the deceased. The prayer never mentions death, but rather praises and glorifies God and the beauty of life he gives to us all. If there really is life after death, in some form, then the spirit of Joe Berman surely came to life during that call.

As a further indication of the life Joe Berman led while on this earth, below are two eulogies given after his untimely death. One was from the president of his Rotary Club, who had succeeded Joe in that position; the other was an editorial in the *Lexington Advertiser,* a weekly newspaper of Lexington and Holmes County.

Given in tribute to Joseph Emile Berman, they are as follows:

Eulogy given at the Lexington Rotary Club by Billy
Martin
who succeeded Joe Berman as its president
Billy Martin was later mayor of Lexington for twelve
years

"Life in our community moves along today in much the same manner as it does every day. But our hearts are saddened by the tragic circumstances which left a void among our citizenry. Lexington will never have quite the same atmosphere it had when Joe Berman hurried around the square laughing and talking with his friends.

He was a busy man but he always had time for a pleasant 'good morning' and a cheery word to those he met. Even the people whose lives were not personally touched by this dedicated man will realize the loss in our community. His every effort was aimed toward the betterment of Lexington and its entire population.

Joe was a person who could produce ideas and reach goals—his civic achievements go unnumbered. His life exemplified 'service above self' in its every phase. There are few such unselfish men in our state and in our country.

Time has a way of healing our wounds and lessening our grief, but time cannot erase the influence of a great man, a true friend, and a devoted heart. Lexington is a better community, our Rotary Club is a stronger organization, and our lives have been deeply enriched because Joe Berman passed this way."

Editorial Page
The Lexington Advertiser

Joe Berman

The smiling face of Joe Berman will be seen on our streets no more.

This genial, popular citizen of Lexington was one of eighty-two persons killed in the tragic air disaster over North Carolina last week. News of his death stunned this community of which he has long been an important part. There are so few persons these days who display good will to everyone—who love their fellowman and hold a genuine concern for his welfare and that of the community.

Joe Berman was such a man.

He was concerned about Lexington and Holmes County and Mississippi. But his interest did not end there—he was a citizen of the world. Perhaps that is why he was able to live a happy, useful life without many of the tensions and frustrations that plague lesser mortals. He wanted nothing for himself. He only wanted to do what he could every day along the way for those with whom he came in contact.

His outward reach and positive constructive attitude, his progressive thinking and innate respect for the dignity and rights of all people, his happy disposition and philosophical manner combined to make him a unique person in our community.

His life was rooted in love for his wife and children and grandchildren—and extended to all his relatives. His faith in his religion was deep and it gave him a solid basis for living. He was proud of his country and served it well in the armed forces.

As Rabbi Perry Nussbaum said at the final rites Sunday afternoon: "It was not how he died that counted, but how he lived."

And Joe Berman's life was a sermon.

Joe left his wife, Fay, and three children; me, married to Sondy; Joan, married to the late Dudley Burwell, of Jackson; and our much younger sister, Brenda, now a radiologist in Birmingham, married to Jake Guercio.

In memory of my father, our family donated a cover for the pulpit bima in Temple Beth El, which we felt personified his life. It was inscribed with a Star of David and the words of the Prophet Micah: "Do justly, love mercy, walk humbly with thy God."

Although a most gregarious individual, Joe Berman never bragged about himself or spoke publicly about his many achievements during his life. He liked to tell the story of Will Rogers, who once said, "I like to hear a man talk about himself, because all he says is something good." Joe Berman's life represented goodness, and I, as his son and author of this book, felt it worthy of relating.

Fay lived for twenty-one years after her loss of Joe, passing away in 1988. During those years she was the family matriarch, using her home on various occasions, as a gathering place with sumptuous meals, for both family and friends

Joseph Emile Berman (top)   Fay Lewis Berman (bottom)

Chapter 15

Dudley Sale Burwell and Joan Berman Burwell
One of the Kindest, Gentlest of Men

Dudley Sale Burwell was born in Ebenezer, Mississippi, in 1931. It is worth mentioning that Joan Fay married Dudley on the front open porch of Faymorcele, overlooking a beautifully landscaped front lawn with large oak trees swaying in a light summer breeze. This was the same place and setting as the wedding of Joan's mother and father, Fay and Joe Berman.

In the home was a family crest on a large multicolored stained glass window. It framed a landing on the front stairs which overlooked a large rose garden, resplendent with a variety of reds, whites and yellows, bordered by a trellis covered with purple wisteria. The flowers accented the colors in the stained glass crest, combining to offer a radiant view from above and below. Ironically, the family crest happened to be that of the Burwell family, which had remained in the home Morris Lewis, Sr., purchased a few years after the home was built. It was purchased from Steve Burwell, a great-uncle to Dudley. Today, that same elegant stained glass window adorns the home of Joan Burwell in Jackson, which she shared until recently with her husband. Dudley passed away in 2005.

In Dudley's early life, he went to school in Ebenezer, a few miles from Lexington, near the old Sontheimer place. He attended high school in Lexington, where he was president of his senior class, a star athlete and represented his school at Boy's State. Joan was confirmed at Temple Beth El. She was the head drum majorette in the Lexington band and held the title of "Miss Lexington." Dudley, upon graduation from high school and Holmes Community College, entered the United States Marine Corps.

After his honorable discharge, his father-in-law, Joe Berman, offered to defray his junior and senior year college expenses in business at Mississippi State University. However, Dudley respectfully refused that offer, saying he intended to earn his own way and support his family without help from anyone else. He studied and obtained his CPA license. Years later, he became president of the Lewis Grocer Company and Sunflower Food Stores. He was also president of his Rotary Club and the chamber of commerce. Additionally Dudley Burwell was chairman of the board of the Retail Association of Mississippi.

Dudley was a Methodist when he married Joan, but they raised their children in the faith of Judaism. Dudley regularly attended Sabbath services with his wife, participating in all the Jewish holidays and customs. On his 70th birthday, he converted to Judaism. Later he became a bar mitzvah, along with Joan as a bat mitzvah. At his bar mitzvah, he took the Jewish name of Yosef—for Joseph, his father-in-law. In his address to the congregation at his bar mitzvah service, he explained why he took that particular name: because Joe Berman was the man he most admired. In his lifetime, Dudley was one of the kindest, gentlest persons who ever walked the face of this earth.

In Jackson, he and Joan were members of Beth Israel Congregation, where she continues to worship. Prior to Dudley's death, he was serving on the Board of Beth Israel and as its controller.

Joan followed in her mother's footsteps by becoming a gourmet cook. It is well-known that one of the very best meals one can savor is in the home of Joan Burwell.

Dudley and Joan Burwell had five children; four sons and one daughter. All four sons became Eagle Scouts. Two are doctors—Dudley, Jr., an orthopedic surgeon, and Joel, a general physician—both on the Mississippi Gulf Coast. During Hurricane Katrina, neither left the coast; they remained to render medical attention and assistance to those in need. Todd is an attorney in Jackson, Troy is a computer analyst in Atlanta, and Lana is a businesswoman in Birmingham.

Dudley Sale Burwell, Sr. (top)   Joan Berman Burwell (bottom)

Chapter 16

Brenda Berman Guercio and Jake Guercio
Leading Radiologist, City Councilwoman

Joe and Fay Berman's other daughter Brenda, was born in 1949 in Lexington after Joe returned from World War II. She kept both her parents young. Joe's tragic death came just after Brenda had graduated high school, as the valedictorian of her class. She was in New York with her mother, Fay, attending modeling school. While in New York, she won several major prizes on the national television show known as "Eye Guess", hosted by Bill Cullen. She generously shared those winnings with her siblings.

She and Fay were waiting for Joe to join them after his planned meeting in Greenbrier, when they received the shocking word of his demise in the tragic air crash.

Brenda continued on to Emory and then the University of Alabama medical school, graduating with honors from both colleges. She recently retired as the senior partner in her radiological group in Birmingham, Alabama. Brenda was confirmed at Temple Beth El in Lexington, and is currently a member of both Emanu-El Congregation in Birmingham and Temple Beth El in Lexington. Following in the footsteps of her beloved father, she is a member of the city council of Indian Springs, Alabama.

She is married to Jake Guercio, a financial advisor, and they reside in the Birmingham area. Together, Brenda and Jake own a multitude of dogs, horses, and an irascible parrot named Chico, whose favorite expression is "Roll Tide." They are major supporters of the animal rescue league. Brenda has one son, "Bo", an attorney, and one daughter, Emily, a medical doctor, married to Matt Casey, an attorney. All reside in Birmingham.

Brenda Berman Guercio at Confirmation, Temple Beth El

Chapter 17

Morris Herrman and Jessie Waterman Herrman
Salesman, Business Manager

Morris Herrman was born in 1876 in Davisborough, Georgia, to Abraham and Celia Sontheimer Herrman. He was one of four sons and three daughters. One of his sisters, Julia, married Morris Lewis, Sr.

When Abraham and Celia moved their family from Davisborough, Georgia to Lexington, Mississippi, Morris became an important member of the Lewis Grocer Company. Starting as a salesman, he climbed the corporate ladder into a managerial position. At the start of World War II, he began managing the Lewis warehouse and sales operations in Lexington.

In his travels while making sales calls, he utilized a chauffeur, since he was not very adept at driving himself.

During one of his trips into Arkansas, he met Jessie Waterman of Dumas, Arkansas. Jessie was the daughter of Gus and Rachel Ulman Waterman. Gus Waterman was born in Breslav, Germany in 1849. He died in 1918. Rachel's family, the Ulmans, came over from Frankfurt, Germany in the early 1800s. Both Gus Waterman's family and Rachel Ulman's family came through the port of New Orleans. Some moved north to Natchez, Mississippi, a big Mississippi River trading port in the early days of settlement. Later, some of the family moved on further north to Jackson, where Rachel was born in 1860. With them, they brought a considerable amount of delicately made artisan furniture, which is now going on 200 years old. Most of this furniture now sits in the Museum of Southern Jewish Experience in Utica, Mississippi, on the site of Henry S. Jacobs Camp.

After Union General Sherman came through Mississippi during the Civil War and ravaged much of Jackson, the Waterman family moved to Memphis, where Rachel's mother's family name was Seessels. Later, they moved to Dumas, Arkansas, where Jessie was born in 1887. Her father, Gus Waterman, was its first mayor. There they had considerable farming interests, growing mostly cotton, which was the "king crop" of the South at that time.

Jessie's older brother, Miles, died a few days after birth. Her two older sisters, Frances and Dora, also died at an early age. Two brothers were born after her; Lawrence Ulman Waterman in 1889 in Dumas, and Julian Seessels Waterman in 1890 in Pine Bluff, Arkansas. Julian Waterman established the School of Law at the University of Arkansas in 1924. He was called upon to both establish a law school and to achieve accreditation, and accomplished both. Waterman Hall at the University Law School is named in his honor. Lawrence was a successful merchant and farmer in Dumas.

Morris Herrman met his wife to be, Jessie Waterman, during his sales travels in Arkansas. Jessie was impressed with Morris, especially since he had a chauffeur, and he was very attentive to her. Morris was attracted to Jessie and had a high regard for the esteem in which her family was held throughout Arkansas. After a brief courtship, they married and settled in Lexington, where they had two sons, Cecil Waterman Herrman and Gus Waterman Herrman.

Rachel, Jessie's mother, was an attractive woman in her youth. During her old age, when she was bent over and fully gray-headed, they referred to her as "Granny." When Jessie and Morris's second son, Gus Herrman, first went into the military service at the beginning of World War II, he was initially sent to Camp Shelby near Hattiesburg, Mississippi. The first letter he received was from Granny. She had never forgotten what the northern soldiers had done to their property during the Civil War. Recalling her turbulent youth in Jackson, Mississippi, and the trials and tribulations their family suffered during those dreadful times that pitted brother against brother, she wrote the following: "Dear Gus, do you have to sleep in the same room with them Yankees?"

Later she lived with her daughter, Jessie, and son-in-law, Morris Herrman, in Lexington. After Morris died in 1949, she and Jessie moved back to Memphis, where she lived until her death in 1950. Jessie died in 1979.

Morris Herrman

Jessie Waterman Herrman

Chapter 18

Brothers in Philanthropy
Cecil Waterman Herrman
Star Salesman, Philanthropist
Gus Waterman Herrman
World War II Hero, Federal Agent
Philanthropist

Morris and Jessie Herrman had two sons; Cecil, born in 1913, and Gus, born in 1920. These two sons went through the Lexington school system and each graduated from Lexington High School. They were both confirmed at Temple Beth El.

It was these two sons, coming from a small Mississippi town, who later in life did more than anyone else before them to support the Hebrew Union College—Jewish Institute of Religion—the center of Reform Judaism. Their remarkable story will follow.

Cecil was a football star for Lexington High, playing on the same teams as Celian Lewis, Herbert Hyman and Herman Flowers. Cecil, Celian and Herbert began as teammates on the 1929 team; however due to a temporary injury, he was not able to be a member of the 1932 undefeated championship team. Cecil was also an excellent tennis player. They had a tennis court in their side yard. In addition, he was musically inclined and played the clarinet.

Cecil was a true gentleman, known for his humility and good cheer. He had the esteem and affection of many friends throughout Mississippi, Tennessee, and other parts of the South.

Gus' interest and athleticism went in a different direction. He wasn't a musician, and was much more mild-mannered than Cecil. Both brothers were thoughtful and loving to their parents and to one another. However, Gus was the tender one, who always adored his mother, next to God. When he was a small child, likely in the first grade, he wrote his mother a note for Mother's Day. In it, he said the following: "It is wonderful how a mother can do. Others can love you but only your mother. She attends to you, looks after you. And the only thing she ever does bad to you is to die and leave you. Mother is so sweet."

Even more than his rough and tumble brother, Gus' forte was tennis and he was an avid player. He wrote in his memoirs that one of the worst times of his early life was when he lost the tennis championship in the finals at the Lexington Country Club. However, he recovered from that disappointment when he went on to become a star tennis player on the University of Alabama tennis team.

At the University of Alabama, Gus was a member of the ZBT Jewish fraternity. He was quiet, but friendly and popular with his fellow students. He took his studies seriously and graduated with high grades in 1941.

In the mid 1930s, when Morris Lewis, Jr., Celian Lewis, and Herbert Hyman moved from Lexington to Indianola to work at Lewis's newly opened warehouse, Cecil also joined them. Shortly after, the Lewis company purchased one-half interest in the Abe Lewis wholesale liquor company in Memphis, Tennessee.

Soon after came World War II. Cecil was unable to serve due to what was then known as "flat feet." That is when Cecil moved to Memphis and became a salesman and key sales representative for the Abe Lewis liquor organization, where he successfully worked until his retirement.

Gus' history took another path. He joined the army and received his commission as a second lieutenant. He was assigned to a tank destroyer battalion. After extensive training in the United States, Gus was promoted to first lieutenant and later captain. Then he and his tank destroyer battalion were shipped overseas to England, to prepare for the invasion of France intended to take back Europe from Nazi Germany and its heavily fortified German positions.

Gus was always reticent about his military service. He never spoke of it, and when questioned, he answered for the most part with a terse yes and no. However, knowing that he had received both the Purple Heart and Bronze Star, I occasionally questioned him about the battles he was in—from Normandy to the Battle of the Bulge, and on into the heart of Germany.

Gus and his battalion were part of the invasion going ashore on Utah Beach, D-Day + 6. They went in attached to the 82nd Airborne, and to the day he died Gus always said how lucky he was to have gotten through Normandy and what followed. At that time, the German forces continued to occupy strategic areas overlooking the beach and nearby, including St-Marcouf, about ten kilometers north of Utah Beach. There, the Germans had four enormous casements, each housing a 205mm cannon, used to shell Utah Beach and the American battleships offshore. These areas were still being secured by the American troops, with the big guns silenced near D-Day + 12. As the Higgins LCVPs (Landing Craft Vehicle Personnel), massed produced in New Orleans, approached the beach, heavy fire from German 88mm and 205mm cannons and mortar fire were hitting all around them. Some took direct hits, destroying all those aboard.

Taking such heavy fire from the imbedded pill boxes and concealed German positions, on the hills above the beach and some miles away, while most commanders (known as coxswains) of the landing crafts exhibited great courage, some were reluctant to approach too close to the beach. They attempted to stay as far out of range of the German guns as possible. What resulted was they opened their front panels to let the troops and equipment out in water that was over the heads of the American troops. With heavy packs on, the American soldiers could not swim in and a number of them drowned before ever being able to fight as part of the landing force.

As the coxswain of Gus' landing craft stopped considerably short of the beach and was about to lower the front steel protective panel into deep water, Gus realized what was happening. Just before the lever was cranked to expose the troops under Gus' command, Gus stopped him and said they were too far offshore and that both the troops and their tank destroyers would sink and drown. The commander told Gus he was not going any closer. Gus pulled out his 45 pistol, pointed it at the landing craft commander's head, and said, "Either you take us to shore, or I will take command of this landing craft and you will never live to see your mother ship again." Nothing more needed to be said, and they were taken as close to the beach as any troops had been.

With that act of heroism, Gus saved the troops under his command and their equipment and brought them safely ashore. They began the fight for freedom, advancing all the way across France into Belgium and Germany to ultimate victory on VE Day.

Growing up in Lexington, Gus Herrman had a warm and quiet demeanor and a sweet, yet manly disposition. He was the type that, as they say down South, would never hurt a fly. Yet when the time came to literally sink or swim, Gus rose to the occasion and did his duty, as duty called.

While fighting across Europe, Gus' 644th tank destroyer battalion was awarded a number of Battle Honors. They were: Five Battle Stars for Normandy, Northern France, Rhineland, Ardennes and Central Europe. They also received the Presidential Citation for action Nov. 21—Nov. 28, 1944 in the Hurtgen Forest. In addition, they received the Belgian Fourragere for actions Dec. 13—Dec. 30 1944 in Rocherath-Krinkelt.

One day while walking down a wooded path, there was a big explosion from an incoming German shell. Gus took a shrapnel hit in the chest, which immediately knocked him to the ground. He happened to be walking with another officer, who heard Gus say, "I'm hit." Later, that same officer wrote Gus how fortunate they had been when Gus was wounded, as they were just a few yards from a front-line medical tent. Gus was promptly taken to surgery. Some shrapnel was taken out, but some was too close to his heart to remove. He was sewn up, and soon after was back at his command in the heat of battle. For Gus' heroics and that shrapnel wound, he was awarded both the Bronze Star and the Purple Heart. The shrapnel remained in Gus' chest for the rest of his life, and prevented him from receiving an MRI examination many years later, when he was seriously ill and needed such a test.

Gus was in the infamous Battle of the Bulge, in Belgium, when the German forces launched their last major do-or-die offense against the American and British forces. The German High Command totally surprised the American and Allied troops in this their last stand, and they almost succeeded in driving the American troops back to the beach. Some of the most important military victories in the history of warfare have come from the element of surprise. The German forces had built up to over 200,000 troops. It was the largest single battle the American forces ever fought.[25]

It was only through bravery and tenacity that the American forces held on until General Patton's Third Army and his tank divisions broke through the German lines to reach Gus' unit and the beleaguered American troops. They then combined to counterattack and defeat the German armed forces in Germany's last major offensive, which almost succeeded.

When asked to talk about it, most all he would say was, "It was very, very cold." Gus remembered his mother telling him "don't go out without a sweater." He said it was so cold that none of the men under his command could catch a cold to go back to the rest area—they couldn't even sneeze. He said it was so cold that even the germs couldn't last. Although the American and allied troops sustained over 85,000 casualties in that battle, the American lines did last and held on. Gus' tank destroyer troops under his command continued to hold their position and fire on the Nazi Panzers once the German tanks had emerged from the small narrow roads of the Ardennes Forest[26], until the Panzers finally ran out of fuel and Patton came with his tanks to relieve the American troops.

But that was all Gus would ever say about the historic Battle of the Bulge at Bastogne. Gus Herrman, who never had a bad word to say about anyone, was one of the most unpretentious souls ever to grace this earth.

After World War II, Gus entered the United States Customs Service and made it a career. However, his career was interrupted once more by military service as he was recalled to duty to serve during the Korean War. After his discharge, Gus retired from military service with the rank of lieutenant colonel.

Gus then resumed his career with the U.S. Customs Service. He moved through the ranks as a customs agent and a customs supervisor, to eventually become a high customs official as a regional customs director. He retired in 1980. Gus passed away twenty-one years later, in 2001, at the age of eighty-one from a brief illness in Houston, Texas, where he was residing. His brother, Cecil, had predeceased him.

There were two events of magnanimity involving both Cecil and Gus, in regard to their philanthropic actions, which were not revealed until after each of their deaths.

The story began many, many years ago when both Cecil and Gus were still living in Lexington. At that time, Temple Beth El utilized the services of student rabbis from the Hebrew Union College in Cincinnati for the Jewish High Holy Days of Rosh Hashanah and Yom Kippur. One such student rabbi was the later renowned Rabbi James Wax, rabbi emeritus of Temple Israel in Memphis, Tennessee.

One evening, on the eve of Rosh Hashanah, Rabbi Wax was having dinner at the home of Morris and Julia Lewis. Cecil and Gus, their parents Morris and Jessie Herrman, their grandmother Rachel Waterman, Joe and Fay Berman, Celian Lewis, Herbert Hyman, Claudia Hyman, Daisy and Aaron Jacobson, and Isadore Herrman and children all were at that family dinner before the services.

As a young student rabbi, James Wax had impressed those attending the dinner with his charm and spirituality, as someone who would go far in the rabbinate. At dinner, Cecil, closer to the age of James Wax, established a good rapport with the rabbi. Their friendship continued and grew throughout Cecil's life, and he became a member of the Memphis Congregation, Temple Israel, when Rabbi Wax was its distinguished spiritual leader. Through Cecil, Gus also developed a close friendship with Rabbi Wax. Rabbi Wax told Gus and Cecil that if they were ever in a financial position to help the Hebrew Union College, which ordained all reform rabbis, it would be a great mitzvah (good deed). He mentioned this not only because of his love and respect for the College that had ordained him, but also because he was aware that the HUC graduates were rabbis, scholars, teachers, cantors, administrators, camp directors and other religious leaders. Its alumni normally would not be the type of professionals who would accumulate a great deal of wealth. Therefore, the school could not look to or depend upon many of its alumni to contribute sizable financial support. Nothing more was ever mentioned, but the two brothers both remembered that conversation. Cecil in particular and Rabbi Wax became even closer friends. In time, their friendship and James Wax's remarks bore great fruit for the Hebrew Union College.

Neither Cecil nor Gus ever married. They were both devoted to their parents, Morris and Jessie, and to their grandmother, Rachel (Granny). When Morris Herrman passed away in 1949, Jessie and Granny moved to Memphis to live with Cecil. Cecil and Gus spent most of their adulthood taking care of their parents, being with friends and, for entertainment, traveling extensively around the world together. Gus' last trip abroad, after Cecil's death, was made to Israel. Accompanying him on that trip, as friends and personal guides, were Macy and Susan Hart and Dr. Walter Berman (son of Dr. Maxwell D. and Flo Berman).

With Cecil in the liquor business, but never owning his own business, and Gus spending many years in the military and with the U.S. Customs Service, neither brother was in a position to accumulate a great deal of wealth—or so it was assumed. They did have some stock in the Lewis Grocer Company passed on to them by their father. Later this stock was converted into SuperValu stock and split many times over the years. With this stock, some other wise investments, and frugality, and without families to support, each brother accumulated considerable wealth.

Upon Cecil's death in 1994, he left all of his estate, with the exception of what he could leave to Gus tax-free, to the Hebrew Union College. That sum amounted to $3,300,000. It was completely unsolicited and gratefully accepted by the president, Alfred Gottchaulk, and his board of trustees.

With that magnanimous gift, the College renovated the oldest building on its Cincinnati campus, including adding air conditioning, and renamed it the Cecil W. Herrman Learning Center. In 1996, Gus, Sondy and I, along with Rabbi Steven Engel of Beth Israel in Jackson and his wife, Beverly, attended the dedication. In the entrance of the building are displayed large pictures of Cecil, his father, Morris, and his mother, Jessie. Gus was named to the HUC board of overseers. The HUC posthumously awarded Cecil the Founders Medallion in gratitude for his generous commitment to the College.

At his own death years later, Gus too left the great majority of his estate—some $7,000,000—to the Hebrew Union College. When I, as Gus' executor, called Rabbi David Ellenson, the newly appointed president of the HUC, to tell him of this gift, he was both amazed and astounded at the magnitude of such a gift to the College—again completely unsolicited and unexpected. Most assumed Cecil's generous gift was all the College would receive from the Herrman family. They were astonished by the next gift the College was to receive from the Herrman brothers.

Rabbi Ellenson acknowledged that Gus' gift alone was the largest single gift ever received by the College. Added to Cecil's gift, it amounted to over $10,000,000 bequeathed to the HUC by the two brothers from the small Mississippi town of Lexington and the congregation of Temple Beth El. Here were two great gifts from two fine men hailing from one of the least expected places.

Besides being unsolicited and a complete surprise to the HUC, the gifts from both Cecil and Gus were completely without reservations or qualifications, with no strings attached. Rabbi Wax had died long before the gifts were made. In addition to other significant gifts from Gus Herrman to Temple Beth El and the Institute of Southern Jewish Life, he also bequeathed to Beth Israel Congregation in Jackson the sum of $100,000, as he knew how dedicated my wife and I, along with our family, were to that synagogue, in addition to Temple Beth El in Lexington.

At my request as Gus' executor, the funds at Beth Israel were put into a trust, the Gus Herrman Fund. The earnings from the principal will be used to promote high-caliber speakers and programs for the annual Holocaust Memorial Service at Beth Israel, known as the Shoah, and other closely related events such as The Jackson Jewish Film Festival. After Gus' experiences in Europe fighting the Nazis, seeing and learning what they did to the Jewish people, he always wanted to make certain the Holocaust and the Nazis' evil deeds of unprecedented genocide would never be forgotten.

Cecil Herrman was a fun-loving, yet reserved southern gentleman. Gus Herrman was a genteel patriot of God and country. Gus loved his Jewish faith, and revered his God with all his heart and soul, which gave him the strength and fortitude to serve his country with all his might, from Utah Beach at Normandy through the Battle of Bastogne and on through Germany. He was the personification of what Tom Brokaw described in his book as "The Greatest Generation."

When he retired as regional director of the Customs Department in the United States Department of the Treasury, in 1980, he received a high commendation and medal from the Treasury Department.

Both Gus and Cecil were unpretentious and unassuming, never asking for any credit, and only had good words to say about everyone. An illustratation of Gus' gentle spirit is that after Cecil passed away, Gus ordered a slab to go over Cecil's grave, to be placed in the Morris and Jessie Herrman plot in Beth El Cemetery in Lexington. Being single, at the same time he also ordered a grave stone for himself to hold until his demise. To Gus's amazement, when the stone on Cecil's grave was unveiled, there was a tombstone next to it, with Gus' name inscribed on it. The next day, Gus called the monument company that made the slabs and asked, "Tell me, when did I die?" The monument company owner was most embarrassed, and offered to pick up the stone over where Gus would someday rest. However, Gus told him that he had never returned anything in his life, and he wasn't going to start then.

In recognition of Gus' $7,000,000 gift, the HUC bestowed upon him the exclusive honor of the Gus Waterman Herrman Presidential Chair.

At the inauguration of Rabbi David Ellenson, as the new president of the Hebrew Union College—Jewish Institute of Religion, accompanied by Sondy and Rabbi Jim Egolf of Beth Israel Congregation in Jackson, I was asked to speak to the board and faculty about the life and achievements of Gus Herrman. It took place in the Cecil Herrman Learning Center, where a large portrait of Gus Herrman was displayed for all to see. It was there on that day that I respectfully and officially proposed that the HUC approve my request, made earlier to Rabbi Ellenson and Chairman Burton Lehman, that $250,000 of the gift given to the College by Gus Herrman be used for the production of a first-class documentary. This production would be dedicated to the memory of Gus Herrman, his family, and the Lexington Jewish community. It was to tell the story of the relationship between the Hebrew Union College, Temple Beth El and the Lexington Jewish community, including the close camaraderie that developed between Cecil, Gus and Rabbi James Wax.

The documentary was to portray the Hebrew Union College and what it has meant to Jewish communities such as Lexington's, where the College sent student rabbis to conduct services when communities did not have full-time rabbis of their own. It also would have told what the Jews of Lexington, including the Herrman family, have meant to both the College and to the promotion of Judaism and ecumenical spirit throughout the state of Mississippi and surrounding states.

It is a remarkable story, how this small southern Jewish community, for over a hundred years, has maintained a high-profile Jewish identity and strong commitment to the faith of Israel within a predominately Christian environment. It's all about keeping the Covenant—about "A House of David in the Land of Jesus"—a compelling story that could have made an impressive documentary.

It was noted in my address to the College that I had assembled a highly qualified, experienced and successful team, consisting of a documentary producer/director and a script writer, both from California, and a research historian—all three of whom were Jewish, with great empathy for the subject. I assured the HUC that it would be proud of the result, since it would ultimately praise and glorify the Lord God.

Rabbi David Ellenson, president of the HUC, and Rabbi Emeritus Alfred Gottchaulk both openly expressed, in writing and verbally, their personal support for the project. However, rather than vote on it at the board meeting during the inauguration, the chairman assigned the proposal to a three-man committee of the board. After two years of effort by myself through phone calls, letters and meetings attempting to persuade the committee and board to act favorably upon the proposal, it was reported that the committee felt the College had more pressing financial needs. That decision was respectfully accepted and the idea for a documentary was then abandoned.

At that time, I decided that a book about this subject could tell the story of Temple Beth El in far more detail than a documentary. The rejection of the documentary idea by the HUC was actually a blessing in disguise, and from it came the reason and motivation for this book, *A House of David in the Land of Jesus.*

When Rabbi Ellenson visited my wife and me in Jackson in 2002, to receive the bequest in person, he was taken to Lexington to see Temple Beth El and the Beth El Cemetery. He also saw Faymorcele. In honor of Temple Beth El, the Cecil and Gus Herrman family, and the Jewish community of Lexington, at my personal request Rabbi Ellenson—a very warm and articulate individual—graciously accepted to be the featured speaker at the centennial celebration of Temple Beth El in December, 2005.

Cecil Waterman Herrman

Robert L. Berman, Sondra S. Berman, Gus W. Herrman,
Dedication of Cecil W. Herrman
Learning Center at Hebrew Union College

Gus Waterman Herrman

Chapter 19

Sam Herrman and Flora Levy Herrman
Early Business and Philanthropic Partner

Born in 1874 to Abraham and Celia Herrman in Davisborough, Georgia, Sam Herrman moved with his family to Lexington, Mississippi, where he met and married Flora Levy of Vicksburg. Sam and Flora had four daughters; Irma, Annette, Edna and Rosa Mae, and one son, Eugene. All of their children grew up in Lexington. Each was confirmed at Temple Beth El and was an important part of the Jewish and overall communities.

Although Sam died in 1934 at the relatively young age of fifty-nine, he accomplished good and successful deeds while he was alive. Besides the beautiful family that he and Flora raised in Lexington as staunch members of Temple Beth El, it was Sam and his brother-in-law, Morris Lewis, Sr., (married to Sam's sister, Julia), who bought and donated the land where Beth El Cemetery and Temple Beth El stand today. Numbering nearly sixty at that time, in the early 1900s, the Lexington congregation grew to eighty-nine in the mid 1930s.

Sam also had the business foresight to partner with Morris Lewis, Sr., and form a wholesale distributorship, which was the beginning of what was known shortly after as the Lewis Grocer Company. Later, Morris Lewis bought out Sam and the rest is history, as described earlier in this book.

Besides being a visionary businessman and philanthropist, Sam was also an entrepreneur. He joined with Jessie Hyman to buy out the historic Sontheimer store and plantation in 1927.

Of the five children Sam and Flora raised in Lexington, marriage eventually took three of the daughters to live in Arkansas and Louisiana. Eugene remained in Lexington all of his life, married to Janet Whitehead Herrman. Irma also remained in Lexington, marrying Leroy H. Paris. Flora passed away in 1963.

Sam Herrman

Chapter 20

Leroy Henry Paris and Irma Herrman Paris
Respected Businessman, Avid Sportsman,
Admired Community Leader

Irma Herrman, born in 1903, remained in Lexington as the wife of Leroy Henry Paris, originally from Sandersville, Georgia. Leroy was born in 1902 in Sandersville to Henry and Pauline Paris. He had one brother, Herman, and one sister, Rachel. He attended the University of Georgia where he played freshman football and was on the wrestling team. His roommate and Phi Epsilon Pi fraternity brother was Joe Berman, who became a lifelong friend.

His second year of college was at Eastman Business College in Poughkeepsie, New York. After that year, he came back to Sandersville to work in his father's general merchandise store and to coach the Sandersville High football team (at no salary).

His mother had a distant cousin who lived in Mississippi and she insisted that Leroy visit this cousin. Leroy's mother, Pauline Herman (spelled with one "r") Paris was distantly related to the Herrman family of Lexington and had heard about the Jewish contingent's business success and acceptance there. While in Mississippi, Leroy Paris met Morris Lewis, Sr., who recognized Leroy's potential due to his education in New York, and asked if he would like to move to Mississippi and work in the Merchants and Farmers Bank in Lexington. This seemed like a great opportunity to Leroy, so he accepted the offer and moved to Lexington for the job. After a few months of working at the bank, the Depression hit and most of the small-town banks were closed, at least temporarily. Morris Lewis asked Leroy if he wanted a job in his wholesale grocery business. Leroy responded, "Or what else?" Morris replied, "Or nothing else." With that, Leroy Paris began his long and successful career of fifty-one years with the Lewis Grocer Company, ending as senior vice president.

While he was a teller in the bank Morris started, Leroy's business acumen had so impressed Morris that he brought him into the Lewis

Grocer Company, first as a salesman, and later as general manager of a major operating warehouse in Durant, Mississippi. Leroy was also a member of the board of the Merchants and Farmers Bank of Lexington and Holmes County, along with Morris Lewis, Sr., founder and chairman.

It was in those days in Lexington that Leroy met, courted and, in 1929, married Irma Herrman, a cousin of Morris, Jr., Celian and Fay Lewis. Leroy and Irma were married in the Methodist Church, which had a Star of David at the entrance, by Rabbi Sol Kory. They had such a large wedding planned that Temple Beth El could not accommodate all those in attendance. Besides, at that time the Lexington temple had no bathroom, so it would have been doubly inconvenient for such a large crowd. They were one of Lexington's most popular couples during the many years they lived there. Leroy was an avid fisherman, hunter, golfer and sports fan. He was active in the business, civic, social and religious circles of Holmes County. He was named "Citizen of the Year" in Holmes County on March 30, 1976.

Irma, a graduate of Lexington High School and confirmed at Temple Beth El, was a charming southern lady with a soft and deep southern accent. She was an excellent bridge player, very charitable and leader of Temple Beth El's Sisterhood and member of its choir. Besides being first cousins, she and Fay Berman were always best of friends, with great respect for one another.

Leroy was active in the Jr. and Sr. Chambers of Commerce, helping to build a strong overall community in the county seat. He was past president of the Mississippi Wholesale Grocers Association, a Shriner, a 32nd Degree Mason, and a member of Temple Beth El in Lexington. Due to the confidence members of all races and religions had in Leroy Paris' sense of fairness and his compassion for his fellow humans, he was selected to be a leading member of the interracial council in Lexington and Holmes County. It was, to a large extent, through his leadership that peace and calm was maintained in that central Mississippi community during the hot and potentially explosive days of the civil rights movement.

Leroy and Irma had a son, their only child, whom they named Henry Paris. Henry turned out to be the shining star of the entire Sam and Flora Herrman clan. The year Henry was born was the same year that Leroy Paris became division manager of the Durant division of Lewis Grocer Company, a post he held until the company consolidated its operations in the one warehouse in Indianola, Mississippi in 1957. He continued to live in Lexington, and as when he worked in Durant, he commuted daily to his office in Indianola. Leroy and his brother, Herman, also owned the highly successful Georgia Gas Company in Atlanta. During his long and successful tenure at Lewis Grocer, he was depended upon to be the human relations leader of the large organization. Many a person, in business and the community, received wise counsel and advice from Leroy Paris.

Leroy passed away at the age of seventy-four in 1976. Irma passed away in 1987.

Leroy Henry Paris (top)
Irma Herrman Paris (bottom)

Chapter 21

Henry Paris and Rose Leonard Paris
Popular Banker, Owner of Supermarket Chain, Humanitarian

Henry Paris, the only child of Leroy and Irma Paris, was born in Lexington in December 1929. He spent his entire youth there, attending elementary, junior high and high school, graduating in 1948. We are close cousins.

Although only 5'8", he was an outstanding athlete in high school, lettering in all three sports of football, basketball and baseball. Henry jokes when he says that in sports he was small, but slow. He was anything but slow. Having a natural athletic ability, he led his teams to many of the victories they achieved.

Henry showed his merit by becoming an Eagle Scout and represented his high school at Boy's State. He was also a talented musician with his trumpet. He admired the great trumpet players Harry James and Charlie Spivak and did his best to emulate them. He was always able to hit the high note and hold it in the tune "In the Mood," which was a featured song in the swing band of which he was a member.

During high school and college, Henry traveled up and down the high roads and throughout the Mississippi Delta as the lead trumpet in a swing band, formed by myself, known as the Dixiekats. (This is not to be confused with the political party known as the Dixiecrats). The band frequently played in a number of illicit casinos at that time, some of which were likely run by the local mafia, unlike today's Mississippi casinos which are legalized and tightly controlled by the state legislature and gaming commission.

The only problem in those earlier casinos was the fact that the band's music was so good, the casino owners had to continually remind the band to take more breaks so their patrons could get off the dance floor and go to the back rooms where gambling flourished.

My cousin Beryl Weiner, from Atlanta, was adopted as an "Honorary Lexingtonian" when he lived with us during the summers in Lexington. He also played with the Dixiekats, as the lead clarinetist, and continues his playing today with the popular Atlanta Concert Band as their lead bass clarinetist. He could give Pete Fountain a run for his money. Incidentally, besides Beryl's closeness to my mother, Fay Lewis Berman's side of the family in Lexington, he is the one person who holds my father, Joseph E. Berman's side of the family together in the Atlanta area and Georgia. Bi-annually, he organizes a Berman family reunion in the Atlanta area, which attracts nearly a hundred members of the Berman family, and even some of the Lewis family, to this nostalgic event. When Henry and Rose Paris were living in Atlanta, while managing the Paris' Georgia gas business, they attended this gala affair as "adopted" members of the Berman family. Beryl, more than anyone else I have ever known, recognizes that family is the very bedrock of civilization.

Other members of the band, besides myself on lead alto sax, Henry Paris on lead trumpet, and Beryl Weiner, clarinetist, were; Johnny Yarborough (now Dr. John Yarborough) and J.B. Robinson, pianists; Ed Tye Neilson, trumpet; Bob Jordan, from Kosciusko, Mississippi, trumpet; "Pepper" Tidwell and "Snorky" Phelps, trombones; Dick Temple on drums; John Garrett Herbert on sax; Jimmy Terry on sax; and occasionally my future brother-in-law, Dudley Burwell, on tenor sax. I can't recall who played the bass fiddle but he, along with the pianists and drummer, gave us a terrific rhythm section. There was the great trumpet player from Greenwood, Mississippi, "Sonny" Hill, who sat in with us on occasion, when he was not playing on the road with the Jimmy Dorsey and Tex Beneke bands. While writing this book, I recently saw "Sonny" when we were both shopping in a Kroger supermarket. He commented to me that he recalled how impressed the dancers were at one of our gigs, when we played the latest pop songs that had just come out on the radio show *Hit Parade* of most popular tunes. Some years after college, when we had long since disbanded, I gave all of our orchestrations to "Sonny" Hill when he was the band director for Jackson Academy. Then came the Easter Flood of 1979, and all of those valuable orchestrations washed down the Pearl River with much of the school's band equipment.

Those were the days of the Big Bands. Besides the Glen Miller, Tommy and Jimmy Dorsey, Tex Beneke and Harry James bands whose music we played, there was also Guy Lombardo. His theme was "The sweetest music this side of heaven." The Dixiekats' theme was "The sweetest music this side of Guy Lombardo." Unlike the rock and country music bands so popular today, our orchestrations were the oldies such as "Star Dust," "Embraceable You," and "Smoke Gets in Your Eyes." When we wanted to liven things up, we would swing into "In the Mood," "Two O'clock Jump," and stand singing "In Old Shanty Town." Then there was the appropriate title "Down Where the Delta Begins," which featured Henry Paris on solo. Few people had ever heard that song until we made it a familiar sound. After the Easter Flood, that orchestration probably ended up at the mouth of the Mississippi at its namesake—exactly down where the delta begins. Our theme song was "Deep Purple" with which we began and ended each performance.

One of the night spots in which we played frequently, known as Rainbow Gardens, was just outside of Durant, Mississippi. I recall that the owner was named "Blackjack" Powell and was a tall, immaculately dressed man with deep-set eyes and slicked back jet-black hair. One more thing I remember about him was he had a gorgeous blonde wife who was responsible for paying me what our band was due at the end of each performance. The transfer of funds was always made in the back room of the house. His wife was the kind of woman that commanded more than one look. However, each time she paid me off while sitting at a counter, "Blackjack" was standing right beside her. Therefore, as tempting as it was, I was absolutely certain never to give her a second look. I just took what we had earned for the evening's performance and said, "Good night, and thank you, ma'am." Henry, Beryl, and the other band members waited patiently outside the door for their split of the evening's take. That nightclub eventually burned down. It was rumored that our music was just "too hot."

One more comment about the Dixiekats; I enticed John Yarborough, currently a leading dermatologist and concert pianist in New Orleans, to be the band's pianist. We also found J.B. Robinson as a backup pianist. Their differences in style were most intriguing. John played beautifully every note as written in each orchestration. He was an earlier version of Van Cliburn. J.B. couldn't read a note of music, but always improvised and filled in wherever needed to enhance the band's sound and beat. He was an earlier Marvin

Hamlisch. We were most fortunate to have both of them with our swing band.

After being confirmed in Temple Beth El and later graduating from high school in Lexington, Henry matriculated to the University of Mississippi, better known as Ole Miss. He always knew he wanted to attend that school because of its beloved perception in the eyes of many Mississippians and elsewhere. There's a sign in the student union building at the school that reads: "The University of Mississippi is respected—Ole Miss is loved." That mystique brought Henry to Ole Miss, (as it did me, a year later). Just as our fathers, Joe Berman and Leroy Paris, had been roommates and fraternity brothers of Phi Epsilon Pi, a Jewish fraternity at the University of Georgia, so Henry and I were at Ole Miss.

During his college days at the University of Mississippi, Henry left deep tracks. As a student known for his Jewish faith, he became the most popular man on campus being elected to the coveted position known as "Colonel Rebel." That was the first time in history that a football player was ever defeated for that honored title. During Henry's campaign for the highly respected campus honor, I was his campaign manager. We had a large sign on campus at the student union building that read: "5 Million Parisians Can't Be Wrong, Vote for Paris"—and they overwhelmingly did!

Henry was president of Phi Epsilon Pi, Jewish social fraternity; a member of ODK, honorary leadership society; a lead trumpet in the Rebel Band; and cheerleader for three years, during which time he was chosen as head cheerleader. But the highest honor he received at the University of Mississippi was being elected to the Hall of Fame, one of six chosen his senior year.

While at the University, Henry's Phi Ep fraternity was the only Jewish fraternity on campus. Of the twenty Jewish students at Ole Miss during those years, thirteen were members of that fraternity. The one Jewish female was ineligible, and most of the others were members of other Jewish fraternities transferred from other colleges. The Phi Ep Jewish fraternity was so small initially it could not afford a fraternity house, and met—of all places—in a room on the third floor of the University's YMCA. Later it moved into a renovated building located on what used to be called "Vets Village," so named for the veterans that returned to or attended college on the GI Bill after World War II.

As small as it was, this Jewish fraternity led by Henry Paris on the campus of Ole Miss, received the award as the leading small Phi Ep Chapter in the nation. Many of its members were outstanding students, and most were active and assumed leadership roles in campus activities; i.e., head cheerleaders, Colonel Rebel, president of Phi Eta Sigma (honorary scholastic society), ODKs (honorary leadership society), chairman of the student judicial council, vice president of the student body and president of the campus senate (students and faculty), co-chair of the University's Religious Emphasis Week, and Sports Editor of the *Mississippian* (campus newspaper). Five members of the Jewish faith, in different years, have been chosen to the Ole Miss Hall of Fame (two from Lexington, both confirmed at Temple Beth El).

At that time, there was a business fraternity on campus known as Delta Sigma Pi. In their national policy, Jews were banned from membership. Three members of that business fraternity, two Lebanese and one of Syrian heritage, went to the national assembly and through their courageous efforts lobbied enough votes to take that discriminatory clause out of their constitution. This was all done to enable the Ole Miss chapter of that business fraternity to accept Jewish members, including myself.

After graduating college, Henry entered the United States Air Force as a second lieutenant. The next year he married Rose Marie Leonard of Kosciusko, Mississippi. They have three children: Lee, Irma and Rachel.

Completing his military tour of duty as a first lieutenant, he was honorably discharged and enrolled in Michigan State's food marketing program, where he graduated magna cum laude with a master's degree.

Henry worked for a number of years as a retail supervisor, and later vice president in charge of produce for Sunflower Food Stores, a subsidiary of the Lewis Grocer Company, now SuperValu.

While writing about Henry's time at the Lewis Grocer Company and Sunflower Food Stores where I also began my business career, I would be remiss if I did not mention a spirited Irishman by the name of Walter Swain. Walter was Henry's and my boss for several years at the company. Walter was hired by Henry's father, Leroy, along with Celian and Morris Lewis. These three individuals were the mainstay and top management of the Lewis Grocer Company and Sunflower Food Stores. They sought out Walter and hired him from the Colonial Food Store chain of Virginia and the east coast. Walter knew retailing and they knew wholesaling. He filled a gap in their organization that was direly needed after they initiated the Sunflower Supermarket Chain of stores following World War II.

Walter was one of the most inspirational persons Henry and I had ever met. He could speak extemporaneously for hours at a time, and what was amazing was the longer he spoke, the more inspiring he became. He always wore a bow tie. You knew he was really getting into the swing of things when he started perspiring on the forehead, unbuttoned his collar, and let his bow tie clip hang to one side. That's when he really picked up the tempo, and became even more exciting to listen to. He literally held us mesmerized, and some of his expressions were memorable.

When he interviewed someone for a job, he would look at them and ask, "Young man, are you married—or are you happy?" He was pleased when they answered, "Both." However, some of his more meaningful expressions were: "nothing great was ever achieved without enthusiasm" and "in order to be successful at anything you do, you must stay everlastingly at it."

Those last two expressions strongly reinforced what we already knew. In other terms, what he meant was that as one goes through life, there will inevitably be bumps in the road. At times one will get knocked off one's horse. However, when that occurs, it is important to saddle up and ride again. In other words, hang in there. More recently, the same philosophy was aptly expressed by Pete Carroll, famous coach of the University of Southern California's two-year national championship football team. After going thirty-four games undefeated, they lost to the University of Texas in the 2006 Rose Bowl, playing for the national championship. Afterwards, Pete Carroll stated words that are the hallmark of a great leader. He said, "I've always said that one day, somebody would take us; but that's not what's important; what is important is how we respond." Henry has always lived by that philosophy of enthusiasm, vigor and determination. Walter Swain repeatedly referred to Henry in the following manner: "That Henry is a damn fine Jew!" Besides being one of the finest compliments one can receive, Henry is unquestionably just that!

Henry left the company to move into banking (the reverse of his father's footsteps, who started in banking and ended his career in the grocery business). Henry became chairman of Planter's Bank in Indianola, which later grew to a chain of five branches operating in the Mississippi Delta. With the food business still in his veins, he opened and owned seventeen supermarkets, later selling all to his former employees. He and his family owned the Georgia Gas Company, a successful operation in Atlanta founded by Henry's father, Leroy Paris, and his uncle, Herman Paris. It has since been sold.

He was president of the Indianola Rotary Club and Chamber of Commerce. Now fully retired, he spends his time with his family, friends and his synagogue, Temple Beth El in Lexington, where he is the lay rabbi for High Holy Day services. He has manned the pulpit and bima for many years, never missing a service, in addition to attending other services there once a month. Henry followed Joe Berman and me as lay rabbi for the temple. I replaced my father for five years after his tragic death, with my wife Sondy continuing as soloist. When I became an officer in Beth Israel Congregation in Jackson, we attended services there and I relinquished my lay rabbi role in Lexington to Henry. He has been faithfully serving in that position ever since, for the past thirty-five years.

Henry, a true humanitarian, also organized and successfully promoted an annual charitable delta tennis tournament, with the proceeds going to cancer research.

One of Henry Paris's greatest accomplishments came only a few years ago, and once again involved his love and devotion to his faith. This achievement personified his belief in the Fatherhood of God and the Brotherhood of Man. While Henry Paris always put his Judaism and family above all else, the University of Mississippi has also always remained one of his true loves. He and his wife Rose were married in her Delta Gamma sorority house on the campus. Rose's grandmother founded that national sorority. A fervent believer in interfaith activities as a means of promoting understanding and goodwill, Henry and his son, Lee, in 1999, made a historic move of long term implications which enhanced the University of Mississippi's policy of tolerance and respect for the religious beliefs of all.

Knowing there was no synagogue in Oxford, home of Ole Miss, and recognizing the need for continued ecumenical understanding and respect for all religions at the college, they together proposed the building of a non-denominational, non-sectarian chapel on campus—one that would be a house of prayer for all people, regardless of their religious beliefs.

When they went to Chancellor Robert Khayat about the idea, they told him they had only one qualification before they would commit a large sum of funds for this building.

Henry Paris had an interfaith marriage to Rose, as she was and continues to be Presbyterian. They wanted to show students, faculty and visitors of the University that the faith of the civilized world evolved from the Judeo-Christian beliefs, and the holy teachings of both these ancient religions, one of which came out of the other. Their only requirement to fund a large part of the new interfaith chapel was that on the top of the front would be mounted a Cross, over which would be a Star of David. This was to be in the form of a large stained glass window over the entrance, clearly seen by all those that approached the building, day and night, from both the inside and outside.

While the Chancellor approved the idea of a non-denominational chapel, he at first denied the placing of any religious symbol on it, as in conflict with this country's longstanding and important doctrine of separation of church and state—especially since the University is a state-supported institution. The Parises were firm in their stance on the issue. They were determined to have this unique religious symbol included as a major part of the non-denominational chapel, or they would not participate in it financially, which effectively would have ended the chance for such a chapel.

Lee had an idea, and spoke with Henry about it. He said the primary source of any objection to their plan for such a symbol on the chapel would most likely come from the American Civil Liberties Union (ACLU), an organization known for its ultra liberal philosophy. Lee told his father, as a last-ditch effort to get such a chapel built for all the religious affiliations on the campus of Ole Miss, "Let's take this matter up with the ACLU itself. If we can sell them, then the University should have no hesitation in accepting our idea and plan." That they did.

When they met with the attorney's for the ACLU, they presented their plan. The ACLU's initial response was the same as the University's Chancellor, which was that there must be a separation of church and state. The non-denominational chapel was a fine idea, they said, but there could be no religious symbols on the building.

That is when Lee Paris told them there was a religious symbol, a Cross, on a building at a state university in Texas. The ACLU was familiar with the situation, and quickly pointed out that such was part of a family crest of the family who had donated that particular building. Henry Paris quickly responded that with his intermarriage, the stained glass Cross with a Star of David over it was his family's crest. To that, one of the ACLU's attorney's said, "Oh, yeah? How long has that been your family crest?" To which Henry replied, "Oh, about thirty seconds." With that answer, the room was filled with laughter, including from the ACLU attorneys, who then removed their objection and agreed to a Judeo-Christian symbol being placed on the new chapel at the University of Mississippi. To his credit, Lee insisted that the ACLU attorneys put their approval in writing, so there would be no misunderstanding about their approval. With letter in hand, the Chancellor approved the chapel and symbol.

The American Civil Liberties Union was formed to protect and defend the constitutional rights of everyone, applied equally. That is a good and noble cause. Unfortunately, at times the organization has defended people and other groups that would virtually destroy the very freedoms the organization aims to protect. Nevertheless, they made a good and wise decision in this instance.

Today this magnificent edifice is situated overlooking a beautifully landscaped courtyard, between the chapel and the library. The Cross and Star of David are there in a large stained glass tower at the entrance to the chapel, with red and blue (Ole Miss colors) on stained glass windows on each side of the sanctuary.

The chapel stands as a tribute to the Chancellor and the University, each of whom has always been extremely tolerant and respectful of all religious beliefs, and to the Paris family as its founders who share those concepts. Thus "by staying everlastingly at it", Henry and his son Lee accomplished their Godly mission. In 2004, at my recommendation and the invitation of Chancellor Robert Khayat, Rabbi David Ellenson, president of the Hebrew Union College, visited the chapel and spoke to the student body in the new and magnificent Gertrude Ford Center for the Performing Arts.

Henry Paris

Chapter 22

Eugene Sperling Herrman
and Janet Whitehead Herrman
Insurance Executive, Community Leader

Eugene Herrman, son of Sam and Flora Herrman, was born in Lexington in 1910. He grew up there, where he graduated high school and was confirmed at Temple Beth El. He was an alumnus of Washington University in St. Louis.

During World War II he served as a sergeant in the Signal Corps in Europe.

After the war, he established and developed a prosperous insurance agency in town, known as Herrman Insurance Agency. His office was adjacent to the Berman Brokerage Company and the law firm of Joe Berman, just off the square in Lexington. It represented a number of large insurance companies such as The Prudential Insurance Company, The Hartford Fire and Casualty Insurance Company and several others.

Gene was an amiable man who never pressured anyone to buy insurance from his agency, or for any other selfish reason. He always was low-key in his approach. While that made him many friends in the local and surrounding communities, including Tchula (thirteen miles from Lexington), where he had another office, perhaps his quiet and unassuming approach to business never allowed him to build a large agency. Nevertheless, he was considered to be a successful businessman, Rotarian, civic worker, an outstanding golfer at the Lexington Country Club, and was well accepted in the overall community. Gene was a member of Temple Beth El.

Eugene Herrman served his community for many years as a member of the Board of Alderman for the city of Lexington. He also served as president of the Lexington Rotary club. While he was president, he purchased and donated a lectern for use by the president and weekly speakers. That same lectern is still used today, and a plaque with Gene Herrman's name is engraved on it.

Gene and his wife, Janet, lived next door to his brother-in-law and sister, Leroy and Irma Paris. They had one daughter, Betty, who also was raised in Lexington and followed in her father's footsteps by being a successful insurance executive with Liberty Mutual Insurance Company in Atlanta.

Gene Herrman died in 1985. Janet followed a number of years afterwards, in 2003.

Eugene Sperling Herrman

Chapter 23

Isadore Herrman
and Mildred Reichburg Herrman
Cattleman

Isadore Herrman was born in 1888 in Davisborough, Georgia. He was the son of Abraham and Celia Herrman and the brother of Morris, Sam, Jake, Julia, Claudia and Daisy. Isadore was a cattleman. He had a driver that would drive him around the countryside and the state of Mississippi, buying and selling cattle. He also for a time managed the Horseshoe Plantation near Tchula, Mississippi, which was at one time owned by Morris Lewis. Here was another type of trade among the Jews of Lexington.

He and his wife, Mildred Reichburg Herrman, were charter members of Temple Beth El. They were later divorced. They had one daughter, Eugenia Herrman Levitch, who resides in Memphis with her husband, Arthur Levitch.

Isadore died in 1945.

Chapter 24

Aaron Jacobson and Daisy Herrman Jacobson
Oil Man

Aaron was born in 1884 in Poland and managed to settle in Lexington, where he was a past master of the Lexington Masonic Lodge. He married Daisy Herrman, born in 1881, the sister of Julia, Claudia, Sam, Morris, Jake and Isadore Herrman.

Aaron worked for an oil company in the Lexington area.

Daisy was one of the sweetest, most loving aunts anyone could ever hope to have. She was a great baker. Some of the most delicious pastries ever served in the Lexington community were made by Daisy Jacobson. The sweetness of her cakes was more than equaled by the sweetness of her disposition.

Aaron and Daisy were members of Temple Beth El. After Aaron died at an early age, Claudia, who was also widowed by that time, moved from Faymorcele to live with her sister, Daisy.

Aaron died in 1949. Daisy died in 1960.

PAST MASTERS AT CENTENARY CELEBRATION, LEXINGTON LODGE NO. 24 F. & A.M., MAY 1935

Top row - left to right: R.A. Stigler, H.W. Watson, W.L. Jordan, P.H. Duke, A. Jacobson and Sessions Povall. (This photo is currently hanging Williams, C.C. Pahlen, J.K. Young and S. Cohen; bottom row: J.L. in the Lexington Lodge No. 24 in Lexington.) McRae, R.T. Kimbrough, W.P. Hammett, E. Cohen, W.B. Kenna, R.O.

Chapter 25

Isaac Flower and Ester Hyman Flower
Skilled Tailor, Clothing Merchant

In 1862, Isaac Kwiat was born in Kolo, Poland. Looking for freedom and escape from the pogroms of eastern Europe, Isaac and his wife, Ester Hyman, born in 1867 (sister of Isadore Hyman), immigrated to the United States from Poland in 1881. The family name in Poland was Kwiat, from the Polish word for flower, so that's the name they chose when they came to America. Another story told by the family about how their name came to be Flower went as follows: When Isaac Kwiat arrived in the United States he spoke very little English. When the immigration authorities asked him his name, he said, "Blum, like a flower." His name was then recorded as Isaac Flower, and became his official Americanized name.

In the same way that most Jewish men who immigrated around that time period started out, Isaac became a peddler and traveled throughout the countryside. He and Ester first moved to Greenwood, Mississippi. Later they moved to Lexington, where they eventually settled and raised a family. They were among the organizers of the Jewish congregation and founders of Temple Beth El.

It was in Lexington that Isaac Flower, who had been a vest cutter in Poland, started a store where he sold misfit clothing. It was said that Isaac was so skilled in his trade that he could take a size 40 suit and cut it to a size 36 in a short period of time. Isaac's store was known as J. & A. Flower Co. Clothing.

Isaac and Ester raised a family in Lexington. Ester bore six children; Millie, Jacob, Aubrey, Louis, Carrie and Julius ("Pinky"). All of them were raised in Lexington.

Isaac died in 1931. Ester predeceased him, dying in 1930.

Chapter 26

Julius "Pinky" Flower and Ruth Boyd Flower
Movie Theater, Clothing and Dress Shop Owners
Jacob and Aubrey Flower
Clothing Store Owners

Two of Isaac and Ester's sons, Jacob and Aubrey Flower, had a clothing store on the square in Lexington, known as J & A Flower Brothers. Their brother, Julius "Pinky" Flower, also had a store on a corner in town, where he sold used clothes and seconds. Pinky's wife, Ruth Boyd Flower, born in Lexington, was an enterprising woman. She had a fashionable dress shop, known as the Smart Shop. It was located in the same building as J & A Flower Brothers, after they had closed. The other half of that store had a theater, known as The Strand, operated by "Pinky" Flower. Before "Pinky" was married, he slept in the back of his store and rented his home out to Ephraim and Joscelyn Cohen. After he married Ruth Boyd, he and his wife moved into his home. Later, after their divorce, Ruth opened and operated a small restaurant, Casa Manana, next to the old Strand theater. The progressive Lexington community is presently renovating the old Strand theater building and the part next door, where Ruth had her Smart Shop, as a Holmes County arts center.

While Judaism does not proselytize, it is in the discretion of the rabbi to reach out to and welcome those who have professed a sincere interest in or have reason to join the faith of Judaism, as well as to raise their children in the Jewish faith, if they are married to a Jew. Here is an example of that outreach approach in the early part of the twentieth century.

During the early days of Ruth's marriage to "Pinky," the following letter was written to her by Rabbi Sol L. Kory, of P.O. Box 356, Vicksburg, Mississippi. It was dated April 4, with the year estimated to be sometime in the early 1930s:

Dear Ruth—

As I promised you I am sending you, as my gift, this copy
of the little book called "Judaism."

Now—I would like you and Julius to study this little book.
I include "Pinky"—because I think it would be interesting
for him too. Of course—what impressed me most was
your sincerity—Ruth and I do hope that you will have a
child by Julius and that you will have the chance to rear the
child as a Jewish child. With this blessing—I do hope that
you will have true joy in your home.

I am going to be in Lexington the third Sunday in April—
ask Morris Lewis, Jr., if this date is satisfactory. Then
I would like you to come to temple and take part in the
activities of the congregation.

Again wishing you and Julius happiness and with best to
you both and all the folks in Lexington—
        Sincerely-
        Sol L. Kory

"Pinky" and Ruth were later divorced, which was unusual in the
early years of the 1900s. During their married life they did have one
daughter, Emilie Flower, whom they raised in the faith of Judaism.
She was confirmed in Temple Beth El in 1952, along with Julia Lewis,
Elaine Schur, Harry Kaplan and Phil Cohen. Today she lives in
Jackson, Mississippi, yet she continues to attend monthly services
and High Holy Day services in Temple Beth El in Lexington. She
also attends services at Beth Israel Congregation in Jackson.

So, in that particular point, Rabbi Kory got his wish. By profession,
Emilie is a veterinary microbiologist.

Julius, born in 1907, died in 1964. Ruth died eleven months later,
in 1965.

Chapter 27

Abram Flowers and Julia Cohen Flowers
Gourmet Baker, Department Store Owner
Sam Flowers and Flora Flowers
Department Store Owner

Shortly after the turn of the century, Isaac Flower arranged to have two of his nephews from Kolo, Poland, a small Polish town on the German border, join him and his family in America. They immigrated through Ellis Island. The oldest of these, Abram, born in 1886, had been trained and apprenticed as a baker in Poland. He had enormous arm muscles that were the results of kneading bread. When he arrived in Lexington as a teenager, he opened a small bakery next to the Lexington Opera House. As the only baker in town, he did quite well. He continued to make bread, especially big loaves of German rye, for those in the town and county who savored it. He also made beautiful and delicious pastries for parties and special events throughout the area.

Abram's younger brother, Sam, born in 1891, soon joined him. They later opened a clothing store known as Flowers Brothers Department Store. When one immigrated, it was easier to enter the United States if one had relatives. When Abram came through immigration, he used his uncle's adopted name of Flower. Again the authorities had difficulty understanding him and recorded his name as Abram Flowers. Sam came over in 1909, and spelled his name ending with an "s" to be like his brother.

In 1909, Abram married Julia Cohen, born in 1892, the daughter of a local merchant, Samuel Cohen, and sister to Ephraim. A few years later, Sam married Julia's younger sister, Flora Cohen, born in 1899.

In 1915, the Flowers Brothers moved their business to the east side of the courthouse square and began a dry goods business in a two-story wood frame building. The second floor was occupied by the telephone exchange. In 1920, this building was torn down, and with a loan from their father-in-law, Samuel Cohen, the Flowers brothers built the brick building that remains today. The business was named Flowers Brothers.

In 1932, at the height of the Depression, the Flowers Brothers partnership was dissolved. Sam, Flora, and their two children, Helen Frances and Philip Harold, moved to Ruleville, Mississippi.

Abram and Julia continued to run the store in Lexington and renamed the business Flowers Dept. Store. They prospered, becoming one of the most successful Jewish merchants in the town of Lexington.

Abram and Julia raised three children in Lexington; Herman, Earl and Phyllis. All graduated from the Lexington schools and were confirmed at Temple Beth El. Phyllis resides with her husband, Bernie Insler, in Connecticut. They have two children, Amy and Ric. Phyllis recalled that during the Great Depression when she was attending Lexington Elementary School, many of the children would come to school barefooted, since their parents could not afford to buy shoes for them. At the beginning of school each year, Abram would send boxes of tennis shoes to the school, so that the children without shoes could have cover for their feet, especially during the cold winter months. A chapter about Herman follows next.

Earl passed away early in life. Abram died in 1945. Julia passed away in 1993. Sam died in 1943. Flora died in 1970.

Front of Flowers Department Store L to R
Abram Flowers, Ruth B. Flower, Sam Flowers

Herman Flowers, in store years later

Chapter 28

Herman Frederick Flowers and Elvera Lamensdorf Flowers Department Store Owner, Sportsman, Beloved Citizen and Leader

Herman Flowers, born in 1915, was the oldest of three children. He excelled in every endeavor throughout his life. He was confirmed in Temple Beth El in Lexington. An honor roll student, he was an active member of his Lexington High School class. He was one of several Jewish students that played in the Lexington High School band, as a first position trombone player. He was quarterback of the Lexington High School football team that went undefeated in 1932.

After graduating from Lexington High School, Herman went to New Orleans to attend Tulane University. He was on an athletic scholarship and scheduled to play football for the Tulane Green Wave. However, he injured his knee during his freshman year, which prematurely ended his college football career.

At Tulane, he distinguished himself by serving as president of his Jewish social fraternity, ZBT (which later merged with the Jewish fraternity Phi Epsilon Pi, with ZBT being the surviving fraternity name). Herman was also elected President of the Tulane Student Body. He was inducted into ODK leadership fraternity, a high honor society.

Upon graduation in 1937, Herman returned to Lexington to join his parents in their clothing business. Shortly after, he married his college sweetheart, who was a student at Sophie Newcomb College in New Orleans. She was Elvera Lamensdorf of Shelby, Mississippi, born in 1915. Elvera and Herman raised two daughters in Lexington, Beth and Anne.

Sports continued to be a big part of Herman's life as an adult. He promoted local players from Holmes and neighboring counties to college coaches, who grew to depend upon him and his Kodak Super 8 films of the action to fill their rosters with quality players.

The legendary Ole Miss football coach, Johnny Vaught, was particularly appreciative of his efforts, and bought gifts for his staff from Herman's store, out of appreciation. Herman believed that if he could get a young man into a college football program, he could help him get a college education and keep him out of the cotton fields. Herman wanted to start young men on the road to a better life, possibly as a professional football player, or as a coach at a high school or college. He never stopped being an avid sports spectator and friend of the sporting world, taking in high school and college games and track meets all over the state. Even in his last years when his health was failing, generous younger friends, including some coaches themselves, drove him to sporting events around the state.

Herman was also deeply concerned about race relations in Lexington, especially as the civil rights movement brought such fervor to the situation. One of his happiest sports moments related to excellence in sports and demonstrated the excellence of his character. It came at the senior Blue/Gray football game in Mobile, Alabama. In that particular game, Glen Griffin, an outstanding Ole Miss quarterback, later drafted by the New York Giants, and Willie Richardson, a standout wide receiver from Jackson State, later with the Baltimore Colts, were teammates on the first integrated Blue/Gray team in history. Herman beamed with pride when those two hooked up for a long touchdown pass—white to black, and black scored. Herman knew that athletics was a great builder of character and teamwork, including respect for one's teammates of all colors and faiths.

Herman had a contagious laugh and was a great storyteller. He was extremely civic-minded, believing firmly that it was each man's duty to serve their community and make it a better place to live, both in the present and future. Besides serving as president of the Rotary Club and the country club, he was also president of the chamber of commerce and a mediator in race relations. He was highly trusted by both the black and white communities, which enabled him to be a calming influence in those troubled days of racial unrest. Herman Flowers could be considered as one of the reasons the Lexington community was spared the racial violence that occurred in other parts of the state, the South and the nation.

Herman was instrumental in finding and convincing owners of Lexington's first factory, Henson-Kickernick (makers of ladies lingerie) to locate in Lexington, thereby providing many jobs to the unemployed citizens.

His devotion to Temple Beth El and to Jewish concerns in the state was always paramount. He was a past president of Temple Beth El and a Sunday school teacher. He drove his daughters, Beth and Anne, to Jackson each week so that they could participate in Beth Israel Congregation's youth group. They both, along with Herman before them, were confirmed in Lexington at Temple Beth El.

Keeping Temple Beth El as part of their Jewish heritage was important to Herman and to his wife, Elvera. Elvera's name was not the only thing uncommon about her. She had an exuberant personality and a nurturing manner with her daughters. She could initiate a project and focus her energies with unrelenting resolve. She took care of her home and gardens with zeal. With her gardener, she cared for Temple Beth El's grounds for years, and was really excited when it won "yard of the month" honors several times. Elvera was southern living personified, and her meals for family gatherings were truly a southern feast.

After Sam Flowers and Abram Flowers died, Herman became a partner in the business of Flowers Dept. Store with his mother, Miss Julia, as she was called, until her retirement in 1978. Herman continued to successfully operate Flowers Dept. Store until his retirement in 1988.

When Herman Flowers finally closed the doors of Flowers Dept. Store, after years of operation on the square in Lexington, it had been one of the five top retail stores in the history of the Jewish community in Lexington. The other four were the well-known R&B Sontheimer Store that preceded it; Nathan Schur's Department Store; Joe Stern's Sunflower Food Store; and Ephraim and Phil Cohen's Department Store, which continues to successfully operate on the square in Lexington.

During his life in Lexington, Herman was a mainstay in both the Jewish and overall communities. He was one of the most well-liked men in the entire community. Herman passed away in 2002 at the age of eighty-six.

Mourners at his funeral packed Temple Beth El. There was the remaining Jewish community, along with members of all faiths in Lexington, and throughout the state of Mississippi that attended. Several eulogies and tributes were given, a number from the Christian community, including Al Povall, who, among others, had the highest respect for Herman Flowers, a most distinguished man of decency and integrity.

One of those attending Herman's funeral came up to Phyllis Insler, his sister, and related a heartwarming story to her. He was actually crying when he told her that many years before, when his own father died, he went to Herman and told him he didn't have a suit to wear to his father's funeral. He only wore overalls. In the same manner in which Herman's father, Abram, had sent shoes to the children at school, Herman told the man to go pick out a suit, and there would be no charge for it. There were also times when Herman showed his generosity by calling impoverished widows and offering a suit for the deceased husband for his funeral. To make them feel better and not embarrassed about it, he would say something like, "It was returned after being altered and I cannot sell it. I think it will fit your husband just fine." These are only a few stories of the many acts of charity and goodwill that Herman and his father rendered during their lifetimes.

Herman had a brother, Joseph Earl Flowers (1920-1971). His sister, Phyllis, continues to reside with her husband, Bernie, in Connecticut. Daughter Beth resides with her husband, Harry Lebow, in Baltimore. Daughter Anne resided with her late husband, Ken Gold, in Savannah, Georgia, where she continues to live.

Elvera predeceased Herman, passing away in 1992.

Herman Flowers (top)   Herman and Elvera Lamensdorf Flowers (bottom)

Chapter 29

Morris Flink and Mildred Flower Flink
Owner/Operator of Meat Market,
Self-Made Man
Dave Flink and Julia Flink
Owner of Clothing Store

Morris Flink, born in 1888, and his brother, Dave Flink, came to Lexington in the early 1900s. Mildred Flower Flink came to this country first, and also used Flower as her last name, taken from Blum ("bloom"). When her brothers, Abram and Sam, arrived, unlike their sister they added an "s" to their last name, Flowers.

Dave Flink had a prominent clothing store next to Schur's Department Store, where the Texaco station was and the *Holmes County Herald* now stands. Morris opened a meat market directly behind Dave's store. When their establishments burned to the ground, Dave moved with his wife, Julia, to Kosciusko, Mississippi. Dave and Julia had three daughters. Morris and his wife, Mildred, stayed in Lexington. He made an agreement with George Patterson, owner of the IGA grocery store. Morris would lease the market space from George and own and operate the meat market within the IGA premises. George Patterson was pleased because Morris' meat market brought a considerable amount of extra business to the popular IGA grocery store.

Morris was a hard worker, working many hours each day except Sundays. He and Mildred, who was born in 1891, had three daughters; Bernice, Inez and Myra. Morris and Mildred were kind, considerate and well respected in the overall community. They always sat in the same pew at Temple Beth El for religious services.

Bernice was a star on the Lexington High School girl's basketball team. Inez was also a basketball star. She recalls that after practice each day, she and her teammates would walk to either Beall's or People's drug store to sip on five-cent Cokes and nibble on five-cent packages of Nabs. They also spent their Saturdays going to the local Strand Theater to see Buck Jones for ten cents a ticket, and five cents for popcorn. Sometimes, if you didn't have a nickel for popcorn, "Pinky" Flower, owner of the theater, would give you a bag anyway, out of the kindness of his heart.

She also recalls excellent relations between the Jewish and Christian communities of Lexington. Neither she nor any of her family ever experienced any form of anti-Semitism.

Bernice and Inez were confirmed at Temple Beth El. Tragically, Myra never made it to confirmation, as she died in 1943 at the age of thirteen of spinal meningitis. She was a lovely young girl. She carved a heart on a tree that may still stand in Lexington, with her name and mine in the center of that carving. By now, some sixty-five years later, that heart must have grown high up that tree, reaching upward toward the heavens where Myra's soul surely remains at peace.

Morris and Mildred were always very proud of their three daughters. It took them many, many years to learn to live with their great loss of Myra. There is a very poignant tribute to Myra in a later chapter about the Jewish community's relationship with the white Christian community. It is written by Billy Ellis of Lexington, former president and owner of the Holmes County Bank and Trust Company, originally organized as Merchants and Farmers Bank by Morris Lewis, Sr. The tribute is entitled "Myra's Legacy" and is well worth reading.

Inez resides with her husband, Gerald Fried, in Memphis. They have two daughters, Miriam and Marilyn, and one son, Gerald, Jr. Bernice resides in New York. She was married to Clarence Beyer, now deceased. They had two sons, Henry and Mike.

Morris died in 1957. Mildred predeceased him and died in 1948.

Morris Flink and Mildred Flower Flink (top)
Myra Flink (bottom)

Chapter 30

Sol Applebaum and Agathyne Applebaum
Owner of Tailor Shop and Laundry
Nathan Applebaum and Rosebud Applebaum

Sol Applebaum, born in 1882, and his wife, Agathyne Applebaum, born in 1888, had two businesses in Lexington, a laundry and a tailor shop. They developed a big trade in the tailoring business. People in Greenwood and the Mississippi Delta would buy train tickets "to Applebaum's tailor shop." When they went to the train station, they only had to ask for a ticket to "Applebaums" to have a suit or a dress made for them. Agathyne also taught Sunday school at Temple Beth El. I was one of her students and recall that she always had a pleasant smile and a twinkle in her eyes. She succeeded Lena Levy and Julia Flowers, who were the first Sunday school teachers at Temple Beth El.

The Applebaums had four children; three sons, Milton, Manuel and Carl Myer, and a daughter, Rosalind. They all four grew up in Lexington and were confirmed in Temple Beth El. Manuel's class had thirteen, which was the largest one in the history of the temple. Both Milton and Manuel were active members of the Lexington band, and helped their parents in the family businesses. Milton was born in 1920 and died in 1996. He was married to Myra Applebaum (1926-1989).

Agathyne's sister died and left three sons whom Agathyne and Sol also raised in Lexington. They were Sadrian, Berthal, and Florian Bernheim. As men, these three served in the U.S. Armed Forces during World War II, along with Milton, Manuel and Carl Myer Applebaum.

Nathan Applebaum was a brother to Sol. His wife's name was Rosebud. He worked in the Applebaum tailor shop with Sol. He was born in 1885 and died in 1939. Rosebud was born in 1890 and died in 1923.

Sol died in 1940. Agathyne died in 1976. Manuel was born in 1916 and died in 2006, outliving his younger brother, Milton. Except for Rosalind, all are buried in Beth El Cemetery.

Chapter 31

Ben Schur and Ida Fine Schur
Department Store Owner

Ben Schur, born in Russia, immigrated from Kuovo, in Lithuania, to America in 1880. He first lived in Boston, where he got a job with Travis Farber Wholesale Jewelry Manufacturing Company on Washington Street. His future wife, Ida, had a sister who was married to one of the Farber family.

In 1890, he moved south to Memphis, Tennessee. There he worked at a dry goods store. In 1899, his parents, Eli and Gurturde, immigrated to the United States from Lithuania. The 1900 U.S. census notes that living together were Ben, his parents, and his siblings Rosa, Annie, Fannie and Joe. Also in the same home was Ida Fine, Ben's future bride, who had arrived in America a few months earlier.

Ben and Ida had known each other as children in the Old World. In 1900, Ben and Ida were married in Memphis.

On July 1, 1901, they had their first child, Nathan, in Memphis. A second child was born in 1903, Hyman, and in 1911 their third child, Ethel, was born.

In 1911, Ben and family moved to Tchula, Mississippi, after his brother-in-law, Samuel Cohen, opened a successful store in Lexington. Tchula was only a few miles away from Lexington, the county seat, and was a likely spot, since it was on the railway route and halfway between Memphis and New Orleans. Things were tough in the early days in Tchula. They rented part of a house from a woman, and the only bathroom was in her side of the house. She would allow the women to use the bathroom, but not the men. The men had to go "downtown" to use the bathroom. Even the old-style outhouse was more convenient than that—although not as sanitary.

In 1922, the Schur family moved from Tchula to the larger town of Lexington. It was there that they opened Schur's Department Store, a dry goods clothing store, at 310 Court Square. This store remained in continuous business from 1911 to 1995, through three generations.

In 1924, Ben was not in good health, so Nathan took over the store at the age of twenty-three. He had quit school after the eighth grade, to go work in the store and help his father. This allowed his brother, Hyman, and sister, Ethel, to finish their schooling.

Ben and Ida lived in Lexington, on North Street first, and later on Race Street. Ida worked in the store every day, and was a neat lady who always wore a dress and her hair in a bun. Ben loved opera and attended performances in the local opera house in Lexington. He was quite deaf and had an early style hearing aid, a box that was kept in one's pocket with a wire to the ear. Ben chewed tobacco and had a gold spittoon, but was quite clean about it. Both Ben and Ida had nice, quiet dispositions and got along well together in their married life and daily working environment.

Being American immigrants, Ben and Ida worked extremely hard in their clothing store. When Ben came home from work for dinner, he liked soup and he liked it hot. He always complained to Ida that it wasn't hot enough, and why couldn't she have it hot for him after a long day's work. One night, tired of his complaints, Ida kept the soup boiling right until she served a bowl to Ben. He took a giant spoonful, turned red, but didn't say anything. He never again complained to Ida that the soup was not hot enough.

Ben retired in 1954. They moved to Memphis, because they wanted to be able to attend an Orthodox temple (Temple Beth El in Lexington being a Reform temple) and to be near more relatives. Ben died in 1958. After Ben's death, Ida moved to Clearwater, Florida, to live with her daughter, Ethel Schur Peltz. Ethel and her husband, Marvin, had four Peltz Shoe Stores in Florida. Both Ben and Ida are buried in Memphis.

Ben and Ida Fine Schur

Chapter 32

Nathan Schur and Ellen Applebaum Schur
Department Store Owner
Edward Schur and Marilyn Kiser Schur

Nathan, born in 1901, the oldest son of Ben and Ida, took over the store's management in 1954 when his parents, Ben and Ida, moved back to Memphis, where they lived until Ben's death. Nathan managed the store from 1954 until his death on November 2, 1978. His wife, Ellen, and son, Edward, managed the store from 1978 until it closed in 1995.

The store building was the only one to burn down twice in Lexington. It burned to the ground in 1962 and was rebuilt. After the Schurs closed the store in 1995, they rented the building to another merchant. It burned to the ground again in 1997.

When Nathan was thirty-two, he met Ellen Applebaum of Yazoo City, Mississippi, about forty miles south of Lexington. After a couple of dates with her older sister, Esther, he dated and married Ellen, who was much younger. At eighteen, she was a high school beauty. To the public they made a cute couple, since she was taller than he. Ellen gave Nathan a pet name, affectionately referring to him as "short-stuff."

Ellen Applebaum Schur's grandfather, Morris, had moved to Yazoo City from Philadelphia, Pennsylvania. He came to Yazoo City after the great flood on a barge coming down the Yazoo River. He was a peddler, and sold shoes as soon as he got off the barge. Later he opened a dry goods clothing store. He and his wife, Annie Glas, were quite successful. They had eight children. Their oldest son, Harry, was Ellen's father. Harry married Bella Simons of Philadelphia. They were both members of Temple Beth El in Lexington since there was no temple in Yazoo City.

Harry worked at the cotton gin as a weigher and manager. Ellen was one of their six children. Harry became a member of the House of Representatives in the state legislature. He was the sponsor of the bill that ended Prohibition in the state of Mississippi. He said he was a teetotaler and drank no alcoholic beverages. However, he knew that liquor was being sold on the black market in Mississippi and that the state could benefit greatly if liquor was legalized, controlled and taxed to improve schools of the state.

After two terms in the state legislature, Ellen's father, a devoted member of Temple Beth El, became a four-term mayor of Yazoo City. His last term ended in 1966.

Eli N. Evans interviewed Harry about Jews in the South for his book *The Provincials*. He was also written about by Yazoo City author Willie Morris. In his book, Morris stated that when he brought friends from New York down to visit in Yazoo City, nobody could believe that a town in the middle of "sticksville" had a Jewish mayor.

He was a tall, thin man whose family referred to him as "Big Daddy." His wife, Bella, Ellen's mother, was a petite woman known as "Big Momma." It was said that "Big Daddy" may have run Yazoo City, but "Big Momma" ran the home.

In Lexington, Nathan and Ellen had three children; Elaine (July 30, 1936), Morris (1940-2005), and Edward (July 27, 1947). Edward is currently president of Temple Beth El in Lexington.

Ellen, born in 1914, was strong-willed and had the tenacity of a bulldog when she came to one's aid. In the store, Ellen did more of the bookwork and Nathan more of the selling because he liked it. If someone came in and wanted a good deal, they knew that Ellen was fair but tough to deal with, so they approached Nathan. He was seen as more of a pushover, especially when it came to helping those less fortunate.

Despite his lack of formal education, Nathan was self-educated through his reading and was quick in math. He and Ellen worked six days a week, and Nathan would come in on Sunday morning for a few hours, in case someone needed anything before church. On Christmas Eve, they never closed the store until customers stopped coming in, regardless of how late it got. They seldom took vacations together because one of them had to be there to manage the store at all times. Ellen would vacation in Atlantic City and Philadelphia, where she had a sister and family. Nathan would travel to Florida to visit his mother. Later when their son, Edward, could manage the store, they were able to travel together to visit their children in many states, including Hawaii.

They believed in instilling a strong work ethic in their children and grandchildren, having them work in the store to help out and also to learn what business was about.

Nathan was one of the few Jewish members of the Lexington community who did not become a Rotarian. Instead, he was a charter member of the Lexington's Lions Club, another fine international civic and charitable organization. He was a member of the Lexington Chamber of Commerce and also a member of the democratic election committee. Ellen, like most Jewish women of Lexington, was an active member of Temple Beth El's Sisterhood.

Nathan and Ellen were avid readers. Nathan mainly kept up with current events and read history and Wild West books; Ellen read mainly romance novels. Nathan got to see the Wild West cowboy life when he traveled to Oklahoma City to visit his son, Morris, who was stationed there while in the Air Force. As a matter of fact, they read so many books that the Lexington library often had to obtain books through an inter-library loan. Reading wasn't expensive and was their main source of entertainment.

Nathan was a light smoker, and smoked one Roi Tan cigar a night. Ellen and Nathan had a longtime cook and maid, Bertha Kirkland, who wore a kerchief around her head and looked just like "Aunt Jemima," the woman pictured on the Aunt Jemima syrup bottle. Their favorite foods of those she cooked were steak, biscuits and cornbread.

Nathan was conservative with his money and was well insured. He always carried a lot of cash, especially when going out of town, in the days before credit cards became so prevalent.

In 1978, CBS News did a two-night TV special called "Blacks in America," with Ed Bradley. Staff from CBS and Ed Bradley came into Schur's store and interviewed Nathan. They chose Holmes County because of its large black population and low per capita income. The show was to be an exposé comparing the inequalities of blacks and whites, and comparing the North to the South. Some merchants they tried to interview said they had no comment and walked away. That's what CBS expected, people hiding something. When the group came to the Schur's store, Nathan answered their questions openly and truthfully, and made Lexington look good. They asked him about opportunities for blacks. He said there were many black-owned businesses, a black sheriff, and other black city officials in town. He told them that he currently employed three blacks and no whites. He also explained there were nice black-owned homes in town and where they could find them. They then interviewed Benny Davis, a black man working in the store, who told Bradley there were job opportunities for blacks if they wanted to work and furthermore, he had been able to raise twelve children in Lexington. While Benny was being interviewed, Nathan could be seen in the background, leaning against the counter and swinging his keys on a long chain. He looked calm and made Lexington look the way it was — hospitable and friendly.

His family was the most important part of his life. He bought a second home for his daughter, Elaine, when she moved back to Lexington with her two children after a divorce. They lived in the house for a dozen years while in Lexington. When Edward and his wife, Marilyn, moved back to Lexington, they lived in the same house for years, until they moved into Ellen and Nathan's home. Today Edward's daughter, Terri, and her husband, Bret, live in that same house. Nathan's foresight provided for his family's security for decades to come.

The high-fat diet of his cook's southern specialties and worries about the boycotts during the civil rights days and lack of business caused Nathan's first heart attack. On the last day of his life, he was doing what he enjoyed the most, being with Ellen and pushing his new granddaughter, Elizabeth, in her stroller. Later that night he died from a sudden second heart attack.

Ellen stayed busy in the store and nurturing her children, grandchildren and great-grandchildren. She died in Lexington in 1995 at the age of eighty-one.

What put an end to Schur's store and other small-town merchants all over the South? In 1900, 95 percent of the population of America were farmers; today less than 1 percent. Regardless of what the merchants did, things would never be the same without the income from the farm workers and farming population.

Elaine married John Martin Rich, a college professor, and had two children; Jeffrey and Suzanne. Elaine, now divorced, and both children all live in Atlanta. Jeffrey, who contributed much of his family's information for the book, is a computer analyst. Suzanne married her high school sweetheart, Scott Brown, of Tuscaloosa, Alabama. They have three children.

Morris went to the University of Mississippi, then to the University of Colorado and the Air Force Academy. He married Stephanie Morris. Morris spent twenty years in the Air Force and retired as a lieutenant colonel. He then worked for Kodak until his retirement. They had two children, Jacqueline and Keith. Morris is recently deceased.

Edward married Marilyn Kiser of Indianola in 1976. Edward and Marilyn both worked for the Lewis Grocer Company in the computer department. They moved to Lexington in 1976 to work in the Schur's family department store until it closed in 1995. They have two daughters, Sara Elizabeth and Terri Crystal, both of whom work in Jackson. Edward has served for several years as president of Temple Beth El and also as president of the Lexington Rotary Club.

L to R in store Nathan Schur, and Ellen Applebaum Schur. Far right Maurice Auerbach

Chapter 33

Samuel Kaplan and Yetta Flower Kaplan
Dry Goods Stores Owner

There also was the Kaplan family, dedicated members of Temple Beth El who had a store in the nearby community of Pickens, a small rural town outside of Lexington.

Samuel Kaplan, born in 1906, immigrated to Mississippi in 1923 from Poland. He was only seventeen years old at the time. He became a partner in Kaplan Brothers, a small dry goods store in Pickens. He had two brothers, Joseph and Jacob, in business in Canton, Mississippi, about thirty-five miles south of Lexington and twenty-five miles south of Pickens, on the way to Jackson.

Samuel was active in Temple Beth El in Lexington from the time he settled in Pickens. He was one of the few members of the congregation able to read Hebrew during the services. He married Yetta Flower, born in 1906 and formerly of Lexington, in Chicago in 1930. In 1936, their first child, Harry, was born, and in 1942 a second son, Roy, was born. Samuel eventually had businesses in Pickens, Goodman and Canton, until he passed away in 1954. He was an active member of the Pickens Masonic Lodge.

Samuel would get up on Sunday morning and drive Harry and Roy to Sunday school in Lexington on the days that it met. Temple Beth El, where Harry and Roy were confirmed, was always an inspiration to each member of their family. Harry commented that the stained glass windows were so beautiful, and when the afternoon sun streamed through them, everyone's heart was filled with joy and holiness.

Samuel's wife, Yetta Flower Kaplan, was also an active member of the congregation in Lexington and in the temple sisterhood for many years. She operated the business in Pickens until 1968, when Harry moved back from Albuquerque, New Mexico, to take over. She continued to come to work each day until she passed away.

Harry and his family worshipped in Lexington at Temple Beth El, in his childhood and as an adult, until Harry and his wife, Sandy, moved to Arizona in 2000. He commented that the congregation was always very small, so that if anyone missed the services it was immediately noticed.

Harry and Sandy have three children; Steven, Seth and Tammy. They now reside in Phoenix. Roy and his wife, Maggie, have two daughters, Deborah Lynn and Sybil Leah. He and his family reside in Virginia.

Sam died in 1954. Yetta died in 1991.

Samuel Kaplan

Chapter 34

The Lowentritt Family
Farmers and Merchants

It was a rare occasion when Morris Lewis, Sr., of Lexington, ever foreclosed on any property. As stated earlier, during the Great Depression he mortgaged everything in order to preclude foreclosing on his debtors. However, in this particular instance, he foreclosed on a plantation near Tchula, Mississippi, situated just thirteen miles from Lexington. No disrespect to Tchula, but I've always thought of that town, which was smaller than Lexington, as a suburb of Lexington, the county seat.

Horseshoe Plantation was so named for being in the shape of a horseshoe, with a large lake of the same name formed in the same manner. Some years later while Morris was building his business empire, the plantation was used for many southern-style galas, with fried fish, cornbread, turnip greens, black-eyed peas, watermelon and a variety of entertainment. In 1929, shortly after taking ownership of the plantation, Morris's only daughter, Fay Lewis, married Joe Berman from Atlanta and a big celebration and picnic was held at Horseshoe Plantation in their honor.

In the late 1930s, Morris Lewis sold the plantation to the Lowentritt family from Winnsboro, Louisiana. The father owned a bank in Winnsboro. There were two brothers who bought the property; one named Leo and the other named Louis.

These two brothers were highly educated. Leo had received a degree in physics from MIT, and Louis had earned an MBA from Columbia. Despite their educational background, they chose to own a mercantile store in Winnsboro, living among their family. Every six months, one brother would tend to the store in Winnsboro with his family, while the other brother and his family would take care of Horseshoe Plantation, just outside of Tchula, where their children would attend school.

As it happened, they apparently had much more success as merchants than farmers. While their children continue to own the plantation, they lease it out to others to farm.

Both families were devoted members of Temple Beth El in Lexington, and faithfully attended services there monthly and during the High Holy Days. Both Louis and Leo are now deceased.

Leo and his wife, "Sis," had three children. Leo Lowentritt, Jr. was a fraternity brother of Phil Cohen at Tulane. He is now a doctor living in Alexandria, Louisiana. His sister, Jean Kaplan, also resides in Alexandria. A brother, Henry, resides in New Orleans, Louisiana, where he owned a shipping line before selling it and retiring.

Louis and his wife, Dot, had three children. Louis, Jr. and his sister, Ann, are now deceased. Their brother, Phil, continues to reside in their former home of Winnsboro, Louisiana.

Chapter 35

Herbert Smullian
Vivacious Salesman, Owner of
Major Building Supply Company

One of the most dashing members of the Lexington Jewish community was Herbert Smullian. He was handsome, with a small mustache, and dressed immaculately. He smoked small cigars known as cigarillos. He owned a yellow convertible car and had an outgoing personality. Herbert grew up in Florida, graduated from the University of Georgia, and was a member of Phi Epsilon Pi fraternity. He was the nephew of Joe Berman. Joe, knowing of Herbert's positive outlook and charming demeanor, convinced him to move to Lexington after graduation and take a sales job with the Lewis Grocer Co. He became a member of Temple Beth El.

Herbert worked there and was a highly productive salesman until just before World War II, when he enlisted in the military. He was a captain and served in the Philippines.

During his return to the United States, Herbert was on a large military transport ship. Like many of the troops who had nothing else to do during the long sea journey home from the Pacific Theater, he became involved in a crap game. On the trip home, Herbert won so much money that he decided to resettle in his original home state of Florida. He used his winnings to open the Smullian Building Supply Company of Jacksonville. There was so much demand for housing after the war, and wisely being in the growth state of Florida, Herbert's company became one of the leading building supply houses in the country and thrived for many years.

Herbert and his wife, Rachelle, from whom he later divorced, had two daughters, Shay and Lisa. Herbert Smullian was born in 1916 and died in 1993.

Herbert Smullian

Chapter 36

Goldberg and Stein Shoot-out
Dueling Pistols on the Square
1919 Shoot-out on the Lexington Square
Between Two Jewish Men

On a Monday in 1919, Jewish grocery store owner Harry Goldberg was shot and killed by Paul Stein. Three different articles in the *Lexington Advertiser* weekly newspaper described the shootout as follows:[27]

"Harry Goldberg Killed by Paul Stein Monday"

"One of the most deplorable occurrences in the history of our city was a shooting affray in the grocery store of Harry Goldberg last Monday afternoon which resulted in the death of Harry Goldberg and the wounding of Paul Stein, the principles in the affair. Mr. Goldberg was shot through the body with a 25 caliber pistol, while Mr. Stein received a glancing shot in the upper portion of the stomach, from which he is recovering. Exact details of the affair are as yet unobtainable, but will probably develop at the preliminary hearing to be held when Mr. Stein has sufficiently recovered from his wounds to justify it.

It appears that Paul Stein, being dissatisfied over some canned goods purchased at Goldberg's, went to the latters store for an adjustment, carrying his pistol with him. Words followed words resulting in the fatal shooting affray. It appears that Mr. Goldberg fired the first shot, which by reason of Mr. Stein, knocking the pistol, caused a glancing instead of a direct shot which necessarily would have been fatal. The pistol used by Mr. Goldberg was of 25 caliber.

After the shooting, Mr. Stein, who believed himself mortally wounded, rushed to the Arlington Hotel and physicians were immediately summoned. Owing to this shot and organic heart trouble, the doctors could not at once determine the full extent of Mr. Stein's injuries which proved not to be fatal.

Immediately after the shooting, Sheriff Beal impaneled a coroner's jury consisting of Morris Lewis, B.R. Stigler, W.M. Hester, Jr., J.Lipsey and J.R. Watson, Jr. And W. Lemon Smith, who after due examination rendered the verdict that "Harry Goldberg came to his death from gunshot wounds inflicted at the hands of Paul Stein."

The body of Harry Goldberg was taken in charge by C.S. Harrell, manager of Barr-Gwinn Co.'s undertaking department, who embalmed it for shipment. Owing to the number of perforations to the body and severances of arteries, he was compelled to cut the body open in order to make the embalming effective. The body was held until Tuesday evening, when a brother of the deceased, Roderick Goldberg of Arkansas, and a brother-in-law arrived and carried it to Memphis where it was buried in the Jewish cemetery.

Mr. Roderick Goldberg turned the keys of the grocery store of the deceased over to C.S. Harrell with the request to sell the fruit and perishables, pending his return Thursday, (yesterday), to take definite action in regard to winding up or continuing the business, as may be desired by the widow of the slain man.

Mrs. Goldberg, who had been ill is completely devastated at the loss of her husband and is at the community hospital for treatment while her two children are being tenderly cared for by Morris Lewis and family.

Harry Goldberg was born in Arkansas, his parents having emigrated from Germany. He is survived by his wife and two children, and by a brother and sister. After a service of six years in the army he went to Durant and opened a restaurant which he shortly afterwards sold, buying a little farm near Mcmilias. This he in turn sold and purchased this stock of goods of W.J. Overstreet and conducted the business at the same stand enjoying a good patronage. He had also purchased a residential lot, and intended to enlarge and improve a small building thereon for a home for himself and family.

The only eye witness to the shooting affair so far known was a little son of the deceased.

The tragedy is deeply deplored by all."

The next article in the Lexington paper appeared the following week:

"Paul Stein acquitted of murder charge"

"The grand jury hearing of Paul Stein charged with murder of Harry Goldberg on Monday afternoon, November 24, was held before Judge G. D. McCaleb, Judge E. E. Brown and Judge J. G. Grace at the Arlington Hotel Wednesday forenoon. Hon. A. M. Pepper represented the defendant and Hon. H. H. Johnson the State. C. S. Harrell and a son of the late Harry Goldberg and Mr. Stein were examined. After hearing the testimony of the witnesses and the argument of the attorneys, the judges retired for consultation, returning in a few minutes with a verdict of acquittal."

An article in the following weekly Lexington newspaper stated:

"Goldberg merchandise sold to J. A. Brown"

"Sam Herrman, as administrator of the estate of the late Harry Goldberg, offered the stock of merchandise for sale to the highest bidder for cash. The highest offer made was $1,550 by Col. John A. Brown, and he was declared the purchaser. Mr. Brown immediately sold one-half of the stock to W. P. Hammett. What disposition messrs. Brown and Hammett will make of the stock has not been made public so far."

Chapter 37

Sam Cohen and Rosa Schur Cohen
Owner of Three Stores

Samuel J. Cohen was born in Kuovo, Russia, in 1862. His father was a grain dealer for the Tsar, and traveled throughout Europe selling grain for the Russian government. At the age of thirteen, Samuel began traveling with his father and became fluent in six languages.

Rosa Schur, sister to Ben Schur, was also born in Russia in the year 1867. Her father was a rabbi. Believing that there was far greater freedom to practice his faith and opportunities for a better life for himself and his family in the United States, he packed up his family and emigrated around 1880.

Shortly after, Samuel Cohen also left Russia in search of his girlfriend, Rosa Schur. Upon arriving in New York City, Samuel found work at the dock unloading ships. When he was able to save up a few dollars, he bought a peddler's pack, as was typical of so many Jewish immigrant men of that time. He ventured out to the wilds of western Pennsylvania and part of Ohio where he could get more money for his merchandise.

After a few years of peddling, he returned to New York and located Rosa. Apparently, she was still waiting for him and they were reunited and married.

Rosa was a sickly person and had always suffered from asthma. They decided that a warmer climate would be better for her. Having relatives that had already settled in Memphis, they moved south to the bluff city.

Their first child, Eva, was born in 1888. Eva made news in 1895 when, according to *The Commercial Appeal,* she was the first person in Memphis to have an appendectomy. The surgery was performed on the kitchen table of the Cohen residence.

Samuel and Rosa had five children by 1900; Eva, Julia, Mollie, Philip and Flora. Samuel operated a small store in the Pinch neighborhood of Memphis.

Things were going well for the family, except that Samuel suffered greatly from an ulcerated stomach. The only known relief at that time was natural spring water containing a large amount of alkaline. So Samuel boarded a train to Mississippi in search of soothing spring water, having heard it existed there.

The train stopped in Tchula, just a few miles west of Lexington, at a round house to be refueled and take on water. When Samuel inquired about a room, someone recognized his accent and said there were several Jewish merchants in Tchula. He was greeted warmly by these merchants because he could speak Yiddish and knew how to play pinochle.

Samuel never made it to the natural spring water for which he was searching, but noted that after a few days in Tchula there was no pain from his ulcers. Anxious to have another member of the faith in their midst, the other Jewish merchants told him they would help him start a business in Tchula if he would move there.

Samuel returned to Memphis, packed up his wife and five children, and moved to Tchula in May of 1900. It was in that town where Rosa Cohen gave birth to two more children. Ephraim was born in 1901 and Estelle was born in 1904.

While Tchula was a bustling town in the early 1900s, there were certain limitations. The public school was a one-room building with one teacher for eight grades. The Cohen's two oldest daughters, Eva and Julia, were sent back to Memphis to live with relatives and attend high school.

A few miles away was Lexington, the county seat of Holmes County. A new, modern school building had been erected there in 1904 and the Temple Beth El synagogue had been built in 1905.

In 1908, Henry Rosenthal convinced Sam Cohen to move to Lexington, not only because of the better school and a new temple, but also because Mr. Rosenthal owned a store building he needed to rent. This turned out well for all parties concerned.

In 1921, Henry Rosenthal passed away. His only son, Jake, was a doctor practicing in Virginia. Dr. Rosenthal returned home to settle his father's estate, and sold the remaining three stores in his father's building to Samuel Cohen, who continued to prosper. Sam was a past master of the Lexington Masonic Lodge.

However, five years later, 1926 was a devastating year for the Cohen family. Eva, the eldest of the Cohen children, had married

Dave Miller of Drew, Mississippi. Eva's younger brother, Phil (1894-1926) had married Rebecca Livingston of Cleveland, Mississippi, and had rented a store building in Drew from his brother-in-law, Dave Miller. Both families resided in Drew. Dave Miller, who suffered from asthma, suffocated during an attack and died, leaving Eva with three small sons to raise by herself. About three weeks earlier, her brother, Philip Cohen, died from a ruptured appendix. At the time of his death, he was taking a train to Memphis for an appendectomy. Shortly after, Samuel Cohen had a heart attack. He was unable to continue working full-time.

Mollie Cohen (1897-1951) was a spinster and helped in the store. Sam died in 1943. Rosa died in 1949.

Sam Cohen and Rosa Schur Cohen

Chapter 38

Ephraim Cohen and Jocelyn Stern Cohen
Founder and Owner of
Cohen's Department Store;
Continues in Business Today

Ephraim Cohen was born in Tchula, Mississippi, in 1901, the son of Samuel and Rosa. He was confirmed at Temple Beth El. He graduated from Lexington High School in 1920 and was offered a track scholarship to the University of Mississippi in Oxford. Instead, he opted to open a clothing store in Tchula with his cousin, Hyman Schur.

After Ephraim's father, Samuel Cohen, became ill and unable to continue his full-time work, Ephraim sold his interest in his store in Tchula and returned to Lexington to operate his father's store. He also opened the Economy Store in the location originally occupied by H. A. Rosenthal as Rosenthal Brothers. Then in 1930, Ephraim bought his father's store and continued to operate both businesses.

Ephraim was active in the Masonic Lodge, serving as master of the lodge in 1930. As a tribute to him, Ephraim's name is engraved on the cornerstone of the old hospital in Lexington, which was built during his term as Lodge Master. Later that year, his friend Julius "Pinky" Flower introduced him to Jocelyn Stern of Greenwood, born in 1910. In 1932, Ephraim and Jocelyn were married. The two resided in Lexington and raised a family. Sylvia Lynn was born in 1933 and Phillip Raymond was born in 1937.

In 1935, Ephraim had new storefronts put on his two stores in Lexington—E. Cohen's Dry Goods and the Economy Store.

A few years later, in 1937, he sold the Economy Store to his nephew, Freddie Miller, who operated it as a variety store. Ephraim remained active in the Masonic Lodge and in 1943 was given an even greater honor, by being elected Grand High Priest of the state of Mississippi. Because of World War II, he agreed to serve two terms. At the same time, J.P. Coleman served as Grand Master of the lodge for the state of Mississippi. Ephraim Cohen and J.P. Coleman became close friends and made many trips together. J.P. Coleman later became governor of Mississippi, and he always cherished his close friendship with Ephraim.

Ephraim became a partner in a real estate firm with two members of the Povall family and two bankers, William Ellis and Will Wilson. They bought and operated the Lexington Compress for about ten years. They also purchased and sold numerous farms.

Jocelyn was an active member of Temple Beth El's sisterhood and was a member of its choir. She was an excellent businesswoman, and was most helpful to Ephraim in his business activities.

Ephraim and Jocelyn's daughter, Sylvia Lynn, was confirmed at Temple Beth El, and was involved in many activities during her days at Lexington High School. She was a straight-A student and a clarinetist. She played in the Lion's All State Band, was a basketball player, and was co-editor of the school annual and school paper. Sylvia later graduated from the University of Texas.

Living in Dallas with her husband, Murray Benenson, Sylvia Lynn served as president of the greater Dallas National Council of Jewish Women and also became a member of the NCJW national board of directors.

Information about their son, Phillip Raymond Cohen, can be found in the next chapter.

Ephraim died in 1986. Jocelyn died in 2000.

Ephraim Cohen (top)
Jocelyn Stern Cohen (bottom)

Chapter 39

Phillip Raymond Cohen and Sally Stein Cohen
Last Remaining Jewish Merchant in Lexington; Continues to Successfully Own and Operate Cohen's Department Store
Historian and Community Leader

Phil Cohen, born in Lexington, enjoyed the advantages of a small town high school by being able to participate and achieve in many school activities. He lettered in football, basketball and, following in the footsteps of his father, Ephraim, he also lettered in track. He sang in the glee club, played drums in the band, and was on the school's annual staff. He was confirmed at Temple Beth El.

After high school, he attended Tulane University in New Orleans and was active in the Zeta Beta Tau Jewish fraternity. He also played the drums in the University's band.

Phil graduated with a BA degree in economics in 1959. In 1960, Phil joined the Mississippi Army National Guard, went through OCS in Fort Sill, Oklahoma, and was commissioned as an officer.

Phil worked with his father, Ephraim, in Lexington until 1964, when he went to New York to interview for a job as a stockbroker. He was hired by Bache and Co. and worked in their San Antonio, Texas office for the next ten years. During most of this time, he served as assistant office manager and represented the firm in civic activities. Phil became active in Toastmasters International, serving as president of his club and area governor. In 1972, he was honored by being elected "outstanding toastmaster of district 56" which encompassed most of Texas and Mexico.

Returning to Lexington in 1975, Phil bought his father's business and became active in civic affairs. He has served as scoutmaster, president of the Lexington Rotary Club, president of the Holmes County Country Club, and president of the Lexington Chamber of Commerce. Additionally, he organized the Holmes County Chamber of Commerce and served as its president for two years. He also is a member of the Central Holmes Academy school board, a member of the arts commission, and is on the board of Main Street. He was chairman of the board of the Mississippi Retail Association in 1994, and served on it for more than twenty years.

Last, but far from least, he was president of Temple Beth El in Lexington, the "House of David in the Land of Jesus."

In 1979, Phil bought a seat on the New Orleans Commodity Exchange, which traded cotton, rice, and soybeans. He had plans to form a commodity brokerage business and move to either New Orleans or Chicago. Later that same year, he met Sara Ann "Sally" Stein from Greenville, and they were married in February 1980. Phil and Sally have three children, "born within four years of one another"—Samuel, Jeffrey and Sarah—and they decided to make Lexington their permanent home.

While Temple Beth El had many confirmations, the largest being in 1929 with thirteen confirmants, the first bar mitzvah was that of Phil and Sally's son, Samuel, on April 23, 1994. Jeffrey Cohen became a bar mitzvah in March 1995, and Sarah Cohen was the first bat mitzvah on April 28, 1998. Capacity crowds consisting of both members of the Jewish and Christian faiths attended each service.

All three of the Cohen children spent most of their summers at the Henry S. Jacobs Camp in Utica, Mississippi. Sam now works with his father in Cohen's Department Store. Jeffrey is with the investment department in Wells Fargo Bank in Minneapolis. Sarah is a recent honors graduate in Judaic studies and sociology at Indiana University.

During the devastating Hurricane Katrina of 2005, Sarah showed her mettle by setting a fine example of community service, not just in the Jewish community, but the community of humankind.

She returned to Bloomington, Indiana, home of the University, on August 25, 2005 for her junior year. Four days later, Hurricane Katrina hit the Mississippi Gulf Coast and New Orleans. True to her Jewish, southern and American spirit, in October she began talking with some of her college friends about spending their Christmas vacation working on the coast to help FEMA. The response was very gratifying. After a number of students agreed to help, Sarah talked with some of the IU faculty about organizing a trip to the coast. She was told that if she could raise funds for transportation,

IU would sponsor the project. This was no easy task, but the funds were raised. Six buses and two vans were chartered to take more than 200 college students to the Mississippi Gulf Coast, to help with the removal of debris from Katrina's destruction. At that time, this created the largest presence of student assistance to the devastated region. When Sarah was asked by her father how she was able to talk so many students into participating, she said she just asked if they would like to spend their Christmas vacation on the beach! Articles appeared in the Bloomington newspaper and the IU newsletter, praising Sarah's efforts, the students who participated in this humanitarian endeavor, and the success of their mission. Sarah also participates in other community projects as well. Quoted in the Indiana University Newsletter, Sarah said, "I had always been an individual—but I wasn't the leader that I am now. All of these experiences have made me step up."

Sally Cohen is a marathon runner, participating in several races. She also is musically talented, playing a bassoon in the Mississippi Symphony and Mississippi Pops orchestras. She is an active member of Temple Beth El's Sisterhood.

Phil Cohen knows more about the Jewish community of Lexington, both past and present, than any other living individual. More about Phil and his contributions to the welfare of Lexington will appear in my interview of Elder James Rodgers of the black community in Lexington and its relationship with the Jewish community.

Phillip Raymond Cohen, front of Cohen's Dept. Store
Phillip Raymond Cohen, inside Store

Chapter 40

Freddie Miller
Variety Store Owner

David Miller, born in 1882, was married to Eva Cohen, sister to Ephraim. Eva was born in 1888. They had three sons; Nathan, Freddie and Herbert, all born in Drew, Mississippi. Herbert was killed in World War II at the Battle of the Bulge in 1944 and was buried in Beth El Cemetery.

Nathan had a variety store in Drew, Mississippi.

Freddie was born in 1914. After returning from military service in World War II, he went into business with his brother in Drew, and also opened a variety store in Lexington, which he bought from his Uncle Ephraim. Freddie married Vera Mundth of Helena, Arkansas. Freddie was an outgoing member of the Lexington community and seemed to always be smiling. He spent time in both Lexington and Drew and would commute between his businesses in the two towns. While in Lexington, he roomed at the home of Mrs. Julia Flowers, mother of Herman Flowers of Flowers Brothers Department Store. Freddie was an active member of Temple Beth El in Lexington.

David Miller died in 1926 and Eva Cohen Miller died in 1972. They are both buried in Beth El Cemetery. Freddie died in 1987.

Chapter 41

Joe Stern and Phyllis Berkower Stern
Owner/Operator of Supermarket

Joe Stern met his future wife, Phyllis Berkower Stern, at a small Masonic USO hall while he was stationed in Staten Island. They dated for about six to nine months after which Joe went overseas. While Joe was overseas, love was stronger than distance, and they became engaged. In his absence, Joe's mother, who lived in Memphis, bought a diamond for him on Memphis' famous Beale Street from someone she knew and had it mounted at Broadnax, a major jewelry store in Memphis.

When the war was over, Joe was honorably discharged from the navy. He and Phyllis were married and honeymooned in Niagara Falls. They returned to Memphis flat broke, according to Joe. His brother, Sol, owned a grocery store in Memphis and loaned Joe $4,000. He was loaned a similar amount by Ephraim Cohen, his brother-in-law, as well as $500 from his grandmother.

Joe was Jocelyn Cohen's younger brother. Ephraim Cohen saw an opportunity and arranged for Joe to rent a store building next to Ephraim's store in order to open a grocery store in Lexington. In June of 1946, Joe opened a small grocery store, spending all the loan money on paint, wiring and shelving, along with refrigeration for a meat market, which was unavailable until September of that year. His store was called Liberty Cash, a large local chain in Memphis. Joe had grown up in Memphis with the sons of the owner of that chain.

The Sterns stayed with Liberty Cash for seventeen years and raised three lovely daughters. About that time, Joe and Phyllis considered moving back to Memphis. His brother suggested that Joe talk to Morris Lewis, Jr., about finding a buyer for his store so Lewis Grocer Co. could get another customer for its wholesale distributorship. Morris Lewis, Jr., listened to Joe and then advised him that he would be making a mistake to sell his store in Lexington since he had spent seventeen years building his business and customer base. Joe had heard that Lewis Grocer Co. wanted to build a big Sunflower Food Store in Lexington. Joe Berman also advised his friend Joe Stern that, rather than sell or compete with Sunflower, Joe should consider becoming a franchisee of Sunflower in Lexington. Such a move would provide all the benefits of that name and Lewis Grocer Company's franchise program.

Lewis was the leading corporate and franchise food chain in the state at the time and the state's largest food distributor. Joe Stern followed the advice he had received and became a member of the fast-growing Sunflower Food Store chain.

In 1963, Joe Stern built his own building just off the square near the Holmes County Bank and Trust Company. There he opened a Sunflower Food Store, the first store of that regional chain in Holmes County. It was the most modern supermarket in the town of Lexington. Joe was a hard worker and an excellent operator, paying meticulous attention to each department of his supermarket. He also treated his customers with care. Joe said that for the first few years of his new operation, it was tough going. However, he then put in S&H green stamps which, while expensive, built his business. His supermarket operation became highly successful.

In the days of the civil rights turmoil, Lexington's grocery stores went through several boycotts. Joe decided to sell his store to another Sunflower franchisee and live off the rent and other income from his investments. He looked at getting a job with a food broker, but there were no openings available. Retail sales representatives had strenuous jobs, working their products onto the shelves of the supermarkets, with long days of traveling and out of town work. He was fifty years old by then, and his age was against him for such work.

After the Sunflower five-year lease term was up, Joe decided to buy his store back from the current owner. Three years later, he had open heart surgery (one bypass). He fully recovered and kept the store for another seven years and then sold out due to labor problems. That time he stayed out, and it was for the best. In 1992, he had a big heart attack, from which he also recovered. He leased his store building once again to a chain dollar store and they have been a solid tenant for the past fifteen years. He recently sold that building.

Joe and Phyllis are very active in the affairs of Temple Beth El. They have three daughters: Amy, Susan and Nancy. Two of his daughters,

Susan and Nancy, got a grant from S&H for college and both went to the University of Texas. The oldest daughter, Amy, went to the University of Alabama.

While at Texas, Susan once caught a ride home with Macy Hart and his sister, Ellen, from Winona, Mississippi. The love affair of Susan and Macy started then and they later married,

Joe and Phyllis told me that, coming from a small country town, they were proud that all three of their daughters were confirmed at Temple Beth El in Lexington. All married fine young Jewish men, to whom each has been happily married for over thirty years. Joe and Phyllis had been successfully married for sixty years as of June 9, 2006. Joe mentioned that he recalled June ninth was the same day Henry Paris and Bob Berman were confirmed in Temple Beth El by Rabbi Stanley Brav of Vicksburg.

To celebrate the auspicious occasion of the 60th anniversary of Joe and Phyllis Stern, forty-five relatives and friends attended Sabbath service at Temple Beth El on that very Friday evening of June 9, 2006. Phil Cohen and his daughter, Sarah, a student in Judaic studies at Indiana University, conducted the services. Afterwards, fifty attendees were entertained for dinner at the home of Phil and Sally Cohen. The next day, seventy-five guests attended a luncheon at Kittrells Restaurant on the Lexington square. The Friday evening Sabbath service at Temple Beth El vividly demonstrated how that little "House of David in the Land of Jesus" continues to serve the community for religious services and life cycle events over one hundred years after it was built.

Joe Stern and Phyllis Berkower Stern (center) with family

Chapter 42

Susan Stern Hart and Macy B. Hart
Henry S. Jacobs Camp
Museum of Southern Jewish Experience
Institute of Southern Jewish Life

Along came a young man named Macy from a small neighboring town of Winona, Mississippi, who won the heart of Susan Stern from Lexington. Together they have accomplished wonders in promoting the recognition, continuity and longevity of the Jewish faith throughout the mid-South. This chapter is a taped interview with Macy about his life with Susan, their life together, the Henry S. Jacobs Camp, the Museum of Southern Jewish Experience, and the Institute of Southern Jewish Life. They have had significant roles in the growth, development and success of each.

Since the interview pertains to the manner in which Macy, with the assistance and full support of Susan, has been dedicated to promoting the faith of Judaism throughout the mid-South, it does not cover their civic activities and contributions to the overall community. One of those other activities is especially worth mentioning. Recognizing that over 90 percent of the school children of Mississippi continue to attend public schools, and how necessary it is to provide them with the best education possible, Macy and Susan are among the founders of Parents for Public Schools, Inc. This organization's first chapter was founded in Jackson, Mississippi in 1989, with the national organization organized in Jackson in 1991. It has now grown to encompass twenty-five chapters in fourteen states. Its purpose is to foster and promote parents' vital involvement in the support of public education.

Below is a transcription of an interview I conducted with Macy Hart, on June 29, 2005, in the private dining room of Nick's Restaurant in Jackson. All three entities—the Henry S. Jacobs Camp, the Museum of Southern Jewish Experience, and the Institute of

Southern Jewish Life—have played such an important role in the lives of so many southern Jewish families that I felt it important enough to record the entire interview.

The interview tells how Susan and Macy met and about their life together. It describes how Macy began his first full-time job with the Henry S. Jacobs Camp, which led to the development of the Museum of Southern Jewish Experience, which further developed into the formation of the Institute of Southern Jewish Life, and what has transpired since.

This saga began in Lexington, Mississippi, the former home of Susan Stern Hart, and where Susan and Macy and their family remain dedicated members of Temple Beth El's congregation. This House of David, surrounded by Christian churches, has been determined to maintain its Jewish identity and continue to conduct services since it first opened in 1905. Susan, Macy, their children, and many other members of their family, including Macy's parents, Reva and Ellis Hart, attend most of the High Holy Day services at Temple Beth El every year.

The following are my questions and Macy Hart's responses.

Author: Macy, where were you born and raised?

Macy: I was born in the old hospital in Greenwood, Mississippi as was Susan, by the way—it was the regional hospital. I was raised in Winona, Mississippi. By the time my siblings and I came along, we were the only Jewish family in Winona, although there had been a sizable Jewish community in Winona at one time, possibly forty to fifty families. Many stores were owned by Jews, but by the time I was born, my family had the biggest department store left in the town that was once mostly Jewishly owned stores. That was a great experience. It really taught me a lot about ecumenicism, about getting to know my neighbors, and wanting them to understand Judaism, and me wanting to understand their religions, so that we could play side by side.

Author: Where did you graduate college and what was your degree?

Macy: I started at LSU, spent two years there and then transferred to the University of Texas. I graduated in May of 1970 with a degree in government, which of course I never got to use. My goal had been to get a law degree, go back to Mississippi, be a part of the changing face of the state, and, at some point, be governor. But I got sidetracked.

Author: When and how did you meet your wife, Susan Stern Hart, from Lexington?

Macy: Susan's parents are Joe and Phyllis Stern. Joe was originally from the Greenwood area. Phyllis came from Staten Island, New York. They met at an officer's club in New York [actually a USO club] and eventually settled in Lexington, Mississippi.

After World War II, a number of folks returned to the South with spouses who were not from the area. They were relatively isolated since there weren't as many Jews in these small towns. This group of adults created this organization called the YJPL, for the Young Jewish Peoples League. Once a month couples from all over the Mississippi Delta would meet, which is how my parents, Ellis and Reva Hart, and the Sterns got to know each other—just like they got to know so many other families across the delta. In my memory as a child, there were usually anywhere from sixty to a hundred people that would come to somebody's house or a local restaurant. So, that's how we knew the Sterns.

Years later, I was a senior at the University of Texas. Susan was a freshman. My sister Ellen and I were both at Texas at that time and we were driving home for the mid-winter break. I had met Susan at a sorority party, where I was the date of the president of the sorority. Susan and I were introduced and I offered her a ride home to Mississippi to save her parents the air fare. So even though we technically knew each other beforehand, that's how we actually met. We basically started dating from that point on. I hired her to be a counselor at Henry S. Jacobs Camp in Utica, Mississippi that first summer of 1970; then we got engaged in October of that year and got married January 3, 1971.

Author: Were you married in Temple Beth El?

Macy: No we were married in Beth Israel [in Jackson], by Rabbi Perry Nussbaum and Rabbi Sol Kaplan. We were the first couple married under a chupah [a traditional religious canopy]; as there had never been a chupah in that synagogue until we got married.

Author: Where did you first settle after you were married?

Macy: I had already been living in Utica since the summer of 1970 since I was the camp "administrator." We got married that next January and moved into the director's lodge, which was just like a little summer temporary quarter. Susan was commuting back and forth to Clinton attending Mississippi College to finish her degree.

Author: Was that your first job?

Macy: That was my first full-time job, but I had jobs all my life. What led to this job was that I was very fortunate in high school and college to be a part of the Southern Federation of Temple Youth, [SOFTY]. It was a lifeline for me and Jewish kids in the area. It was being a part of SOFTY that gave me an opportunity to meet a lot of other Jewish kids. I became active, and then an officer. I became a national board member for the National Federation of Temple Youth [NFTY]. In 1966 and 1967 I was elected first vice president of NFTY and in 1968 I was elected president. That introduced me to a whole new world, not just the Jewish world of the United States but international as well. I was selected as one of ten American Jewish youth to represent NFTY at an international conference and I got to meet people from all over the world. It was a wonderful experience. When I was finishing college, I wanted to give something back to the reform movement. I approached Rabbi Hank Skirball, NFTY director, at the national office about going to work in New York for NFTY for a couple of years before going to law school. They welcomed me, but said they were going to open a camp in Mississippi. Jewish families and people of my own age had been holding car washes, auctions and all sort of stuff to help raise money [for the Henry S. Jacobs Camp in Utica]. Rabbi Skirball said, "We are going to open it this coming summer when you are graduating, so why don't you go there?" I thought that would be a great idea, so I went and met with Rabbi Sol Kaplan and he hired me to be the "administrator." He was in the Dallas office of the UAHC [Union of American Hebrew Congregations]. That's how I got to camp.

Initially, I was going to do it, as I said, for two years. By the next summer I had decided I would do it a little bit longer. I never had a contract. It was always like year to year. But the challenges just kept getting bigger and bigger, so two years led to five to ten to twenty to thirty. I loved every minute of it! It was a great opportunity because, truth be known, I believed that the leadership of the [Jewish] reform movement had no expectations that this camp would ever succeed and since there were no expectations, we got a chance to do things as a southern community that were innovative in camping. The camp really became the center of Jewish life. There were forty-eight reform congregations in the territory that Jacobs Camp served. Of these forty-eight congregations, only twelve had rabbis, so the camp needed to take on a greater role than just being a summer camp for kids. It needed to be a year-round conference and retreat facility and we set about to make it that way.

Author: So you were the first director.

Macy: I was really the first hired director. [Rabbi] Sol Kaplan, who was the regional director of UAHC, really only served as the director in name because I was only twenty-two years old. So, officially, he was the director and I was the administrator, but by the second summer I had been named the director.

Author: Tell me about the beginning of Henry S. Jacobs Camp, a brief history and how Utica [Mississippi] was selected.

Macy: The history goes back to the late 1940s and early 1950s. Celeste Orkin of Jackson started this youth group called Mississippi Temple Teens. It started with the Jackson youth group because she had heard about NFTY in other regions of the country. Henry Jacobs was the temple administrator for Temple Sinai in New Orleans and he had heard about the success of this Mississippi Temple Teens group that Celeste was running and brought a group of young people up to Jackson for a retreat. He went back to New Orleans and formed Louisiana Temple Teens. Then the Mississippi group and the Louisiana group merged. With the encouragement of the national office and Rabbi Sam Cook, the Southern Federation of Temple Youth was begun around 1950 or 1951.

After the success of SOFTY, Celeste and Henry decided the teenagers needed a camp experience, too.

At first a camp in North Carolina was rented for SOFTY camp, but they soon decided they needed a camp in the area and founded the Camp Association of Southern Temples. Since Mississippi was so central for the rest of the region, they literally drew a line on a map between Monroe, Louisiana, and Meridian, Mississippi, and started looking at properties along the line. And somebody, I believe Andrew Orkin of Jackson notified them about this 140-acre piece of land in Utica. They first bought that 140 acres and then bought another forty acres and then I bought another hundred acres later on—eventually totaling 280 acres.

Author: Who bought the land?

Macy: A group of folks from New Orleans, Little Rock and Memphis put some money up for the land. In 1966 or 1967, Henry Jacobs died and they decided to change the name "the Camp Association of Southern Temples" to "the Henry S. Jacobs Camp" as a means of memorializing Henry, as well as to try to get more impetus going in the New Orleans and Louisiana area and to let the rest of the world know that they were serious about this camp.

The '67 war in Israel broke out and lots of things changed. People in the Jewish community seemed to be more energized and empowered to stand up for things that they had been quiet about before. I think that there is a direct relationship between the war and the amount of money raised for the camp. Only $20,000 had been raised before the Six Day War began, and by the time the camp opened in June of 1970, $420,000. They built a shell of a camp, and over the next thirty years we added approximately $7,000,000 worth of new buildings, including the building that memorialized your [the author's] parents; Joe and Fay Berman. That magnificent center was actually a Godsend to the camp. I always want you, Sondy and your family, [Joan and Dudley Burwell and Brenda Guercio] to know how much I appreciated that.

Author: Macy, didn't you tell me at one time the UAHC didn't want the camp?

Macy: The UAHC was, at first, opposed to the camp in Mississippi. These were tough times, at the height of the civil rights era [movement], as you know in the 1950s and 1960s. There were great divisions everywhere; in the Jewish community, north and south, east and west, and within each area. So the UAHC just didn't feel like there was a Jewish presence significant enough [in Mississippi]. Maybe they were stereotyping the Jewish community in the South as all being racist and bigots. Who knows what the real reasons were? But in 1965 and 1967 some groups from the camp movement had gone to the UAHC biennial and appeared before the National Committee of Camps and Institutes, and asked the union to take ownership of the camp and were declined.

In 1969 another group went to Miami—Celeste Orkin, Joe Harris and Dr. Julian Wiener from Jackson, Bernie Bennett from New Orleans, Sol Mintz from Monroe, and Julian Allenberg from

Memphis—and appeared before the NCCI in November 1969, and again asked for permission and were again denied.

Then, one in the group representing the camp made a motion for a recess. They [the group from the camp] took the UAHC committee leadership behind closed doors, and stated, "It's too bad you don't want the camp because we actually broke ground in 1967 and 1968. We're building the camp. We're going to open it in June of 1970 with or without you! If you go back in, call this matter up for reconsideration, bring it back off the table, and vote to accept the camp, we will give you the camp debt-free in the summer of 1970, completely paid for." They came back in, the meeting was called back to order, the motion was brought back to the table, and this time passed for some strange reason. There is no question in my mind that the Union, in its wisdom at that point, decided to accept the camp. They had nothing invested in it, so they had nothing to lose. If the camp folded in two or three or four years like they suspected it would, they had a debt-free property that they could sell and use those dollars for the UAHC.

Obviously that never happened. By the time all remaining charitable trusts are paid there will be a million and a half from endowments. At that time no other camp in the UAHC system, even in the bigger cities, had any endowment at all. We were the only one.

Author: I believe there are about four hundred children that go through the camp each summer.

Macy: We had to get one out of every four eligible children to fill our beds, whereas the next camp to us would have been six out of one hundred, which seemed like an impossible recruitment task. But as I've always said, one should never underestimate the determination of a southern Jewish parent to provide their child with an opportunity! Now there are somewhere between 400 and 500 in the summer by counting all the various groups and sessions.

Author: Tell me more about the endowment and growth of the camp.

Macy: From 1994, when we had our twenty-five-year anniversary to 1999, our thirtieth year, we were determined to tear down the old camp, build a new one, and have an endowment for two things: scholarships and long term maintenance. We raised five and a half million dollars. We had a little over 4.4 million dollars in new construction, and we were going to have a million and a half endowment when all the trust paid in. It was the first endowment the camp really had and again, none of the other camps had any.

Author: What kind of endowment is there today?

Macy: As I am no longer the director, I really don't know what their financial status is.

Author: Tell me more about activities at the camp unrelated to summer sessions for campers. What about "Dream Street," which I believe is also called the "Mitzvah [to do a good deed] Corps?"

Macy: We started that at the camp as an opportunity for the softyites to be able to be a part of making the world they live in better. There were lots of things going on in those times, but nothing for children with severe physical handicaps. Today the politically correct words are physically challenged. There were Special Olympics for the children who were mentally challenged, you had all sorts of things for muscular dystrophy, but you had nothing for children with cerebral palsy, spina bifida, and birth defects in general. So SOFTY [Southern Federation of Temple Youth] and Mississippi Easter Seals came together and founded this camp called "Camp Funalot." They would bring the patients to the camp and we provided all the staff. It created this wonderful relationship between the SOFTY kids and kids with disabilities.

Easter Seals, at first, was concerned that we would make the camp religious, but I assured them that there would be no Judaism taught during this time. For us, the Jewish value of serving was a great education in itself for our kids. It would be reflective of kids going out and playing. We lived on that and still do. The camp will be thirty years old this coming summer with only one year of interruption.

Easter Seals left us and we got Bill's Dollar Stores, which has now gone under, to pick up the funding. It costs about $45,000 a year to run the program. All the staff worked for free and all the campers come for free. But it costs a lot of money to run the camp because of the specialized staff needed. In addition to food, supplies and housing, there have to be doctors, nurses, physical therapists, occupational therapists, social workers, horseback people, art people and so on. Some of the children unfortunately are of such an economic condition that we even end up buying clothes, paying transportation just to be able to give them an outdoor experience.

The camp staff are members of the Southern Federation of Temple Youth, now called NFTY southern. There is a one-to-one camper/counselor ratio, but in addition to that, there is the upper staff, who are the people that help with all sorts of projects and run programs. Now, all of those people are former staff members from SOFTY, whereas in the earlier days we had to go out and solicit people to help us. It is a marvelous, marvelous program.

Author: Is Easter Seals back with you now?

Macy: No. Easter Seals went another way, and after Bill's place went under, I went to some friends in California who were running a system of camps called "Dream Street" for kids with cancer. They wanted to participate with Camp Rainbow in Mississippi. But they didn't need the money and didn't want to change their name to Dream Street. We did need the money and we were willing to change our name. So we approached Dream Street, asked them to give us the money and we would change the name if they would contribute the $10,000. Every year we have to raise the rest. Part of my plan for the future, after we got the camp rebuilt and got the endowment done, was to try to raise a half a million dollar endowment just for Dream Street so it could sustain itself every year instead of having to raise the money themselves every year. The dollars we did not raise, I just absorbed from the camp's overall budget.

Author: I understand adults come for programs also.

Macy: The new camp is a complete year-round conference and retreat facility, instead of having a lot of congregations like you do in the bigger areas where they just rent [the camp] and bring their own staff, we knew we needed to plan, run and staff the programs and started doing regional grade level weekends, for teens as well as adult weekends. We've had some of the most well-known Jewish scholars, authors and leaders come for a weekend to be with people from small towns all over the region to meet, study and learn. For many of these people, this was the only opportunity to gain exposure to some of these well-known luminaries.

Author: Do any other denominations have access to the camp?

Macy: Absolutely! We were [and still are] always open. I remember when I first started at the camp, one of the first calls I got was from a church group that wanted to come use the facility. They asked me would we have a problem if they had blacks in the group. I said absolutely not; we are open to church groups and civic groups and education groups. It is important that we took a stand on that issue as racial tensions were high at that time in history.

Author: Where do you get your counselors?

Macy: They have been recruited from all over the country, Israel and other countries, annually.

Author: Why, Macy, did you leave the camp?

Macy: In the 1970s I recognized there was a need for more Jewish opportunities than the reform movement offered. I began talking and pushing the leadership in the UAHC camping department to start doing more through the camp. One example was to come up with a curriculum that all the regional Sunday schools could use. When I was growing up, there was no rabbi and no educator. My parents did a great job, as did my uncles and aunts and friends, in trying to give us an education [in Judaism]; but they didn't have any training; they didn't have a curriculum—they just had to figure it out for themselves what they should teach.

So I had been pushing the reform movement to come up with a curriculum we could hand to the Lexingtons, the Greenwoods, and places like that. This was an idea I hoped whose time had come, but it was just something they were not interested in. So in the early 1980s, I did a series of books through the camp's educational program that resulted in seven years of work so that each year the kids got one of those volumes called *Tochnit: project in Judaica.* Each year built upon something from before. Because I wanted to give our kids what I call a "common body of Jewish knowledge."

Author: Exactly what is the definition of "tochnit"?

Macy: Tochnit means project in Hebrew. So it means a project in Judaica. It was a great overall glimpse into Judaism that every camper could learn and build upon each year with a new volume. Then the campers became the teachers of their parents which we thought would help us accomplish the goal of putting Jewish education back into the home.

Then I started approaching the UAHC about this need for me—and for the camps—to do more. I came up with this idea called "the UAHC center for Jewish life/southern region." My hope was that the Union would view this as an opportunity to look at how they might better serve so many of their smaller congregations.

In 1985 we were finishing the Berman building [activity center] and I had this next idea of building an indoor sanctuary/museum. I thought the camp needed an indoor place, and I had been collecting artifacts from congregations and families that had this "stuff" [Jewish religious items of value] and didn't know what to do with it. Somebody heard about the idea in early 1986 and basically gave us the opportunity to build the building [sanctuary/museum] in Utica. It was a programmatic concept for which I gave the UAHC the master plan in April of 1986. It is quite a document.

This concept included a Sunday school curriculum that was user friendly and grade-oriented from kindergarten through tenth grade so that our kids who grew up in these small towns with volunteer teachers could have the same opportunities as larger communities with professional resources. I continued to develop the institute from 1986 to 1999 while the museum became quite an entity unto itself. We also expanded the museum and came into ownership of an old synagogue building in Natchez. We are continuing to expand the Museum of Southern Jewish Experience so it will never be in just one place, but rather a series of satellites.

Author: Initially the museum was owned by the UAHC?

Macy: Well the building [museum and sanctuary] is still owned by the UAHC because money was given to UAHC for the purpose of building the facility in Utica. All of the contents, however, are owned by the museum. The leadership of the Union wanted a separate organization with its own 501c3 status. I was the director of both organizations—the camp and the museum—but finally realized I wasn't getting anywhere with regard to moving forward with the master plan of itinerant Jewish educators and rabbis to serve the underserved and isolated communities as well as larger ones, besides the full Sunday school curriculum we had developed.

Finally, the president of the UAHC gave me the ultimatum of either giving all of this up and go back to being just a camp director or leave altogether. I chose to leave because the camp was already thirty years old and had a life of its own. The 4.4-million-dollar renovations were complete. The only two buildings that are standing today that were there in 1994 are the Berman activity center and the museum/sanctuary itself. Every other building was completely torn to the ground or gutted all the way down to the stud walls and slab and rebuilt. We had also bought another hundred acres of land and had an endowment. I knew the camp would make it without me, but I wasn't convinced that anybody would pickup the issue of small and isolated and underserved communities. I really believed that this is what we should be focused on, so I left and became the president of what was then still known as the Museum of Southern Jewish Experience. We quickly changed our name to the Institute of Southern Jewish Life, in order to reflect what our future would look like. We would still be involved in gathering history and preservation, but we would also develop a Sunday school curriculum, have traveling rabbis, educators, authors and scholars, and cultural programs like the [Jewish] film festival. So that's why I left. I am really sad that the UAHC did not, in its wisdom, seek to find ways to serve their smaller congregations better. I think that was a big mistake on their part and I was unhappy about it, but I am so thrilled about what I am doing now and what I get to do. This is the only thing I could do that I could possibly love any more than I did the camp because it's the next step. The camp prepared me and the community for this job.

Author: What part of the Camp directorship, the Museum, and the Institute of Southern Jewish Life has your wife, Susan Stern Hart, played?

Macy: Susan is from Lexington, so she understood what it was like to grow up in a small town with a small congregation where the Sunday school teachers were her parents. She was my partner from day one! Even with all my travels she never once asked me to stop what I was doing to spend more time with her or the kids. She believed enough in what we were doing, so that her close support, dedication and assistance were her contributions. She was a counselor the first summer of the camp, she did resource stuff and then took over the important job of the kitchen management, and ended up running the entire food service program for nine years [a major job]. Then I had to "fire" her because we opened another business. She just couldn't do it all.

Author: What are your other businesses?

Macy: Susan has the Sylvan Learning Center. And the Thomson Prometric Testing Center. We decided that she would be at home until our youngest daughter, Hannah, was in kindergarten. We knew that my non-profit salary would require some secondary income. But, at the same time, we were looking for something that satisfied some of our own goals. She was an educator and I was as a camp director so we were interested in youth, and we saw the Sylvan Learning Center as an opportunity and opened it. She's been at it almost twenty years now.

Author: Do you have an honorary degree from the HUC [Hebrew Union College]?

Macy: I was the first camp director ever honored with this degree, and they gave it to me to acknowledge the innovation and work we were doing for the small communities. I also was very fortunate to receive the "covenant" award, which is similar to the McArthur award in the secular world. They tap three people a year they think have made important contributions to the good of the Jewish people. It was a great honor, because I've been told several hundred people are nominated each year, and they only select three. I was the first sitting UAHC staff member to ever receive one so it was another milestone for my work as part of the reform movement.

Author: Who sponsored the covenant award?

Macy: The Crown family from Chicago set up the covenant foundation to give in two areas; one is the covenant award and the other is the covenant grants for innovative work. The foundation gets a hundred or so requests and they choose anywhere from six to eight recipients a year. Last year we were funded by the covenant foundation for $160,000 over a three-year period for our work in education and curriculum building. This is a major grant that acknowledged the work we are doing.

Author: Macy, that's quite an honor and you have received a number of them.

Tell me, why do you feel Temple Beth El in Lexington has remained active for one hundred years instead of closing like so many other synagogues have done throughout Mississippi, and the South; and why are you and Susan still members, and why do you and your family attend services for the High Holy Days in Temple Beth El in Lexington, instead of here in Jackson at Beth Israel where you are a past president?

Macy: It's a great question. I will tell you that I think Temple Beth El continues to thrive, even though it may not look like it when you are in the pews. It is a matter of dignity and pride in the legacy of the Jewish community of Lexington. We live in the Bible belt where religion is very important to people. The synagogue became the center of life for the Jews of Lexington, as it has in many other communities. While I was an officer of Beth Israel Congregation in Jackson, we stayed in Jackson for the High Holy Days. Prior to that, we would do one holiday in Jackson and one in Lexington. As soon as my presidency was over, we started doing all of our High Holy Holidays in Lexington at Temple Beth El. Jackson is not such a large community itself, but we wanted our kids to be able to feel and touch and be a part of the service. We felt like they would have extraordinary memories if they grew up being a part of helping the service happen. Our kids were all raised with a different Judaism than we were because we wanted our children to have more than we had. My parents wanted us to have more than they had. They now have these memories of being a part of the service so we continue to go there. Jackson does not need us. They need us in Lexington, and we need them. It helps add to the intimacy of the experience, and I think being Jewish is a very intimate experience.

Author: I understand even today about twenty to thirty people attend those High Holy Day services each year in Lexington.

Macy: On a good night we'll have twenty-five or thirty. We always bring a bunch of people because I love for people to see Lexington. I like for people to experience it.

Three years ago, an institute staff member brought her daughter and her daughter's boyfriend [who is now her son-in-law] to the synagogue for services. The boyfriend, a college student wanting to become a rabbi, led the service because of his experience in BBYO [B'nai B'rith Youth Organization]. When he got back to school, he published a paper about his experience in Lexington and what it meant to him. His name is Daniel Septimus and he will be ordained as a rabbi, I believe in three years.

Author: I have a copy of a sermon about Temple Beth El that same Daniel Septimus delivered at Hillel Yom Kippur services at Tulane University in New Orleans on September 27, 2001. I intend to include it verbatim as the next chapter of this book.

What do you see as the future of Temple Beth El in Lexington — as a historic site, or a monument to the Jewish community there of Lexington and Judaism, or what else?

Macy: I'm hoping that some point we will all be able to sit down with the Lexington [Jewish] community; that means people that live there now and people that have long gone away and decide how we want to look at Lexington. We have had lots of conversations about the building becoming one of the satellites of the Museum of

Southern Jewish Experience. We would tell the story and celebrate the Jewish influence and contribution to the town of Lexington and Holmes County. Lexington seems to have hit a very progressive chord of late, as they've created an organization called Main Street, which is tied to a statewide organization and are starting to look at tourism as something that could help the economic development. We want to be in Lexington if there is an opportunity for us to use the synagogue as a catalyst for refinement of tourism, economic development, bringing people together—blacks and whites, people of different faiths—for the betterment of the town and its children. There won't be any more factories coming to these little towns because of inexpensive labor. Those jobs are going south of the border and to China. Tourism is a positive way to develop a future today. Mississippi is very committed to tourism and long ago recognized the importance of getting people into Mississippi—to see Mississippi and to spend dollars in our hotels, restaurants, stores and our shops. That's what we hope we would do with the satellite of the Museum of Southern Jewish Experience—have a permanent exhibit there celebrating the Jews of Lexington and their role as a part of the community. As long as there are any Jews there, we're going to do services. But, even thinking towards the future when there aren't any Jews left, our itinerant rabbi or other community members could still lead services. We could invite other communities to take a Lexington week, and bring their rabbi and community down to see Lexington, tour around and have it open to the community as a way to teach Jews and non-Jews about each other. It could be a site for recruitment as a seminar center or we could do one of our traveling authors, or lectures. I would say that's a part of our [Institute of Southern Jewish Life] long-range goal.

Author: I'd love to see the home in which I was raised, known as Faymorcele, someday be a part of that; where they could house people. They could stay up there. It belongs to a doctor now and unfortunately age has taken its toll on that beautiful southern mansion.

Macy: You know historic preservation dollars are the hardest dollars to raise. You asked me the question about why Lexington is still here and others [synagogues in small towns] have ceased. Take Canton's temple, for example. It's no longer there. It's just a plaque on the corner of a block because when it got down to the last four or five people there was no plan for the future; nobody to plan for the future. Everything in the synagogue, including the synagogue itself, was sold at an auction. At least now we have the opportunity to plan for the future [of Temple Beth El]. People are not giving dollars to historic preservation on sentiment. Sentiment may motivate someone to give if they see there is a program ready to be in place.

Take Selma, for example. Selma was once a much larger community than Lexington; but they've got the same issue. The building was built in 1899, four blocks from the Pettus Bridge, across which the civil rights march from Selma to Montgomery took place. The Selma [Jewish] population was well over a hundred, maybe 200 families. They had more than one cemetery and the downtown area was dotted with all sorts of Jewish merchants. Now they are down to about twelve to fifteen Jewish people living there. They need a million dollars or more just to renovate the building and would need another two million dollars as an endowment for maintenance, and to have a part-time staff person for tour groups and things like that. Funders won't give money solely for preservation. That's where we come in with a program. People want to know that there is a use for a building and a reason for the building to continue to exist. It's not just about the building anymore because of all the other things like long-term maintenance and liability insurance to consider.

Author: What do you think it would take to do the same in Lexington?

Macy: I hadn't taken it to that step, but I'm thinking that just now off the top of my head that we probably ought to arrange for at least somewhere between $750,000 and a million dollars which would yield $50,000 per year.

Author: Macy, let's digress just moment; tell me more about your plans for the Institute [of Southern Jewish Life]; the rabbinic program, the archives, the educational program. You are still trying to raise money to establish it.

Macy: All of that. Today I would say we are five years old and we are quite healthy for a five-year-old organization. Our budget ranges between 1.1 and 1.3 million dollars and we have thirteen full-time staff and six part-time people. Beyond that, we get this wonderful group of interns from graduate schools and programs all over the country in the summer. I'm in the midst of hiring three to four more staff members between now and the end of this calendar year. We have a rabbi who has been on our staff and has served over thirty congregations. She has done funerals, weddings, worked with conversion students, and now she has bar and bat mitzvah students. The families have contacted her from little communities that don't have rabbis or educators. I'm hoping that not only will we fund her replacement in 2006, but maybe we will find the dollars to hire a second. Actually there is a need for more than that in our twelve state region. We've also completed a full curriculum now. We've invested over $800,000 in a Sunday school curriculum that is from early childhood all the way through tenth grade. We thought we needed a common body of Jewish knowledge, and that's what our curriculum is—a script that could guide a smaller community that has nothing other than great dedicated volunteers or to improve resources for larger congregations so that our fifth graders are learning the same things. The goal is that a kid leaving us after ten years has a good, solid, Jewish education and is hopefully motivated to go on and be a part of the next community they join.

We're basically trying to level the playing field. If you had gone from your Sunday school in Lexington to one in another state with a rabbi and an educator, there would be absolutely no connection between what you were learning here and what you would have learned there. Our program has developed; not only do we have the curriculum but we have the delivery system. So we created these two-year fellowships where the fellows travel twice a month to a different community to work with those communities on their religious school, to lead Shabbat services and Torah study, and to visit people that are homebound. They are young Jewish professionals in a community for a weekend. The program has since matured, and now we have three fellows.

Author: So they supplement the traveling rabbi.

Macy: No. Those are actually different departments, although they complement each other. The rabbi serves any congregation. These fellows are only going to congregations that have a Sunday school using our curriculum. We now have twenty-seven communities using our curriculum in a four-state pilot area of Mississippi, Alabama, Arkansas and Louisiana. That means instead of a big synagogue with six or seven sections of the fifth grade, the Institute might have sixteen sections of the fifth grade; all learning the same thing but in sixteen different communities spread over several states.

Author: This is all through the Institute?

Macy: All institute.

Author: Macy, tell me more about the rabbinic chair; the educators chair; the archives chair that you have planned for the Institute.

Macy: Those are endowments.

Author: I understand none of them have been filled yet, but you are moving forward without those goals being reached at this time.

Macy: We have already raised six and a half million dollars. But the people that have given us the money have so far elected not to take any of the boxes [chairs]. They wanted to leave those available to help us grow the organization. We are hoping that some new funders will sponsor the rabbinic chair or any other chair. I think it's just a matter of time before someone will endow the education and the rabbinic piece.

We also have a history department doing research in twelve states that the Institute covers. We are also focusing on oral history and developing a cultural program that is designed to create dialogue and build bridges among races and religions.

Author: Macy, in my opinion, with Susan's continued support and close assistance, you have done as much, and perhaps even more, to spread the word of Judaism throughout the South than anyone I have ever known! Thank you for the time you have taken to give me this interesting interview.

Macy: Thank you Bob. I appreciate that and I'm really excited about the work you are doing. I'm asking you now to make sure that we get not only a copy, but I would like to have your tapes when you are through, so that we can have that as the original part of the original stuff; and any notes that you have taken, for I suspect that you're not going to get everything in the book that you've come across.

Author: Probably not but I'll be glad to give you whatever I've got after my work is finished.

Macy: This is important work you are doing.

Author: We'll just see how it comes out. I hope to get it published. I've come a long way. It will not be a long book because there is just so much you can write about the Jewish community of Lexington, even with its outreach. But I am not only writing about someone having a store. I'm writing about the depth of their family, as much as I can gather. I'm writing about the outreach, not just what they have done and do for Lexington and Holmes County, but where they have gone out like you and Susan, whose influence extends far beyond Lexington itself. I mentioned about the Paris family, what they did about the nondenominational chapel at Ole Miss. It does have a Cross on it, but over the Cross is this Big Star of David. Things of that sort which emanate from Lexington go far beyond it in influence and accomplishments.

Macy: Well, Lexington has created a lot of extraordinary people! And I think small towns have a way of being character builders.

Author: I believe that, and Lexington has its good share of them, through the military and elsewhere, what was done in World War II, including the history of Lt. Colonel Gus Herrman and Colonel Joe Berman and a good many other Jews with their rank and decorations in defense of their country, the United States of America.

Susan Stern Hart and Macy B. Hart

Chapter 43

A Sermon About Temple Beth El
Rabbi Daniel Septimus

In the previous chapter describing how Macy and Susan Hart have worked together as partners to preserve and spread Judaism throughout the mid-South, in an interview with Macy, he referred to a young rabbinic student named Daniel Septimus.

In the fall of 2001 during the beginning of the High Holy Days, Daniel had heard about the synagogue, Temple Beth El, in Lexington and visited it on Rosh Hashanah. Since he was a rabbinic student, he was asked to read the Torah service there. Ten days later, he delivered a sermon at Hillel, Tulane University in New Orleans for Yom Kippur. That sermon vividly described the commitment, dedication and spirit of the Lexington Jewish community, which has kept that temple and congregation alive for over the past one hundred years, celebrating its centennial in 2005.

Below is a transcription of the sermon:

Sermon Delivered at Hillel Yom Kippur Services
Tulane University
September 27, 2001
By Daniel Septimus

Good Yom Tov: As I sat down on Rosh Hashanah, ten days ago, with twenty other participants of the Temple Beth El in the small town of Lexington, Mississippi, I was overcome with admiration for a tiny community's will to keep Judaism alive. The volunteer leader of the congregation began the service, which he drives an hour every year to lead, with the opening prayers. Around three minutes into the service an elderly woman, who is one of the six members of the congregation, interrupts and yells out to the honorary rabbi, "Uh...Rabbi, wait a minute, I think I have the *old* Hebrew union prayer book, can someone give me the *new* Hebrew union prayer book!"

The guests and congregation laugh as her husband helps to exchange the 1941 Hebrew union prayer books, which we were accidentally reading out of, with the 1945 *new* Hebrew union prayer books. Can you imagine someone sitting in your congregation, which probably has hundreds to thousands of people, blurting out in the middle of the rabbi speaking, "Excuse me, Rabbi, I have the wrong prayer book, can you wait a minute?" As you can see, Temple Beth El of Lexington, Mississippi, is not your typical synagogue.

The town of Lexington is about an hour away from Jackson, Mississippi. Today, the town has a population of about 2,200 people and at its height it had about 3,200 citizens. As you are driving into the town square, it looks like you are in a movie. The center of the town has a town clock and many distinctive stores, sorry no chains or corporations! What is interesting about the stores is that most of them have Jewish names or originally were owned by Jews according to the people that lived there. You are probably asking now, how did Jews arrive in Mississippi and especially in the town of Lexington?

I spoke with this amazing and very interesting congregant, Herman Flowers, who is over eighty years old, and he gave me the most detailed account of the history of the town. I will spare you the long version. Apparently, Jews settled in the town as early as the late 1820s. However, the largest migration of Jews was in the 1890s. Jews in New York became concerned that a high volume of Jews below the poverty level would result in an outbreak of anti-Semitism and decided to divert many of them to Galveston, TX. Since there were Jews in Lexington already, many came to the town to start their own business or engage in farming. The first Jews that came to the town were German, but the majority that came at the end of the nineteenth and early twentieth centuries were Polish and Russian Jews escaping anti-Semitism.

In 1898, a group of Jews got together to form Temple Beth El. The temple, if you haven't picked up on it yet, was following classical reform Judaism. Many Jews of the time period wished to assimilate into society. Therefore, these Jews built a synagogue that blended in with the town and is very hard to recognize as a Jewish place of worship from the outside, but when you walk into the doors, it is a completely different story. It is what we would think of as a sanctuary today. There are beautiful stained glass windows that have all been dedicated in memory of its earliest congregants. There are also yartzeit plaques [memorials], which were lit up for Rosh Hashanah and I am sure the same goes for this holiday as well. At the height of the synagogue, there were twenty-three families [authors note: eighty-nine "Jewish souls" according to Ephraim Cohen, which corroborates twenty-three Jewish families], and as a matter of fact, they sent twenty-one men off to World War II. As you know, many Jews, like the rest of America, have moved away from small towns and into larger cities for economic and social reasons; therefore, the town's Jewish population has almost completely left.

But what I really want to draw your attention to is the significance of these remaining Jews having such a service over a hundred years later celebrating the Jewish New Year. As I mentioned previously, the service is led by their honorary rabbi, Henry Paris, who has been conducting the service for over thirty years out of respect to his family. Mr. Paris fills in for a full-time rabbi since the congregation no longer has enough members to support one. When we entered the synagogue, you could see their admiration and happiness for us being there and participating in the service. They followed the old reform service, which is almost entirely in English and ironically is very foreign to us today. I was asked to read Torah because no one in the congregation ever learned Hebrew. I really felt like an honored guest within this small congregation. We attended services on Monday evening and Tuesday morning. Today, there are only two full-time rabbis in the whole state of Mississippi. The wonderful people in charge of keeping these congregations' spirits alive and preserved for the future generations is the Institute of Southern Jewish Life, which is based out of Jackson, Mississippi. They are dedicated to providing educational and rabbinic services to isolated Jewish communities, documenting and preserving the rich history of the southern Jewish experience, and promoting a Jewish cultural presence throughout a twelve-state region. I am thankful to them for their invitation and kind hospitality while visiting the congregation.

What I hope that you have learned is that there were and still are Jews in almost every town throughout the southern states, even if there are just a few like the six members in Lexington, Mississippi. [Authors note: consisting of three families, plus approximately seventeen additional members living elsewhere that continue to support the congregation]. They played a significant role in their respective communities and are proud of their Judaism. It means a lot to these people to be able to worship in their congregations. I hope that each one of you has the opportunity and experience to be a part of your history as Jews in this country and feel the same pride and patriotism for America, and love for Judaism as these many congregants do to this day. Today, they are an everlasting spirit of Jews' success and prosperity in the United States, which they don't take for granted.

On this Day of Atonement we as Jews begin with a new slate. Imagine how the first generation of Jewish families in Lexington felt when they were able to escape religious persecution in their countries and were able not only to worship freely, but also live as *equal* citizens in the greatest country in the world. They genuinely appreciate the willingness of visitors to help keep their traditions and dreams alive. I ask today that we, as college students and the future leaders of our religion, remember and emulate these Jews in Lexington, Mississippi, for their dedication and pride not only for Judaism, but also for the United States of America, and that we will carry on the everlasting light of Judaism with pride and honor for our religion and country.

The above sermon succinctly summarizes almost everything in this book, *A House of David in the Land of Jesus.* The story of the Jewish community of Lexington, Mississippi is simply all about "keeping the Covenant."

Chapter 44

Other Members of the Lexington Jewish Community

Ben and Maurice Auerbach and their sons, Phil and Larry, were relative newcomers to Lexington. They moved from Greenwood, Mississippi, to Lexington in the late 1950s and resided there until the late 1960s. Maurice Stern Auerbach was born and raised in Glen Allen, Mississippi, and after marrying Ben, they lived in Greenwood until moving to Lexington. Their family was a member of Temple Beth El.

Ben owned a scrap metal business and bought and sold old furniture and appliances in Lexington. He later was a partner in a small loan company.

Phil Auerbach was in high school when they came to Lexington and Larry was in junior high. Larry attended Sunday school at Temple Beth El with Phil Cohen as one of his teachers. Larry was confirmed there in 1964, along with Brenda Berman and Amy Stern.

After their sons had gone to college, Ben and Maurice moved to the Mississippi Gulf Coast.

Phil passed away at about fifty years of age, and Larry still resides in Atlanta. Ben died a few years ago, but Maurice continues to live in Biloxi.

Other Members

There were other members of the Lexington Jewish community and members of Temple Beth El about which little is known by this author. Most of them are part of the ninety-six Jewish souls presently resting in tranquil Beth El Cemetery on the outskirts of town. They are mentioned here as part of Lexington's Jewish history so they too will not be forgotten. Those below with dates listed are buried in Beth El Cemetery.

Among these former members of Temple Beth El were other

noteworthy organizers and founders of the temple. They were Mr. and Mrs. L. Dobroski, Sol Auerbach, and Isadore Levy (1856-1932).

Lena Levy (1865-1942) was a sister to Flora Levy Herrman. Lena, as stated earlier, was one of the first two Sunday school teachers of Temple Beth El and helped raise funds to build the temple.

Other Levys, perhaps related to Isadore, are buried in Beth El Cemetery. They are Joseph S. Levy (1886-1939), Herman B. Levy (1889-1936), Morton Levy (1891-1929), and Arthur Earl Levy (1904-1986).

Then there was Miss Harriett Riteman (1870-1951), a nice but eccentric and loquacious lady, who had a penchant for gossip. She lived alone. However, it has been said that somehow she was related to the Henry Rosenthal family. As a matter of fact, Miss Harriett actually lived with Henry Rosenthal's widow, Carrie Sontheimer Rosenthal, after Henry passed away. Their home was at the corner of Carrollton and Cedar Streets, just a few blocks from the square. Carrollton Street is one of the main streets leading into the square from the north of town. The name of Cedar Street has been changed by the city council to Martin Luther King Drive. Ironically, it runs all the way to intersect with another street named Robert E. Lee Drive. Miss Harriett Riteman is vividly recalled, later in this book, in an interview with a member of the Lexington's white Christian community.

There was the Hargon family, who resided in Tchula and were merchants and members of Temple Beth El. They were Otis Reed Hargon (1859-1932), Rosa Marks Hargon (1874-1976), Morris Reed Hargon (1894-1976), and Ida H. Hargon (1894-1923).

There were other Applebaums, including Harry Applebaum, Jr. (1918-2001) and his son, Larry Michael Applebaum (1951-2004). They were the brother and nephew of Ellen Schur. Abe Applebaum (1890-1928) was related to Sol and Agathyne Applebaum, about which an earlier chapter has been written.

Flora Kern (1863-1939) was the mother of Agathyne Applebaum, and Nathan Kern (1889-1964) was a brother to Agathyne.

Joe Shure was a brother to Rosa Schur Cohen and Ben Schur. However, it is reported that he marched to the tune of a different drummer, even choosing to spell his name differently. From all indications, he lived a carefree life.

May these Jewish souls also be remembered as part of the Lexington Jewish community.

Relationships of the Lexington Jewish Community with the Lexington Christian Communities

Why write separately about the Lexington Jewish community's relationships with the white and the black Christian communities? It was not done as a veiled attempt to segregate or discriminate. It was written in this manner only because the black Christian community has had a distinctly different life experience from the white Christian community of the South, from slavery to segregation, to the civil rights era, to even a certain degree in the present. Therefore, I felt it significant for the reader to view the Lexington Jewish community, past and present, from both the white Christian and the black Christian perspectives.

Chapter 45

The Jewish Community and the White Christian Community of Lexington

Ever since the first member of the Jewish faith settled in Lexington, Jews and Christians have respected and befriended one another and worked together for the betterment of their entire community.

Even when the Lexington Jewish community grew from one, Jacob Sontheimer in the mid 1800s, to eighty-nine "Jewish souls" in the 1930s, anti-Semitism was never manifested openly or surreptitiously, to the best of my knowledge, as a longtime resident with deep family roots in the community. By all historical accounts, anti-Semitism did not exist and was never a problem in Lexington, past or present.

While the Jews of Lexington definitely assimilated into the community, they always strongly and proudly maintained their Jewish identity. They were just as much active members of the overall community of Lexington as were the Christian citizens. But they never attempted to hide the fact that religiously they were first, last and always Jews.

An article in the *Jewish Journal*, September 5, 2003, characterized Alfred Uhry, highly regarded author of the Pulitzer Prize-winning play *Driving Miss Daisy* and the documentaries *Shalom Y'all* and *Delta Jews*, as growing up in the South ashamed of being Jewish. Uhry was raised in Atlanta, Georgia. He was quoted as saying about his 1997 play *The Last Night of Ballyhoo*—"It just like my childhood community, where we felt so negative about being Jewish. We should have tried to hold onto our heritage, but we tried to run away from it, which was like pretending you don't have a lame leg. For years, I felt ashamed of being Jewish. I regarded myself as a southerner first." As he grew into adulthood, that feeling was obviously reversed, as seen from his popular writings.

The renowned author Eli N. Evans wrote brilliantly about Jews in the South in his books *The Provincials* (1973) and *The Lonely Days Were Sundays* (1993). In *The Provincials*, he states: "The question that

I have sought to explore is whether it is indeed true that the south is the most anti-Semitic part of the United States. I don't think that most Jews in the south would agree with the findings of the polls and studies, for most Jews live their lives in a placid atmosphere as part of the white majority. It is my view that the studies have never taken into account the special character of the southerner and the complexity of the south." Yet in his later book *The Lonely Days Were Sundays*, he expresses a somewhat different point of view about the self-consciousness and self-confidence of the southern Jew. In that second book about Jews of the South, he wrote the following: "Moreover Jews in the south have acquired the habit of maintaining a low profile, an instinctive shyness. It's something that we grow up with, a deep-seated reticence internalized from one's early years...now that the south is merging as a major regional force in America, Jews in the south may be experiencing an end of the sense of inferiority and inadequacy, the ingrained lack of confidence that has been a part of Jewish life in the south all these years." In another chapter of that same book, he wrote about a young Jewish woman who was Miss North Carolina, and how he was amazed at her enthusiasm and openness about being Jewish. He goes on to say: "In my day, southern Jewish kids were private and defensive about their religion, often ashamed that they were different. Some would do anything to blend in and belong, pretending they were whatever seemed convenient."

In these two books, his descriptions of southern Jews and how they feel about themselves appear, at least to some degree, ambivalent, although not entirely inconsistent.

Surely Eli Evans himself had no sensible reason to grow up with any negative feelings of being Jewish in the South since he was the son of a prominent Jewish family. His father, "Mutt" Evans, an avowed Jew and president of his synagogue, served as mayor of Durham, North Carolina, for six terms in the 1950s and 1960s. At least a majority of the citizens of that city thought enough of Jews, and his father in particular, to have a well-known, devout Jew as their mayor for several years. Furthermore, Eli Evans himself, as a student at the University of North Carolina in Chapel Hill, and member of a Jewish fraternity, was elected president of the student body.

Let us assume Mr. Evans did experience that sense of "inferiority and inadequacy" from some southern Jews he met and interviewed.

But irrespective of his popular and successful writings about Jews of the South, it is apparent that he did not study the complete history, nor interview any of the eighty-nine "Jewish souls" of Lexington, Mississippi, neither past nor present, with one exception. For *The Provincials*, he interviewed Harry Applebaum of Yazoo City, Mississippi. Besides Harry and his wife, Bella, being members of Temple Beth El in Lexington, Harry served two terms in the Mississippi state legislature and four terms as mayor of Yazoo City. That record was certainly not one of a member of the Jewish faith who was apologetic or ashamed of his Judaism. Perhaps Mr. Evans thought that record was atypical of Jews of the South. If so, he should have looked deeper into the lives of those that were members of the same congregation as Harry and Bella—in that House of David in Lexington, Mississippi.

I believe this widely acclaimed author missed the boat by not including the Jews of Lexington in one of his books. But then had he done so, there would be no need for this book, except the Jews of Lexington deserve more than one chapter.

Similar negative feelings about being Jewish, while living in the South and Jackson, Mississippi, were expressed in Edward Cohen's book *The Peddler's Grandson*. In his book, he states that he always felt himself to be an "outsider." He continues by saying: "Some people never realize they'll never fit in. They spend their lives trying to fit in with the 'in' crowd changing themselves, doing whatever they think is necessary to be accepted. Some of the luckier ones come to terms with it and say 'hey, I'm different, and that's ok.' "

Not so for the Lexingtonian Jews. In all deference to Mr. Uhry and Mr. Evans, and the high esteem in which they are held in the literary world and to Mr. Cohen—as successful as each have been, none of them spoke for me or any of my relatives and friends or the Jews of Lexington individually and as a whole.

Maybe the experience of Lexington's Jews has been an anomaly. If that be so, it is a fine one and either way, it's a story worthy of relating. Contrary to the experiences of these three authors, most if not all of the Jews of Lexington had a diametrically opposite experience living as an American Jew in a small southern community. Life was totally different in my personal experience, growing up in both the small town of Lexington and the large Atlanta community. In neither was I, nor any member of my family, nor any of my friends, ashamed of being Jewish; nor did we feel ourselves to be "outsiders." To the contrary, we displayed our Jewishness with openess and pride. We all knew that we were Americans, a nation to which we proudly pledged our allegiance both as civilians and as members of the United States Armed Forces. We knew that America was and is our country, which gave us the freedom to openly be Jewish. We knew we were and continue to be Jewish—that was and is our treasured religion and way of life. We knew that we were and remain southerners—that was and is our regional heritage. We have been and continue to be devotedly loyal to each aspect of our lives. We were and are sensitive, confident and proud enough to combine all three; as Americans, southerners and Jews, identifying openly and being an integral part of each.

Growing up in Lexington, there was no Jewish youth group, so most were asked to join and did join the Methodist youth group. As a matter of fact, Henry Paris was elected president of the Methodist youth group and served for one hour, until his mother, Irma, heard about it and made him march right back up to the square and the church and respectfully resign his new position. She rightly felt such an honor belonged to a member of the church, not the synagogue.

When it came to celebrating the Jewish High Holy Days, everything else was put aside, including high school football games, regardless of how important a Jewish athlete was to the team, and there were a fair number of them.

During my four years at the University of Mississippi, as a member of the Jewish fraternity, I never experienced one single anti-Semitic incident from any students, faculty, the administration, workers on campus, or in the town of Oxford. As a matter of fact, it was at Ole Miss—not New York, Miami or other areas heavily populated by Jews—that the members of Hillel learned to enjoy lox and bagels from a visiting rabbi from Clarksdale, Mississippi. As someone who openly identified with the Jewish faith, I was chosen to co-chair "Religious Emphasis Week," which was held annually. Ministers, rabbis and lay leaders were invited to speak during this week, which was completely non-denominational and non-sectarian. The other co-chair was Polly Franklin, now Dr. Polly Franklin Williams, wife of Dr. Parham H. Williams, another former Lexingtonian and Ole Miss Hall of Famer, who was at one time Dean of the Ole Miss School of Law. Both remain dear friends of mine and my wife, Sondy.

Yes, there were those Jews of Lexington who celebrated Christmas and Chanukah, who hunted Easter eggs and ate matzos and matzo ball soup at Passover Seders with their Christian friends. Some even had Christmas trees and Santa Claus, but they were celebrating the "spirit" of Christmas, not the birth of Jesus. Nowhere was this more vividly demonstrated than an essay written by one of our daughters, Sheri Berman Spector, for the *Clarion-Ledger,* for an essay contest entitled "What Does Christmas Mean To Me?" The essay, written by a young person who openly identified herself as Jewish, won the contest. Below is a December 1983 article that appeared in Jackson, Mississippi's daily newspaper, the *Clarion-Ledger,* written by noted columnist Joe Rogers, that pertained to the essay:

"Sometimes distance helps provide perspective for Christmas"

What does Christmas mean to you?

Maybe it gets you down. Christmas, after all, is a hectic time of year.

There are gifts to be bought and crowds to be fought. The bad side of the tree shows no matter which way you turn it, none of the clothes you'll get as presents will fit, none of the clothes you give as presents will fit, junior will trash the $800 home computer you got him before he figures out how to plug it in and the bill for the whole mess will put you in hock through mid-1984.

But surely there's more to Christmas than that.

The Central Kiwanis Club of Jackson decided to pose the question to local public high school students in the form of an essay contest.

The rules were simple: each student had 200 words to describe "What Christmas Means To Me." The winner would receive a $200 savings bond.

Some 300 entries came in.

Sheri Berman won.

That's a pretty fair achievement in and of itself, beating out several hundred people to claim the prize.

Then the more you find out about it, the nicer it seems. Remember, the theme of the contest was "What Christmas Means To Me."

Sheri Berman, who summed up Christmas best, is Jewish.

"I read all 300 of them and Sheri's was the first essay I read," said Dell Cullum, a Kiwanis Club member who helped judge the contest. "Sheri's just jumped out at me."

"It was from the heart, it was well written and I think she got her point across."

Sheri, when advised of her victory and the 200-buck prize, responded with proper ecumenical glee.

"You just made my Christmas, my Hannukkah, whatever."

Sheri is a junior at Murrah, daughter of Mr.and Mrs. Robert L. Berman. She enjoys writing, but it isn't her favorite pastime.

"I'm not going to major in journalism or anything [like that]" she said.

Perhaps that qualifies her as a genius.

In any event, she used popular Christmas songs and the promise of extra credit in her advanced English class as inspiration for her efforts.

Then she sat down and searched for her own true feelings about one of Christianity's greatest celebrations.

"I really had to go deep down inside to get that," she said.

The trip was worth the effort. This is what she got:

"As a member of the Jewish faith, while I do not celebrate Christmas as a religious holiday honoring the birth of Jesus Christ, I do join with my Christian friends in celebrating the spirit of that holiday as it applies to all human beings.

Christmas to me means "peace on earth and good will to all." While this does not have the same original religious meaning as the Christian belief, it does carry forward from it, and develops from both the Jewish and Christian beliefs exemplified by Moses when he presented God's ten commandment to the Israelites, and through the teachings of love and compassion by Jesus.

"Joy to the World" is a wonderful expression in itself. Throughout the ages there has been so much suffering and misery inflicted upon humanity by man himself; Christmas is a wonderful time of the year when we can commonly join together in spreading a little cheer and share a bit of happiness with one another.

I truly believe that peace on earth is one of God's greatest gifts. If the spirit of Christmas can do nothing more than bring humanity closer together united toward that one great goal of peace, then it more than serves a worthwhile purpose for all mankind."

Merry Christmas, folks.

And Shalom.

There have been so many close Christian friends of the Jews of Lexington, it would be difficult to name them all. However, at the risk of missing the names of dear friends, there are some whose stories, in particular, stand out and are worth relating.

The Barrett Family

Don Barrett

"To say that there was a wonderful relationship between the Christian community and the Jewish community doesn't accurately say what the situation was and is, because there were not really two communities."

In 1957, I first brought my fiancée, Sondra Ann Shindell from New Haven, Connecticut, to Lexington, Mississippi, to visit. The first persons to entertain us and celebrate our engagement were dear friends of my family, Pat and Sarah Barrett.

Forty-seven years later, when Rabbi David Ellenson, president of the Hebrew Union College, visited Lexington and Temple Beth El for the first time, he, Henry Paris, Phil Cohen and I were guests at the mansion of Don and Nancy Barrett for a southern-style dinner at the noon hour. Don was one of Pat and Sarah Barrett's sons. Most every delectable vegetable from the garden of the Barrett's, along with southern fried chicken, other meats and delicacies were elegantly served, along with hot biscuits and cornbread, the traditional "sweet" iced tea, and homemade apple pie.

Pat Barrett, Don's father, was a highly regarded attorney in Lexington and a man of great character and integrity. He was the personal attorney of our family. His sons, Pat, Jr., and Don, followed suit, and today they are the general partners in their prestigious law firm. They and their sister, Sally, and eleven other partners make up their firm. In Lexington there are nine, with five others in their Nashville office. Of the fourteen attorneys in their firm, eight are Barretts, including a number of their children.

Don Barrett was the first attorney to represent a client in the suit against a tobacco company. That one suit grew to gigantic proportions, which later resulted in one of the largest damage awards ever in the courts of America. He personally negotiated the tobacco settlement with Liggett, which was the breakthrough settlement that allowed the plaintiffs to settle with the rest of the tobacco companies, i.e., R.J.R. (the big boys). For his good services, Don alone earned a legal fee of substantial proportions. There were ten Mississippi attorneys involved in the tobacco suit. For their expertise, they earned a combined legal fee of $1.3 billion. I expressed to him that not only did he earn that fee, but in Jewish terms he did a mitzvah for the health of our nation and its citizens.

For some years, Don Barrett has urged me to write about the history of the Jewish community of Lexington and its close relationship with the Christian community in that town. He was active in attempting to convince the HUC to agree to produce the documentary I proposed.

The Barrett family has always been good and supportive friends of the Lexington Jewish community, both former and present. Don's grandfather, William Oliver Barrett, moved to Lexington in 1896 and founded the Barrett Grocery Company, which later merged with his good friend Morris Lewis, Sr. and the Lewis Grocer Company. W.O. Barrett originally owned the land, along with Morris Lewis, where Temple Beth El now sits. Additionally, W.O. Barrett married Rachel Burwell of Ebenezer, who was related to my future brother-in-law, Dudley Sale Burwell, now deceased.

Don Barrett

"One thing, Bob; I would start by saying that I have two photographs on my wall, and both of them I am proud of. The first one, the earlier photograph, speaks to really what we are talking about. To say that there was a wonderful relationship between the Christian community and the Jewish community doesn't accurately say what the situation was and is, because there were not really two communities. At least to my knowing, and I am sixty years old and I grew up here in the '40s and '50s and '60s, and I know that there was one community. The photograph I am talking about is the undefeated Lexington High 1932 football team. My uncle, 'Jelly' Thompson, was the coach, and there were only about sixteen boys on the team, four of whom—or 25 percent—were members of the Jewish faith. They were Herman Flowers, who was the star as quarterback; Herbert Hyman, who was said to be a very good and fast backfield player; Celian Lewis and Cecil Herrman, who were solid linemen, [Cecil was injured and could not participate for the full 1932 season]. That's a pretty good representation for any one religious group on that little team. But it just shows how thoroughly together we were; how we operated as one group.

"There are so many things I would like to say. I remember when I came of age in the 1950s and '60s, with all that was going on during those years, like the civil rights movement. There were some tough times politically and socially all over the country and the South especially, even here in Lexington. I remember when Mr. Ready Ellis died—he was at the Holmes County Bank, one of the 'godfathers of the bank'—the family asked my grandfather, J.E. Stevens, who was a Methodist minister and superintendent of the church who lived in Greenwood, to preach the funeral. He was my mother's father. At that funeral, the Jewish community was there en masse. It was at the Baptist Church. I recall that most of the Jewish community was seated together; not all, but most. They were over on the left-hand side, down close to the front. During the service, my grandfather had a lot to say about how much better the situation was in Lexington than any other place he had ever seen. And how well the Jewish community and the Christian community worked together and lived together. I never had thought about it. He mentioned that he had experienced in other towns a virulent anti-Semitism. I am telling you the truth, it was the first time I had ever heard anybody I knew even say the word anti-Semitism. I hardly knew what it meant. That shows what a wonderful place we had and still have here in Lexington.

"I remember at that time my grandfather was visiting and staying with us for the funeral at my mother and father's home. After the funeral, it seems like every one of the Jewish mothers sent food out, as a gesture, and I asked, 'What was that about?' And Daddy said that was just a gesture because they all appreciated my grandfather mentioning that [the part about a total lack of anti-Semitism in Lexington]. In later years, I think back that I was struck by the fact that I didn't know, because we were so insulated from that kind of junk here in Lexington, the very heart of the Deep South.

"My grandfather actually preached here in the 1930s. The Methodist Church has a communion table where we commemorate the last supper of Christ, his last Passover meal. We commemorate it once a month and we have a communion table where we put the elements—the bread and the wine—on, that is part of our faith. That communion table was given to us by the members of Temple Beth El in Lexington. Now if that doesn't say a lot [nothing will]. I don't know whether or not you knew that, but it's a fact. The fact that we accepted it and loved it, and thought how wonderful it was. I remember my parents talking about it and saying how thoughtful it was. That was back in the '50s.

"I remember your dad [Joe Berman], his enthusiasm and joy for living, or at least apparent to the world and to me. He would take time, when I was a kid, to visit with me. What a neat man your father was.

"Herman Flowers was so good to me. I played high school football, and I was a pretty good high school football player. I wasn't good enough to play in college, but I thought I was, and Herman Flowers thought I was. Herman, by himself, got me a scholarship offer to play at Tulane. Herman had been the student body president at Tulane. Although Herman had no sons, he was the biggest booster of our football team. He was one of the fans that went to the away games. It didn't matter who was playing for Lexington, he just supported the teams. He understood high school football teams, having been the star of the undefeated Lexington team. He followed it all of his life, and he was good to me. Herman was a funny man. He was quick-witted, bright. When I was in high school, I would go down to his store and hang out with him during slow times and just visit. And we would talk about Lexington back in the '20s and '30s and the things that he remembered, and the stories he would tell. Herman was always the person at the Lexington Rotary club who would induct new members because Herman could speak on his feet better. There he was, who ran a clothing store, and all these lawyers in the Rotary club; there was no question that Herman was a better speaker than all of them put together, including my father, who was a good lawyer.

"I have such fond memories of Leroy Paris. He and Dad were great friends. Wilburn Hooker, Harold Hammett, Pat Barrett and Leroy Paris—as unlikely a group as you would think in the world, and they were great buddies. Daddy talked them into buying a boat together. At the time I thought it was the most wonderful yacht there ever was. It was actually about a twenty-foot, homemade wooden cabin cruiser. They kept it at Grenada Lake and would go on these fishing trips. They would always come back with ice-bucket loads of crappie, a wonderful fish to eat. It didn't make sense that they were this good a fishermen to catch all of those fish. We found out later that they would buy the fish. They had great times. The boat sank numerous times; forgetting to take out the drain plug, or for one reason or the other, it sank about four times. Each time they would resurrect it and go again. They were such great friends. I would go and visit Leroy when he had cancer. What a wise man he was, and such a man of goodwill.

"I have thought about this a lot, but it's a fact that Lexington, as small a country town as it is, has, over the past century, produced a lot of men and women that have made a mark in business, law, medicine—not only around the state but around the country. So many people ask me: What is it about Lexington? Why are there so many people that come out and do well, at the top? What causes that? I am absolutely convinced that a big part of it is the fact that we had a vibrant Jewish community influence on our town. What I am saying is that the Jewish community of Temple Beth El, by jumping in and being an integral part of the operation of the community, brought a sophistication, raised the level of intelligent discourse that you don't see, which moderated the lesser angels of the southern nature. This is especially during the bad times, when we were going through the throes of a social revolution that really did change the way we lived, and changed it in many ways for the better. It was a stressful time. And the Jewish community quietly, and not so quietly when you needed not to be quiet, was able to influence and lead and make that transition period work.

"Right now in Lexington, our little town is doing just fine economically. I'll ride you around and show you. We have just raised $300,000 to renovate the old Strand Theater as an arts center. Phil Cohen told me he had the best quarter he ever had last quarter, and this is after struggling for a few years. But we have full employment pretty much here, and I think we have a bright future.

"I think we are different than many little towns in the delta and many towns our size in the South, and I am absolutely convinced that a huge influence on that has been the Jewish community. We are different because you helped make us different. We are better for that and I think it is true. It's been a great and rewarding experience for us. Lexington, I think, and have told everybody this anyway, that I believe Lexington is the smallest town in the United States that has an active synagogue, and it still is.

"Small towns are shrinking around the country, owed to a lot of different things—from Mr. Sam Walton, to better highways, to better opportunities for people in the larger cities. So the Jewish populations in small towns have dried up, and it's happened here. But it's not because the relationships weren't there. The relationships have always been there. And through no fault of Lexington, it's now a different world economically; merchandising is different. The Jewish community is just a shadow of what it was, but I don't know of anybody that left that didn't love Lexington when they left, and still have a warm spot in their heart for Lexington.

"I recall Beth Flowers [Herman's daughter]; wow, what a beautiful girl she was. She was a little older than I, so I could have a crush on her. I'd been in love with her since I was about five years old. I saw Beth at Herman's funeral, and to me she is just as pretty as she ever was. Her husband, Harry Lebow, would come and hunt with us at our hunting club. It was sort of funny having the eastern seaboard Jewish background mixing with the 'bubbas' out in the woods. We had fun, and I think he enjoyed it a great deal. One of our duck blinds is named for Harry, in his honor.

"If I had to pick out three or four people who would stick with me if I ever got in trouble or when things weren't going well, Henry Paris would be one of those. He owns a place in Destin, Florida, and he owns it because I talked him into it. I was his partner. I called him one day and said the market is just terrible, and the market in Destin is in a depression, and that is the prettiest place in the world. I bet we could buy us a place there. Shortly thereafter, we were in his airplane that same day, flying to Destin, and bought a place before sundown. I kept it with him for about six years. All of a sudden I needed to raise some money and I had to sell my interest. Any decision we ever made he would say, whatever you want to do, that would be great with him. When I had to sell it, I said, 'Henry, I know when we bought into it, it was a permanent deal and it's been great, but I've just got to have the money.' He said, 'What do you want me to do? Do you want to sell it or I would buy your half interest? Whatever you want.' I said, 'What's my half interest worth?' And he said, 'Just whatever you say it's worth. I'll cut you a check.' Now, how is that? I love him. He was a great addition to Lexington growing up and I think Henry loves Lexington.

"To summarize: it's not accurate to say I had good relations with the Jewish community. Again, it was so much closer than that. Some of them were my best friends, some of them were good friends. I was so totally integrated into the group that they were integrated into, the social group that we had and have in Lexington, that I am so at ease in that society. My wife, Nancy, and I went to the Holy Land in

1996 with a Jewish attorney and my dear friend, Bob Llieff, senior partner in a major law firm in San Francisco, and his wife. Bob's firm, in my opinion, is the best plaintiff firm in America. We went to all the biblical sites in both the Old and the New Testaments. What a wonderful place."

During this personal interview with Don Barrett at his law offices in Lexington, he made one of the most profound statements made to me by anyone in the Lexington community. To reiterate, he stated that there never has been a Jewish community in Lexington, nor has there been a Christian community in Lexington. He continued that there has, instead, always been one community in Lexington—all working together in concert for the betterment of the entire community and society as a whole. That statement in itself summarizes nearly everything this book is about.

In conclusion, Don Barrett agreed with me that in Lexington, while the Jewish and the Christian communities were distinct in themselves, he and his family were part of the Jewish community and the Jewish community was part of his family, and how proud and honored each was to be a loving part of the other.

The Povall Family

Al Povall

"Our lives and the life of the town were infinitely richer because of the presence of our wonderful Jewish friends and neighbors, and I have said many times since that Lexington was held together by the wonderful Jewish families and the leaders that they produced."

Allie and Betty Povall and their family lived in a beautiful southern mansion on a hill opposite Faymorcele, our family home. Their family, too, were outstanding citizens of Lexington and the state. Allie, now deceased, was the first high school football coach I ever had. He not only taught the basics of the sport, he also taught what courage, honor and integrity were all about. Later, Allie was a fine mayor of the town of Lexington. All of their children went on to successful careers. Al, Patty, Amanda, their families, and their dear mother, Betty, now reside in Oxford, Mississippi, home to the

University they all attended. Betty is as radiantly beautiful as she ever was.

Al, now retired, was formerly the general counsel and vice president of BellSouth. Patty works with her husband, Will Lewis, in the operation of Neilsons, the town's largest department store, along with their gourmet restaurant on the square. Amanda, a member of the Hall of Fame at the University of Mississippi, lives with her husband, William Tailyour, in Oxford, where she practices law. Their brother Kirkham is an attorney in Cleveland, Mississippi.

Below are excerpts of verbatim statements made to me by members of their family.

Al Povall

"Patty forwarded to me a copy of your letter of October 5, 2005, concerning your history of the Jewish community of Lexington. I have long thought that topic worthy of a book, and I am delighted that you are pursuing it. I am happy to contribute what little I can to your effort, the result of which I can look forward with much anticipation.

"We moved 'up on the hill,' as we called it, in March of 1947. I was five, and my first memory of the new house was standing on the sun porch and looking out at a sunny, chilly and very windy day. A kite was flying across the road in what was then a pasture, and later was the home of the Terrys, at the corner of Clifton and North Streets. Warmer weather brought exposure to other sights and sounds, many of them due north of our house, at your home. I remember the peacocks and going over to see them, cutting through our back 'pasture,' and watching the majestic birds fan their tails as I approached. Later, Herman Flowers told me that the birds used to go over to Edwin Neilson's home on North Street, the former home of Governor Noel, and awaken Edwin at daybreak with an avian ruckus—which always infuriated him and engendered a call to your father and a threat to 'shoot the damn things.'

"Your grandfather was alive then, and we could hear the five o'clock news on, I believe, your grandfather's radio—as he was, it was said, hard of hearing. No one thought anything about it; it was just the way it was.

"As you know, the rabbi came up from Jackson for services; usually, it seems, on Sunday afternoons, but I may be mistaken about that. Our organist and my cousin, Fanny Eggleston Lumpkin, whom we called, 'cuddin' to the older generation, played the organ at the temple, and several of our choristers sung in the choir there, including my Aunt Emily, and my sister, Patty. Emily had a prayer book from the temple, marked to include the appropriate choral responses, and I remember reading it at their house and remarking how similar the Episcopal and reformed Jewish services were.

"Our lives and the life of the town were infinitely richer because of the presence of our wonderful Jewish friends and neighbors, and I have said many times since that Lexington was held together by the wonderful Jewish families and the leaders that they produced. Your father was a particular leader and a man to whom everyone looked up and whom everyone loved. Happy, outgoing, full of life and energy, Joe Berman was the kind of person who could and did make everyone feel good about themselves.

"When I was about six, I got my first big bicycle, a 26-inch Schwinn from Thurmond's. I was too short to ride it, really, but undeterred, I came roaring down out of my drive one day after midday dinner, made the first turn onto Clifton, but then hit the loose gravel at the corner of Clifton and the highway and lost it, scattering myself all over the road. Your father had stopped there, before pulling out onto the highway, and he observed the whole thing. He scooped me up and drove me back up to my house for medical treatment and emotional support, which he rendered enroute.

"Many years later, when I was in the navy, I came home following my first Vietnam cruise and Herman [Flowers] asked me to speak at Rotary, which I did. It wasn't much of a talk, but your father made me feel like I had just delivered the Gettysburg Address. I also recall later during that leave, a girlfriend and I somehow ended up at your house, with your mother trying to entice a doodlebug out of its hole by spitting on the end of a broom straw and chanting 'doodlebug, doodlebug.' My girlfriend was absolutely fascinated with your mother and her expertise at the doodlebug hunt.

"There are so many other memories: my first Christmas parade, on the square on a cold December day, and the LHS band leading the parade then ending around in front of the old Strand Theater, just off the square and next to Pep Tidwell's grocery. Your sister, Joan, was the drum majorette, and had on one of those little majorette outfits that looked to me like a bathing suit, and I remember thinking how pretty she was—and still is—and how cold she must be, wearing a bathing suit in December.

"Herman, of course, was my great and good friend, and he told me many, many stories about how the first Jews got to Lexington and how they got started in the various businesses there. I'm sure you have access to all of that, and I look forward to reading it in an organized presentation. One of the things that I have told so many, many people through the years, as I traveled through the United States, is that not only were there absolutely no distinctions—socially or otherwise—between Jews and Christian, as children we actually went to temple—my sister, Amanda, went every time Anne Flowers and Edward Louis Schur went—and Beth and Anne and others came to our church from time to time. Moreover, I tell them that the two choirs contained many interchangeable parts. Frankly, people from other parts of the country simply do not believe me when I tell them these things; but they are true, of course, and constitute, I believe, some of the many unique characteristics of the Lexington in which we grew up that made Lexington such a wonderful place in which to live."

Patty Povall Lewis

"So many lovely families, both Jewish and Gentile, who cared about the community and worked together to make it a very special place to live."

"First and foremost, I consider my years in Lexington during the forties and fifties as pretty wonderful. In this town of 3,200, there were few social lines that I can remember, other than those of black and white. There were so many lovely families, both Jewish and Gentile, who cared about the community and worked together to make it a very special place to live. A sound education was always important to my Jewish friends, and it made me work a lot harder, lest I be left behind. As Mother said, the Jewish families in Lexington set the bar high, and we all strived to do the same.

"St. Mary's Episcopal Church and Temple Beth El shared an organist, Mrs. Fannie Eggleston Lumpkin. Both had small congregations compared to the Methodist, Baptist and Presbyterian Churches. Our choirs were also small, so I was pressed into service at a very young age. She had me singing solos when I was eight or nine—a painful experience for all, I am sure. One Sunday a month, the choir from St. Mary's would join the choir at the temple for an afternoon service. We would sing with Fay [Berman], Irma [Paris], Henrietta [Hyman], Phyllis [Stern] and Jocelyn [Cohen]. My Aunt Emily's voice was always heard above the others, and I can hear her singing the responses, some of which I can still sing to this day.

"Sometimes Rabbi Nussbaum would come up from Jackson, but Joe Berman would most often conduct the service. I always looked forward to the wonderful receptions that followed the service. The food was divine—I had my first tongue sandwich at the temple. My last visit to Temple Beth El was for darling Herman Flower's funeral. The light that filtered through the [stained glass] windows was just as I had remembered it during those afternoon services long ago. When St. Mary's had a special music at Christmas, Fay and Irma would always join our choir for the midnight service. The temple and St. Mary's enjoyed a beautiful and meaningful friendship.

"The Povall and Flowers' families have shared a long friendship. We loved our visits to their home where there was central air conditioning and lots of cold Coca-Colas in the icebox. We made many trips to the delta during high school to hear the Red Tops and danced the night away. I marvel that our parents allowed us to drive all over the delta, returning home in the wee hours of the morning. Herman gave me my first job as a gift wrapper during the Christmas holidays. Little did I know that in married life I would often be pressed into service at the gift wrapping station at my husband's department store.

"The day that Joan and Dudley married, I dragged a chair to the backyard so that I could watch the proceedings. There had been so much excitement about their wedding and I had a ringside seat. I remember someone stood on the balcony and sang something romantic before the vows were exchanged. It was a fairy tale!

"The square was a vibrant place, and I looked forward to Saturdays when I could visit the various stores. So many of the businesses were owned and operated by Jewish families, and their presence was the backbone of Lexington commerce. Today, I can only find my old friend, Phil Cohen, still operating on the south side of the square.

"Bob, I am so happy that you are doing this. It will be a lasting history of a most precious place that I remember with much affection."

Amanda Povall Tailyour

"I have incredibly fond memories of my visits to Temple Beth El, and am grateful that it was a part of my growing up in Lexington."

"My dearest friend growing up in Lexington was Anne Flowers. I cannot remember not having her as a friend, and to this day, we remain close friends, despite the distance that our lives have taken us. We go for long periods without communicating in our busy lives, and another birthday rolls round and one of us will pick up the phone and it becomes a marathon call.

"Growing up in Lexington, I often joined Anne for services at Temple Beth El. Compared to the Anglican service at St. Mary's, the service in Hebrew seemed exotic and filled with mystery to my young mind. At the end of the service, Rabbi Nussbaum would invite the children to come down to the front of the temple to kiss the rabbi. At this point, Anne would whisper in my ear, 'I am not going to kiss the rabbi.' Being the obedient child, always eager to please, I would turn to Anne and say, 'Don't worry, Anne, I will kiss the rabbi for you.' I would then line up with the other children, take my turn in the queue, and plant a kiss on Rabbi Nussbaum's cheek. After the service, there would be a reception in a room that I remember dimly lit with candlelight. The fading sunlight of the late afternoon streamed in through the [stained glass] windows on a table filled with delicious tea sandwiches, cakes and sweets. I have incredibly fond memories of my visits to Temple Beth El, and am grateful that it was a part of my growing up in Lexington.

"I also have memories of your home on the hill, a home that I often visited with Anne. We would pass through an arbor at the back of the Flowers' property, through a secret passage to your home to visit Brenda [Berman]. Much earlier than those visits, I was aware of the peacocks that patrolled the grounds. They must have made a huge impression on me, for at a very young age, I developed an imaginary friend I named 'Mr. Peacock.' I also remember the mynah bird, Sabu, that called out 'Brenda,' imitating your mother, Fay.

"We look forward to joining the celebration of the centennial of Temple Beth El."

Betty Povall

"When I read Edward Cohen's book about growing up in Jackson, I was sorry he did not grow up in Lexington."

"We enjoyed seeing Barbara and Gina Hyman recently. They were attending the Southern Foodways Symposium at the university, and stopped by for a short visit before heading back to Dallas. The visit brought back memories of when Herbert [Hyman] brought Henrietta to Lexington. There was a beautiful reception at Faymorcele for Henrietta. She wore a red chiffon dress, which I can clearly see to this very day. The Jewish families always set a standard of entertaining that we all tried to emulate.

"Eph Cohen lived where the Lehman family lived when you were growing up. The Povalls lived on the hill up the highway, and as soon as Sessions Povall was allowed to leave the yard, he would come down to play with Eph. They were best friends throughout their lives, and Eph was a pallbearer at Sessions' funeral.

"I remember when Celian Lewis came home from military service and retrieved his convertible from storage. I can see him now, going up the hill with the top down—so incredibly handsome. He was home from Australia. Later, Norma and her family came for her and Celian's wedding and reception. We were all thrilled to be invited.

"I remember when Joan and Dudley married also. It was on the lawn at Faymorcele [author's note: the same setting for the wedding of my parents, Joe and Fay Berman, in 1929], where the tables were scattered about so beautifully. The most gorgeous food I had ever seen!

"When Brenda had a birthday—maybe the second or third year—Joe had a miniature train come, and Kirkham was invited. They also included Amanda, who was a bit older.

"Allie always thought the temple had a wonderful way of meeting financial needs. Joe Berman and Leroy Paris would get together and make a budget. They would then decide what each family should pay as their share, and each family did indeed pay that amount.

"I remember the cakes Miss Claudie Hyman made. They were much bigger than the cakes of today. She made the most wonderful white layer coconut cake. She put a pinch of rosemary in the batter.

White cakes were always iced and were 'company cakes.' The yolks were then used to make everyday cakes, which were not iced but always served with sauce. Actually, I liked the yellow cakes better.

"I still use Jocelyn's [Cohen] recipe for spaghetti sauce and Fay's [Berman] recipe for Swedish meatballs.

"I remember the summer parties outside Irma's [Paris] before we had air-conditioning. Chairs were set up in the backyard in a circle. They did not cook out at those gatherings, but always served lovely summer food.

"I remember how beautiful the temple was when Beth Flowers married Harry Lebow. Elvera [Flowers] had it decorated with the most beautiful pink peonies.

"Do you remember Miss Fannie Eggleston Lumpkin, who was the organist for St. Mary's and Temple Beth El? On holidays she would combine the choirs. Special music was Miss Fannie's life, and she had a great time on those occasions.

"When I read Edward Cohen's book about growing up in Jackson, I was sorry he did not grow up in Lexington. Oh, I remember my aunt in Canton and going to dances with the Wiener brothers, William [Bill] and Julian.

"There is a proverb I like:

"Life is short, and we do not have much time to gladden the hearts of those who travel the way with us—so be quick to love and make haste to be kind."

The Watson Family

Julian Watson

"Jed, pass the roast beef down, will ya?"

Morris Lewis, Morris Herrman, Leroy Paris, and others spent many a Wednesday night at Jed Powers' home in Franklin, Mississippi, a close suburb of Lexington, playing poker, drinking beer, and enjoying a delectable midnight dinner made by Jed's wife, Sadie, and their daughter, the ever-lovely Juanita Powers Watson, wife of the late Julian Beall Watson, Sr. Even late in life, Jaunita has kept her beauty. There is something in Lexington—the water, the air, the climate, or maybe the great tradition of love and tolerance among its citizens—that seems to allow its ladies to maintain their youthful beauty, spirit and appearance, even as they age; or just perhaps "Innocence and purity retain its eternal youth."[28]

On those Wednesday nights when they would play poker, Jed would send out the word the day before, by a black man that worked on his place. He would pass the word that on Wednesday night there was to be a meeting of the 'Self Improvement Club,' a euphemism for a Wednesday night poker game where they gambled and feasted the night away.

He did not call over the telephone, since those were the days when a local operator would dial the number called. Frequently, some of those operators would enjoy listening in on conversations between the calling and receiving parties. That's how they would learn of the local gossip. Sometime they would even join in the conversation. Jed did not want any of them to know about the friendly gambling that went on in his household. That was the reason behind the name of the club and the person-to-person communication of the time and date of the get-together.

At about midnight, Miss (Miz) Sadie would take a broomstick; using the handle, she would pound it on the floor, signaling that the midnight dinner was ready to be served. Then she would say, "Come and get it," and that they did. One of her delicacies would always be a big smoked ham. Knowing the Jewish tradition of staying away from pork, Julian Watson related that Leroy Paris would always say, "Jed, pass the roast beef down, will ya?" While Leroy was no orthodox Jew, and highly reform, he loved to kid, having a good sense of humor.

The Watson family was also most generous in allowing many of their Jewish neighbors to hunt quail and dove on their spacious plantation-like setting in Franklin. That's when the quail were plentiful, and with the bird dogs pointing, they could be found in the open sage grass and more easily banged, even if you weren't the best shooter. Today, in that area, the few that remain have gotten smart and alight in trees, staying in the more wooded areas for protection. Henry Paris and I, along with our good friend John McRae, used to hunt every hill and valley in that large tract of land. We knew where every covered sinkhole was, in order to avoid them. One time I even shot a rabbit that had just run between the legs of John McRae, directly in front of him. After that, while we continued to remain close friends, John always kept a wary eye on me as we followed close behind the white and black English setters, red Irish setters, and spotted black and white pointers through the tall sage grass, with shotguns at the ready.

Mr. Jed Powers had a general country store in Franklin, the only store there. Before each hunt, we would go in and get some crackling bread (that's cornbread with pork rinds baked in it; not very kosher, but neither did we practice it, and it tasted mighty fine) to keep us warm during the cold winter days of the hunt. Afterwards, we would return to that store for some Snickers, Hershey bars and Cokes to refresh us.

Juanita Watson, and the Powers and Watson families, were close favorites of the Lewis, Herrman, Paris and Berman families of Lexington. Later in life, Julian B. Watson, Jr., son of Juanita and Julian Sr., who was several years younger, became a close and trusted friend of mine. He is a highly successful insurance agent with Prudential, and also a fellow Rotarian in the Rotary Club of Jackson. Clara Watson, recently deceased, was Julian's aunt. She taught me history in Lexington High School. Some fifty years later, ninety-year-old Clara—dressed so elegantly and looking her beautiful self—attended a Rotary district conference banquet, where she stood and paid tribute to me in front of several hundred Rotarians and spouses when I was completing my term as a district governor. What a wonderful example of true friendship, from a former Lexingtonian lady of the Christian faith to a former Lexingtonian male of the Jewish faith.

The Tahir Family

Abe Tahir

"I am the only Arab I ever knew that bought Israeli bonds."

Then there was the family of Abraham and Mary Tahir, who were of Syrian heritage. They lived in Tchula, Mississippi, just about twelve miles from Lexington, which I have referred to as a suburb of Lexington. Abraham was born in Syria and Mary was born in Greenwood, Mississippi. They were both Muslims. They had a son they named Abe and a daughter they named Mary Elizabeth. Abe and I were friends in high school, and became even closer at the University of Mississippi. Abe and his sister Liz were raised in the Catholic faith, since there were no mosques in the Tchula-Greenwood area. Mrs. Mary Tahir is a lovely lady of much grace and good common sense, with a laugh that can tickle one's soul. Later she was baptized in New Orleans. She and Jocelyn Stern Cohen (mother of Phil Cohen) went to high school together in Greenwood and were lifelong friends. Abe is a former owner of art galleries in New Orleans, Houston and Beverly Hills. He continues to operate out of his home. Mary Elizabeth is a former vice president of D.H. Holmes department store in New Orleans (the first woman in that position), and is now a fashion consultant. All resided in New Orleans, until Hurricane Katrina. They have all now returned to New Orleans.

Incidentally, Abe Tahir says, "I am the only Arab I ever knew that bought Israeli bonds."

A few years ago, when New Orleans was threatened by another of the hurricanes that come through the Gulf of Mexico each year, the Tahir family took refuge in Jackson with some friends. That was at the same time of the High Holy Days. What a blessing it was that they shared the Rosh Hashanah eve dinner at Sondy's and my home, with other members of our family. Here were two families of opposite heritage—one Syrian and one Jewish—sitting down together, in mutual love and respect, on a major Jewish holiday and breaking bread together. A prayer was given before the evening meal which stated: "With so much strife and conflict in this world today, oh, if only the world could witness the love, affection and respect shared for one another this evening between two families of such different mid-eastern backgrounds." Yes, there is hope for peace in this world of ours.

During Hurricane Katrina in August 2005, they had to once again evacuate their homes in New Orleans. This time, at our invitation, they moved in with our family. We were sympathetic of their losses, yet delighted to have them share our home in Jackson for as long as necessary.

What was done by our family for the Tahir family was done out of love and respect for each of them. Had the situation been reversed, they would have, without hesitation, done the same for our family. They are such fine people.

An Aside

As an aside, when Hurricane Katrina slammed into the

Mississippi Gulf Coast and New Orleans, two of our daughters, Deborah Silver and Marjorie Block, didn't wait for the federal and state governments, including FEMA, to send help. Deborah and her husband, Larry, from their home in Boca Raton, Florida, donated and solicited enough funds to send eight full tractor-trailer loads of much needed food, water and supplies to the stricken areas of Mississippi. Debbie was on the telephone all night long making certain that the items sent reached their destination. She even cleared them through Homeland Security.

Marjie, from Manhattan Beach, California, and her husband, Mark, donated, and she almost single-handedly solicited from others to send another tractor-trailer load of food, water, diapers and other supplies from Los Angeles to Gulfport, Mississippi. For this and other efforts, she later received the Humanitarian Award of the Year from her Temple Menorah in Redondo Beach, California, and a Certificate of Appreciation from the County of Los Angeles. Excerpts from her acceptance speech at the lavish awards banquet are as follows:

"As a native Mississippian, I was horrified—like we all were—at the devastation of Hurricane Katrina. Our relief effort started out as a grassroots idea inspired by my sister, Debbie, who lives in Florida. When she saw that no help was going into the Gulf Coast area that first weekend, she decided to take matters into her own hands. Through extremely generous donations, Debbie arranged for eight fully loaded, eighteen-wheeler tractor-trailers to be sent to the devastated areas.

"I thought: if she could do it, I should try as well. So, with contacts made through my other sister, Sheri, in San Diego, I arranged for a donated truck and driver through Feed the Children, to pick up a collection of goods to take to Mississippi.

"It wasn't as easy as it seemed. This project would not have happened without the help of many other people. My friend, Tami Brothers, helped me the most. We realized that in order to fill a full eighteen-wheeler tractor-trailer, it was going to take longer than we had hoped for.

"We held a full weekend drive, and Temple Menorah and Tuvia parents were generous with bags of clothing, shoes, diapers, hygiene products, water, toys and many canned goods, which I loaded up in my van to take to Pennekamp Elementary on a daily basis. It's really all about tzedakah, which is the Jewish way [of giving].

"Finally, on the morning of Yom Kippur eve, thirty volunteers showed up to help load this huge truck. It was an awesome sight.

"The deal I had made with Feed the Children was that we would completely fill this truck. There was some space left after loading these carefully packed boxes, which we meticulously went through to fold the clothes and label according to sex and sizes. We had also received some generous monetary donations. So with this money, I drove with the truck driver and went shopping at Costco. As we loaded the pallets, other customers passing by donated more money. We loaded three pallets of corn, green beans and tuna fish.

"The truck driver was terrific. He kept in touch with me as he drove across the country; and I actually spoke with the relief center director in Gulfport, where your donated items arrived with deep appreciation.

"I also thank Rabbi Silver for his support of this project, and all the families for your generous donations. All of you made a difference in the lives of those who so desperately needed help."

She concluded by saying, "There are so many people around the country who responded to this disaster in so many ways. I share this honor with all of those people."

Our daughters, Debbie and Marjie, did these mitzvahs (Jewish for "good deeds"), along with our daughter, Sheri Spector's, Christmas essay when she was a teenager, because of what they have been taught and have always lived—to do what is good, just, merciful, and do it humbly.

Our daughters' efforts made a big difference in the lives of many people who were without homes and desperately needed supplies due to the devastation caused by Hurricanes Katrina and Rita—and they did these things in the general sense of love for humankind.

The P.H. Williams Family

Parham Henry Williams, Jr.

"I have often thought that Lexington's Jewish community lifted that little town from the commonplace to an enviable level of culture and business entrepreneurship."

There was also the P.H. Williams family. Mr. P.H. Williams was the highly respected chancery clerk of Holmes County. He and his wife, Mary "Sis" Williams, and their children, Parham, Jr. and Nancy, were always close to the Jewish community and were mutually respected. They were outstanding citizens of Lexington and continued in that same manner in their future careers.

Parham and I have been very close friends for many years. We went through high school and the University of Mississippi together. At Ole Miss, Parham was an outstanding student and president of the campus YMCA. He was one of three Lexingtonians elected to the Ole Miss Hall of Fame within a two-year period. I have always referred to him as a "walking encyclopedia." Parham received his law degree from Ole Miss and his LLM from Yale. After his service in the United States Air Force, he became a district attorney. Afterwards, he was a professor of law at the University of Mississippi, and later dean of the law school there. He was dean of law at Samford University in Birmingham, and was then called upon by Chapman University in Orange County, California, to become dean of law there and assist their law school in becoming accredited. His lovely wife, Polly Franklin Williams, also is a graduate of the University of Mississippi and, as mentioned earlier, co-chaired Religious Emphasis Week at Ole Miss with me. She received her Ph.D. in higher education from the University of Mississippi. She is now an English professor at Chapman University, teaching southern literature. She and Parham reside in Orange County, California. Our families have always remained dear friends.

Nancy Williams Murrill is married to Paul Murrill, who is the former Chancellor of LSU. This is another great family from Lexington and close friends of the Lexington Jewish community.

In Parham Williams' contribution to this book, he initially describes his recollection of how the Jewish community started in Lexington. While somewhat redundant to what has already been written, it nevertheless is stated so succinctly, and with such clarity, that I felt it important to record it, along with his other descriptive statements about his family's long and close association with the Jewish community of Lexington.

Parham Henry Williams, Jr.

"As a modest level of prosperity returned to the South in the 1880s and 1890s, Lexington became the principal trade center for Holmes County. Recognizing the business opportunities that awaited them, entrepreneurial Jewish tradesmen migrated to Lexington and energetically sought their fortunes. Most began as itinerant peddlers, hiking the unpaved country roads, rain or shine, their heavy back packs bulging with necessities for their rural customers. These diligent and enterprising peddlers soon acquired sufficient capital to open stores on the square in Lexington. The first and most important of these was the store opened, at an even earlier time in the mid 1800s, by Jacob Sontheimer, on the south side of the square. Sontheimer and the other Jewish merchants that followed stocked their stores with every item needed by the hill country cotton farmers: clothing for men, women and children; boots; shoes of all kinds; seed; feed; grocery staples; cotton sacks; plow lines and a variety of similar items. The merchants also engaged in a 'furnish' business with their customers, furnishing the farmer seed, fertilizer, tools and the necessities for living during the crop year, then collecting the debt, plus interest, in the fall when the farmer sold his cotton.

"By the early 1900s, prosperous Jewish merchants were thriving in Lexington, and a strong Jewish community of more than twenty families constituted the core of the town's cultural and economic life. Tangible evidence of the economic, social and religious strength of the Jewish community came in 1905 with the dedication of Temple Beth El, the first—and still the only—synagogue in Holmes County. When Mr. Sontheimer died, the business continued to prosper under the proprietorship of two of his daughters, Miss Rosa and Miss Bettie. To correctly identify the new owners, the name was changed to R & B Sontheimer.

"Not all of the Jewish entrepreneurs were retail merchants. Morris Lewis made the judicious decision to open a wholesale business, specializing in groceries. The Lewis Grocer Company, with headquarters in Lexington and distribution warehouses in Durant and Lexington, became the most important commercial enterprise in the county.

"By the time I was old enough to remember things, the square bustled with successful Jewish businesses. Sadly, Miss Rosa and Miss

Bettie had died by then, and R & B Sontheimer was sold. Not too long afterwards, it existed only in the faded sign painted across the brick wall of the building. But Applebaum's department store, E. Cohen's, B. Schur's and Flowers department store were flourishing businesses. A block north of the square, on Carrollton Street, a large buff brick building contained the headquarters of the Lewis Grocer Company. Earlier, it occupied a smaller brick building on Beale Street, opposite the train depot.

"Also housed in the latter building on Carrolton Street, in another section, was the food brokerage firm owned and operated by Joseph E. Berman, attorney and son-in-law of Morris Lewis, who moved to Lexington from Atlanta in the mid 1930s.

"I occasionally wondered whether any evidences of anti-Semitism—unkind words or acts—were ever directed toward Lexington's Jewish community. Perhaps there were, but I was not aware of them. Fortunately, I was blessed with parents who appreciated and respected all sorts of people, and who numbered many in the Jewish community as cherished friends. My father, for example, was active in the local Masonic Lodge, where he shared the arcane secrets with several Jewish brother masons, including Sol Applebaum and Eph Cohen. I shall always be grateful that my parents instilled in me that same quality of appreciation and respect.

"My earliest and closest friendship was with Bob Berman [known as Bobby in his earlier days]. He was the oldest child of Joe and Fay Lewis Berman, and I spent many a happy hour in their home. And what a beautiful home it was! Named Faymorcele in honor of the three Lewis children—Fay, Morris and Celian—the massive two-story brick home stood atop a high hill on Lexington's north side. The towering mansion and its fifteen acres of spacious grounds were a child's delight. Arrogant peafowl, resplendent in their rainbow-hued tail feathers, roamed the rolling lawns, raucously challenging the unwary intruder. A bevy of maids and yard men maintained the premises in pristine condition, while a wonderfully talented cook, named Ruth, brought forth meals of succulent quality.

"Mr. Lewis also employed the only chauffeur in Lexington—perhaps in Mississippi—a suave black man dressed impeccably in a black suit, white shirt, black tie and black chauffeur's cap. In addition to driving Mr. Lewis to and from his office, the chauffeur also delivered Bobby [Bob] to the Lexington Grammar School at

7:45 a.m. and picked him up when school let out at 3:00 p.m. Often I would go home with him for an afternoon of play. Climbing into the giant black limousine—I remember it as being a LaSalle—was a special thrill. During these frequent visits, I came to know the Lewis and Berman families quite well, and developed a sincere and abiding friendship for them. Mr. Lewis, somewhat reserved but kind, courteous and dignified, was the deeply respected patriarch of the family that I knew. Other family members included Mrs. Lewis, her sister Aunt Claudia Hyman, Joe and Fay Berman, and the three Berman children—Bob, Joan, and years later, Brenda. In addition to the peafowl, a beautiful red Chinese chow, appropriately named Shanghai, and a remarkably articulate mynah bird named Sabu completed the household.

"My father both respected and admired Morris Lewis and considered him a personal friend. In his position as a public official, my father had occasion from time to time to be helpful to Mr. Lewis and, of course, never accepted any compensation for his work. I well remember a time when my father worked several days on a matter ultimately resolving favorably for Mr. Lewis. When my father refused to accept any payment for the work, Mr. Lewis devised a unique— and much appreciated—means of expressing his gratitude. One day, the big limousine drew up in my parents' driveway and the chauffeur carefully removed a huge carton from the trunk and laid it gently on our front porch. When my mother opened it, she found an exquisite Cambridge crystal punch bowl set—a huge bowl, a heavy ladle, a beautiful tray and twelve cups. Folded in one of the cups was a note in Mr. Lewis's handwriting that read simply: 'Thank you for being a friend.' My mother treasured the set of crystal for the remainder of her life, and served many a festive cup of punch from it.

"On another occasion she received a much different sort of gift from Faymorcele. It seems that Brenda had a magnificent blue Persian cat with an impressive pedigree and a lengthy and quite formal name. Despite its noble breeding, the cat was not the cuddly variety. In fact, it made the unfortunate mistake of scratching its little mistress. The decision immediately was made to give the cat to someone—anyone. But who could be the lucky recipient? Remembering that my mother loved Persians—we always had at least two, of such pedestrian but usefully descriptive names as Snowball and Blue Boy—Joe Berman decided that she would be the one person who would most likely accept the irascible cat. Accordingly, Joe himself delivered the miscreant, handling gingerly to avoid its keenly honed claws. Joe was right. My mother fell in love with the cat, and the creature seemed to reciprocate, or at least tolerate, her affection. In any event, it never bit or scratched her! However, my mother quickly decided that the cat's lengthy formal name was much too cumbersome for everyday use. So, since Joe had delivered it to her, she simply named it Joe. And so, Joe the Persian was a much pampered resident of our home for many years afterward.

"One of my earliest memories is of Bob's fifth birthday party, a grand event staged on the sweeping front lawn of Faymorcele. A fabulous merry-go-round had been imported for the occasion, complete with calliope music and colorful wooden horses that cantered majestically in endless circles, delighting their squealing riders. After daubing our insides and outsides with ice cream and chocolate goodies, we gathered and lustily sang 'Happy Birthday' to Bobby as—like our Saturday matinee hero, Gene Autry—he made a grand solo ride on the merry-go-round's largest horse.

"Although most of Lexington's Jewish households were successful and prosperous, there were two notable exceptions: those of Morris Flink and Miss Harriett Riteman. To the public's eye, Mr. Flink never achieved any greater distinction than being the butcher in George Patterson's IGA grocery store. Unbeknownst to many, he actually owned the market in that grocery store and leased it from the IGA owner. Taciturn and remote, he rarely conversed with his customers for any purpose other than to learn which cut of meat they wished to purchase. When accompanying my mother on grocery shopping expeditions, I always wandered to the back of the store to watch in fascination as Mr. Flink wrestled a side of beef or pork onto the butcher's block and began hacking off prime cuts with a monstrous cleaver. My wonder grew as he slapped the cut on a sheet of waxed paper and laid it on the scales. For only then one became aware that the thumb and two fingers were missing from his left hand, victims of errant strokes of the razor-sharp cleaver.

"Mr. and Mrs. Flink lived with their three daughters in two large rented rooms in a shabby boarding house south of the square. They dearly loved each of their daughters, although their youngest daughter, Myra, who was perhaps a year or two older than I, was the pride and joy of their lives. Tragically, at age thirteen, she was stricken with spinal meningitis. Most unfortunately, this was before the discovery of modern day miracle drugs. She died an agonizing death a few days later. The tragedy affected the whole town and the funeral was crowded with mourners, including Myra's little playmates. The following morning Mr. Flink was back at his butcher's block, stolidly hacking away. I followed my mother back to the meat counter, where she leaned over and said softly, 'Mr. Flink, I want you to know that we prayed for Myra, and we are praying that God will give you and Mrs. Flink his peace.'

"Mr. Flink's back was turned to us and, for a moment, he continued the methodical hacking, the heavy cleaver rising and falling like a metronome. Then his hand became still and his head bent forward. As I watched, a single tear splashed on the bloodstained wood of the butcher's block, and I heard him murmur, 'Mrs. Flink and I thank you, Mrs. Williams.'

"My mother had great empathy with the less fortunate in our world—the poor, the neurotic, the egregiously eccentric—and eagerly took them under her wing when all others ignored them. Miss Harriet Riteman was a prime example of this passionate altruism. An aging spinster with an irascible temperament, Miss Harriet lived alone in a large rambling house a few blocks north of the square. To supplement her meager income, she rented one or two bedrooms, usually for questionable purposes to persons who sought the anonymity not found in a hotel, especially in such a small town as Lexington. I occasionally was in the back seat when my mother drove Miss Harriet, who had no automobile, to buy groceries. During these trips, Miss Harriet would gleefully relate how Mr.____ _____ had brought Miss (or Mrs.) _____ to one of her bedrooms the night before. 'Got there at eight and left at ten,' she would chuckle. 'Paid me three dollars in advance!' Mindful of my presence in the back seat, my mother would hurriedly direct the conversation to a less salacious topic. Over the years, however, I developed a pretty good picture of the nocturnal activities of several of Lexington's leading male citizens.

"Because of her eccentricities, Miss Harriet occasionally was the target of practical jokes and mild vandalism. For example, every Halloween night teenage boys would remove the wrought iron gate guarding Miss Harriet's side yard and hide it in some obscure location. Early the next morning, our phone would ring and Miss Harriet, her voice trembling with indignation, would inform my mother of the missing gate. She never reported the theft to the town marshal because, as she eloquently phrased it, 'that lazy son of a bitch wouldn't lift a finger to find it.' Each time, my mother would load my little sister and me into our car, go pick up Miss Harriet, then drive slowly around town searching for the missing gate. We always found it, though in varied and bizarre locations—twice in Odd Fellows Cemetery, once on the front steps of the First Baptist Church, and once in the watering trough on the courthouse lawn. Having found the gate, my mother would have Baker, our colored handyman, rescue it and return it to its proper location, there to remain in rusting dignity until the next Halloween.

"I have often thought that Lexington's Jewish community lifted that little town from the commonplace to an enviable level of culture and business entrepreneurship. I shall always be grateful for the opportunity to know, and to claim as friends, so many of my Jewish neighbors."

The McRae Family

Murrell and Mildred McRae, along with their children, John and Sybil, were close friends of the Jewish community and highly respected citizens of Lexington and Holmes County. They were, each in their own right, popular and well liked. John was one year ahead of me in school, but we were always good friends. Even past Ole Miss, our paths crossed again later in Boston, when he was enrolled in the Harvard Medical School while I was at the Harvard Business School.

Many years later, when "Dr. John" retired from the practice of medicine, Sondy and I attended his gala retirement party in Hattiesburg, Mississippi. At that affair they presented John with a "This Is Your Life" program. The organizers asked me to be one of those persons from his past, who would stay behind the curtain and give him a hint, over the microphone, of who I was, without him knowing my identity until he heard the words and sound of my voice. I had found a photo of John, along with my sister, Joan Burwell and myself, as young kids dressed in cowboy and cowgirl outfits, probably taken before going to see Gene Autry on a Saturday afternoon at the local Strand Theater. I had that photo enlarged to a three-foot by four-foot size and was to present it to him after I came on stage. I practiced singing Gene Autry's theme song, "Back In The Saddle Again" many times, coached by Sondy, a great vocalist herself. Well, when it came time to sing those words from behind the curtain, I had a "senior moment" and couldn't remember exactly how it went—words or tune. Fortunately, my dear wife was standing nearby behind the curtain. I ran over to her and asked for the cue. That's all I needed to give a splendid Gene Autry impersonation. Then I came out on stage and presented John with the large photograph. He never knew that I almost botched the whole performance—had it not been for Sondy, who saved me from a potentially embarrassing faux pas.

Dr. John M. McRae

"I was aware that my best friend was Jewish, but I didn't think anything about it."

"My best friend when I was growing up in Lexington was Henry Paris. I was aware that my best friend was Jewish, but I didn't think anything about it. My immediate crowd of friends were Henry Paris, Bob Berman, Edwin Ellis and Donald Boatwright. Two of our fivesome were Jewish.

"Henry was my very closest and best friend for years—grammar school, junior high, high school, and into college at Ole Miss. Growing up in Lexington, we lived about four houses apart on Spring Street, and spent many nights together. We were almost inseparable. We had the run of the town, day and night, walking everywhere together, including to the Lexington Country Club, which was over a mile away. Later we did the same in cars. He knew all of my secrets and I knew all of his.

"My father, Murrell, was the general manager of a sugar plantation in Cuba. Thus, he was in Cuba during the fall hunting season, so Henry's father, Leroy Paris, taught me to hunt quail. He had a beautiful trained English setter named Ric. He taught me how to hunt quail behind a dog, until the dog stopped perfectly still, crouched and pointed with his nose forward toward the covey of quail concealed on the ground in the sage grass. At times they would be running on the ground, and it was a thrilling sight to see Ric follow them so deftly and quietly, as if tiptoeing through the high grass. When they would stop running he would stop again. Then we knew it was time to move forward, with shotguns ready, until the quail took off flying. I can still hear the fluttering sound of the covey when they began to fly. That was the time to take aim and fire. We could get out of school at 3:00 p.m. (during bird season) and be on two coveys of birds within an hour. In those days, if you had a good dog like Ric, they were easy to locate. Today, they are scarce and usually in wooded areas, often traveling alone.

"One summer Henry went to Cuba with my family and me, and stayed there in our Cuban home for almost two months.

"In high school, my senior year, Henry and I played all sports together. I was fullback on the football team and he was quarterback. I recall our group even had a 1925 Chevrolet for which we paid sixty-five dollars. We named it Jezebelle. The first night we took it out for a spin, we burned up the motor going so fast down a steep hill past the Lexington Country Club. However, one of our group, Donald Boatwright, later an aeronautical engineer and professor at Mississippi State University, kept it going for years.

"Our parents were a tight-knit crowd, including my mother and father, Mildred and Murrell McRae, Joe and Fay Berman, Leroy and Irma Paris, and Eugene and Janet Herrman. My mother was crazy about your mother, Fay Berman, and thought she was the cutest lady in their crowd.

"Bob Berman had significant uncles in Morris and Celian Lewis, who were highly successful businessmen. They eventually left Lexington to manage the Lewis Grocer Company operation in Indianola, Mississippi, in the heart of the Mississippi Delta. Bob's grandfather, Morris Lewis, founded the business, which later became SuperValu, now on the New York Stock Exchange and one of, if not the largest, wholesale food distributors in the nation. I understand with its recent purchase of Albertsons, along with its co-purchaser CVS, they are also now the third largest retail food operation in America, behind Wal-Mart and Kroger. Incidentally, my grandfather, Mr. Rainwater, was the chief accountant and bookkeeper for the Lewis Grocer Company. He would drive back and forth to Durant, Mississippi with Leroy Paris every business day.

"As I look back, there was a large Jewish contingent in Lexington, including the Herman Flowers, the Ephraim Cohens, the Nathan Schurs, the Morris Flinks, and a good number of others. I just never really thought much about the fact that they were Jewish."

Sybil McRae Child

"I am so grateful that I grew up in a town in which there was no divide between the Jewish and Christian community."

Sybil McRae Child has always been a beautiful, vibrant and talented lady. With a terrific voice, she has starred in many musicals for Jackson's New Stage Theater.

"One of my best friends growing up in Lexington was Beth Flowers. I spent many hours at her home, spending the night, playing bridge, dancing to forty-five records, and in her backyard playhouse.

"I adored both her parents, Elvera and Herman, who were as sweet and loving to me as anybody could be. Beth and I were in each others' weddings; she went to Cuba with me, along with several other friends, after we graduated from high school. Although we don't get to see each other often, we still feel close.

"Of course, Mama and Daddy [Mildred and Murrell] were great friends of your mom and dad's [Joe and Fay Berman]. I remember being taken to their imposing house as a little girl to see the mynah bird. And I remember how sad we were at the sudden and unexpected [airline] death of Joe.

"We were proud that Lexington had a temple. My mother used to sing there on occasion.

"There are many funny stories about the Paris family. One of my favorites is about Irma getting a day pass from the hospital, to come home to supervise her kitchen help in making homemade mayonnaise for a cocktail party that somebody else was giving because she just didn't believe the party could be held without her mayo. Fortunately, my relationship with the Parises continues as Henry's daughter, Rachel, and I are on the same tennis team.

"I am so grateful that I grew up in a town in which there was no divide between the Jewish and the Christian community. I know I am a better person because of my many interfacings with individuals from the Jewish community."

The Hammett Family

Gwendolyn Hammett

"Your book entitled A House of David in the Land of Jesus has really touched my heart."

Gwendolyn Hammett has kept her rare beauty throughout all her years. She and her husband, Harold, lived on Spring Street near Temple Beth El, where she still resides. It is also across the street from the former home of John McRae and Sybil McRae Child, mentioned earlier. Gwendolyn's family has always been good friends of the Jewish community.

"Your book entitled *A House of David in the Land of Jesus* has really touched my heart. Thank you for giving me the opportunity to reminisce about so many wonderful Jewish friends. Hopefully this writing expresses my utmost love for each of them.

"My early years in Lexington began as a young bride when I married Harold Pinkney Hammett on November 5, 1940, at the Presbyterian Manse in Lexington. We were members of the First United Methodist Church where our six children were christened and confirmed.

"Harold passed away at an early age. He would have elaborated more than I about his love for his many Jewish friends. Many times he spoke of his happy childhood in Lexington, and especially of his close friendships with Herman Flowers, Celian Lewis and Gene Herrman. His stories about football and band were so entertaining to hear. Although these boys had different religious beliefs, it never seemed to interfere with their relationships.

"My earliest memory of socializing with members of the Jewish faith was in the late 1940s. What fond memories I have going to eat supper at the home of Janet and Gene Herrman. Irma and Leroy Paris lived next door to Gene and Janet and seemed to sincerely welcome Harold and me to the Lexington social life.

"It was during this time I remember being lavishly entertained in the Berman home. How sad Harold and I were when we heard the tragic news about your father, Joe Berman. The Christian and Jewish communities came together as we all mourned his death.

What a void this left in our group of friends. Your mother, Fay, and I remained friends for the rest of her life. She was always so kind to include me in trips to her beach home on Santa Rosa Island.

"Elvera and Herman Flowers were a big part of our lives and so important to the Jewish community. I have so many wonderful memories of being entertained in their home on North Street. She and I became regular bridge buddies for forty years or more. Her daughter, Anne, and my daughter, Sandra, were dear friends during their school years and remain very close to this day. I love to think about the simple way of life in Lexington, when I could go uptown and shop for my five daughters at Flowers department store. What a great department store Herman owned. He was such a kind businessman to everyone in our town. After Elvera's death, Herman was such a gentleman to me and to all the widows in town.

"One of my fondest memories occurred a few years before his death. He organized and furnished the most delicious picnic on the Natchez Trace for Barbara Ervin, Katherine Foose and me. We were all saddened the day we heard Herman had passed away.

"Phyllis and Joe Stern have been good friends to me throughout the years. Phyllis and I have had many bridge games."

The Hooker Family

Ed Wilburn Hooker, Jr.

"One of the most moving services I recall in our church [Lexington's Methodist Church] was when we invited your rabbi to preach."

The Hooker family has always been close to the members of the Jewish community in Lexington. Wilburn Hooker was a state legislator for many years. He and his wife, Mary Elizabeth, had many Jewish friends in the Lexington community. Their three sons—Ed Wilburn, Bootsy and Wyche—as community leaders, have continued to follow suit.

"Our family has been dear friends of the Jewish community in Lexington for many years. My parents, Wilburn and Mary Elizabeth, had closest ties with Leroy and Irma Paris, Joe and Fay Berman, Herman and Elvera Flowers, and Janet and Gene Herrman.

"As I grew older, I considered Leroy Paris to be one of my most cherished friends. What a wonderful man he was.

"Phil Cohen was my classmate. We have worked together for the betterment of Lexington all our lives. We serve now on the Lexington Historic Preservation Commission.

"The Lexington Methodist Church and Temple Beth El have a strong record of cooperation. More than one of the prominent Jewish weddings took place in our sanctuary.

"One of the most moving services I recall in our church was when we invited your rabbi to preach. He was an excellent speaker with a strong message. The statement that he made in closing has stuck in my mind after all these years. He said: 'Temple Beth El has always been aware of the love shared between members of our congregation and yours. We are honored to be invited here tonight. I feel confident in saying that nowhere else in the world is a rabbi standing in a pulpit in a Christian church this evening.'

"Our church presented a small table to Temple Beth El, which was placed right in front of your pulpit and was still there the last time I visited. As chairman of the board of the First Methodist Church, I know I speak for our whole congregation in congratulating Temple Beth El for one hundred years of service to God in Lexington."

The Beall and Yates Families

Beth Beall Yates

"After we both lost our parents to cancer, Henry [Paris] set up a cancer benefit tennis tournament in Indianola."

The Beall and Yates families have always been leaders and prominent in the Lexington community. Their long-term friendship with the Jewish community there has been well-known and reciprocated.

"My earliest memories of experiences relative to members of the Jewish community were when Triana Wilson and I were five years old. We were asked to be mascots of the Lexington High School band. Joan Berman Burwell was the drum majorette. Those were the days when the band went to the Cotton Carnival in Memphis.

"I remember on Christmas mornings, Leroy Paris would bring me a huge sack of bubble gum. I thought that he was just like Santa Claus.

"Beth Flowers and I were best friends, probably from when we started school, and always played together as children. She meant so much to me, but I always looked up to Joan.

"We went to Ole Miss ball games and saw Henry [Paris] cheering [as head cheerleader] and later become Colonel Rebel [the most popular student on campus]. Al Povall and I followed in his footsteps as cheerleaders.

"I also recall that remarkable mynah bird which Joe and Fay Berman owned. The story goes that one day the bird was in its cage, speaking the "Queen's English." On that day, the regular housekeeper was off and a new one had taken her place for just that day. Your dad, Joe, asked if she knew how to clean the bird. Her reply was, 'Yes, sir, you just put it in the boiling water and pick it.'

"It saddened us all so when your dad, Joe Berman, was in the plane crash. I was not in Lexington at the time, but small towns are wonderful in that everybody is like one big family—and it was as if everyone had lost a member of their own family.

"When I would visit my mother and daddy, I would always try to get a visit with your mother [Fay Berman]. She was such a dear lady. I remember toward the end for Mother, when she had leukemia, your mother didn't miss a day coming by and checking on her. They were very close, dear friends.

"After we both lost our parents to cancer, Henry [Paris] set up a cancer benefit tennis tournament in Indianola. He called me to help, which I did. It has been a major success, now in its thirty-first year, in raising money to fight and someday hopefully defeat that dreaded disease."

The Charles Carson Family

Jean McClellan Carson

"The Jewish people have helped to make Lexington what it is and keep us going through the years."

Charles and Jean McClellan Carson

Charles Carson spent his working career in the retail and wholesale food business, along with the food brokerage business. Charles, through his working at the Lewis Grocer Company and then the Berman Brokerage Company, renamed Southern Food Brokerage, most likely had more association with the Jewish community than most anyone else in Lexington.

His wife, Jean, put together a book entitled *The History of Holmes County.* It is also noteworthy that Jean's daughter, Robyn McCrory, is the current mayor of Lexington, which she won irrespective of the fact that the majority of Lexington's citizens are African-American.

Charles was working for his first wife, Loyce's, father in his general mercantile store in Eden, Mississippi. Loyce passed away many years later. A Lewis Grocer Company salesman was calling on that store out of the Lewis Durant operation. He convinced Charles to interview for a job at Lewis. He subsequently was interviewed by Morris Lewis, Sr., and Leroy Paris, in a car sitting in front of the old Welcome Inn Café on the square in Lexington and was hired to go to work for Lewis in January 1949. He worked at Lewis for six years, and then left to work for a food broker in Jackson for about a year. Leroy Paris recommended Charles to Joe Berman and he was hired to work as a salesman for Berman Brokerage in 1955, to call on both the retail stores and the wholesale warehouses. His combined time working for Lewis and the Brokerage was forty-two years.

Phil Cohen and Charles have been very close, playing golf together and going to golf tournaments. Herman Flowers used to be one of Charlie's golfing buddies also. He said Herman was such a prince of a person and they miss him so. "He was such a great person to be around."

Charles said he was supposed to be on the same plane as my father, Joe Berman, when it crashed. However, they had a new secretary, so he was assigned to stay behind and help the new employee. After the accident, a friend of the family, Dick Barrett, flew Charles down to Jackson to pick up my father's car that was parked at the airport.

Jean said that my dad, Joe, while a professed member of the Jewish faith, was as close to being a Christian as anyone ever was, especially when he went to the Holy Land and came back and delivered all those talks to various churches, clubs and synagogues. Charles went with my father on his many talks to assist with the slide presentations. He went to almost every church in Holmes County, Jackson, Greenwood, Drew and elsewhere. They said Joe Berman brought the Holy Land to those people in Mississippi who not only had never been, but who most likely would never get to go. He not only visited Israel, but also Egypt, Jordan and Lebanon, so he was able to describe and show scenes of vast areas and holy sites in the land of Jews, Christians and Muslims. Those talks were very much appreciated by everyone who heard them.

Jean stated that when she grew up, she was thankful that her parents taught her to be tolerant of all faiths, which was the way it was throughout the Lexington community. She said she really did not know the difference in Lexington's citizens. "You would hear about divisions in other communities, but not so in Lexington. Phyllis Flowers and I were very close in high school." She also remembered Henry Paris, Joan Berman Burwell, Phil Cohen, and his sister Sylvia Lynn and others.

Also, when Jean got married to Bob McClellan, her first husband, she said Phyllis and Joe Stern had built a home near them. "They had three daughters and we had three daughters. I picked up their two older daughters and my three about the same age, and took them to school for years. Our families were very close." Her husband, Bob McClellan, had a service station on the square, with Nathan Schur's store on one side and Herman Flower's store on the other side, across the street. "They were all good buddies and we traded a lot with them."

She continued that, "Mr. Flowers, bless his heart [a typical southern expression of endearment] was so wonderful. I think he helped to send millions of children to school by giving credit to their parents, both black and white, and taking a long time to ever get his money back. Maybe some of it was never repaid." Jean said she grew so fond of Mr. Flowers. "He was the historian of Lexington and got it on the historic register. He served on so many committees to help the town. If the town had more men like him, it would have been even better off today." It has been, she said, a real privilege for her to know the Flowers and the Cohen families. Phil Cohen and she have worked together for years on the chamber of commerce. "He is such a fine person, and so was Herman Flowers."

Jean expressed that "the Jewish people have helped to make Lexington what it is, and to keep us going through the years." She said she knew it was hard for the Jewish merchants during the civil rights movement and boycotts, as was with her husband, Bob, but they all weathered it together. "I remember also Ephraim Cohen's parents, as well as Freddie Miller and his five-and-ten-cent store. Eugene Herrman and my husband, Bob, were good friends." Jean said she still had a copy of my dad's book, *With Apologies To No One.*

She remembered that after so many of the ladies became widows, Herman Flowers and Pat Barrett picked them up and took them all to the country club once a week for a big game of "boo ray [a southern style card game]." They all enjoyed one another immensely. Later, Charles Carson would pick them up for the big weekly game.

The Mike Lammons Family

Mike Lammons

"So that preacher wanted to put a Cross up somewhere so people would know it was a church, but that didn't happen because we like that Star!"

Mike moved to Lexington in 1932. During World War II, he fought in the Battle of the Bulge in Europe with the 26th Division. Afterwards, he returned to Lexington in 1947 and was an outstanding jeweler in the town and Holmes County. When you purchased from Mike Lammons, you knew you would receive the true quality and value that he had described when he sold it to you. It was a matter of complete confidence and trust in him by his patrons. Mike stayed in business for forty-nine years before retiring and turning the business over to his daughter and son-in-law. Mike and his wife, Helen, had, and still have, many Jewish friends and customers.

"One of the things I would like to mention in regard to Jewish friendship, is that through Eph Cohen—who was a very good friend of mine—had it not been for him, I don't know whether or not I would have been able to buy the building that I finally bought to house the business, because at the time I had no finances or guarantee of a loan payment. But he was willing to loan me the money, and we paid it off in a ten-year note. I will always remember that because if it had not been for him and his friendship, some of the things I might not have been able to do. Actually, I could not negotiate to buy the building from the owner. So I asked Eph if he would go over there and buy the building for me and then sell it to me. That he did.

"Eph and I were good Masonic buddies, too. I actually conducted his funeral service as a Masonic service here in Lexington.

"I was in grammar school and high school with Gus Herrman. I recall they had a service in honor of Gus at the Lexington Country Club. It was a tribute to him for bequeathing a considerable amount of money to the Institute of Southern Jewish Life.

"I also knew Gus' brother, Cecil. And I knew their dad, Morris Herrman, who was a likeable person. I will always remember him as smoking a long cigar. At one time, in my earlier days, when I was about nineteen years of age, I was the driver for Morris Herrman when he was a salesman for the Lewis Grocer Co. I recall driving him one day when the roads were very bumpy and I seemed to hit every one of them. That's when he said, 'You missed one; go back and get it.'

"I also recall working on the grandfather clock in your grandfather, Morris Lewis' home, Faymorcele. It was a Herschede clock that sat majestically on the landing of his home. It was a real headache to work on. That was a good clock, but a pain to work on. I took the movement out and took it down to the store, set it up in vises to be sure it would chime and run before screwing it back into the clock. I was up at that home a lot of times working on that clock. The clock has a small metal plaque on the inside of the door that reads 'grand prize.' " [Author's note: It still is in the family, having been handed down to my mother, Fay, and father, Joe Berman, and later to the home of Sondy and myself; and now it has come to rest in the home of our daughter, Sheri, and her husband, Steven Spector, and family. The clock has melodic Westminster chimes that sounded at 7:00 p.m. at each of our three daughters' weddings, announcing their entrance into the sanctuary of Beth Israel Congregation just before they walked down the aisle. That was a family tradition. Therefore, Mike must have kept it in good working condition all those years.]

Mike continued, "I remember vividly when Joe Berman's airline accident occurred. That news was all over town. Your dad was a likeable person. He used to come by my store and we would talk. I recall when he went to the Holy Land and came back with many color slides, which he showed many times, along with a very descriptive talk about the various places in the Holy Land, including many Christian places along where Christ traveled. The community all appreciated what he did in bringing so much of the Holy Land to us.

"There are two churches in Lexington, the Baptist and the Methodist, that prominently display the Star of David on their fronts. We had a preacher here at one time in Lexington who said we want to identify our church as a Christian church, because somebody came through town and recognized our church as a Jewish synagogue, with the Star, and we said, 'Oh, no, that's the Baptist church!' So that preacher wanted to put a Cross up somewhere on the building so people would know it was a church, but that didn't happen because we like that Star! Jesus descended from the House of David; thus, there is no reason not to have the Star of David prominently visible on our church.

"With reference to Lexington history, it was a sad thing when Eph Cohen and Herman Flowers died, not only because they were fine gentlemen, but also because they had more knowledge of the history of Lexington, of all faiths, wrapped up in them than anyone else I know. So when they died, so died a lot of Lexington history. [Author's note: A lot of the history in this book has come from Eph Cohen's son, Phil Cohen, who had been told those stories by his father and by Herman Flowers.]

"I want to tell you one thing about you and your dad, Joe. When I was running my business, I was out selling while I managed my store. And you had just graduated from college. We had just gotten in some brand-new, fourteen carat, solid gold Elgin watches. I said to myself, 'Now, that's the perfect gift for Joe to give Bob.' So I looked him up and said, 'Joe, I've got the perfect gift for you and Fay to give Bob on his graduation from Ole Miss.' And I want to tell you, he took the wind out of my sails when I told him, 'I've got the sharpest watch you have ever seen.' Joe said, 'Well, I've already given him a car.' I said, 'Glory hallelujah, I can't compete with that.' "

[Author's note: I really did need a car at that time as I was on my way to Fort Benning, Georgia, for the Basic Infantry Officers Course. While most young people today get a car in high school, I was happy to receive one after my college graduation. However, next to a car, I couldn't have asked for anything nicer than that gold Elgin watch.]

The William Ellis Family

Billy Ellis

"How wonderful it would be if we could all be wrapped up in that simple love that characterized the life of Myra Flink."

The William Ellis family have been leading citizens of Lexington and friends of the Jewish community from one generation to the next. Their banking interest and success has been noteworthy and a tribute to their business acumen, character and integrity. Billy Ellis is a former president and chairman of the Holmes County Bank and Trust Company in Lexington. He is also a successful author, having written a number of nonfiction books.

William, Sara Elizabeth, Billy, Sarabeth, and their family that preceded them loved their community, and such love and affection can readily be seen continuing unabated in the following descriptive and poignant essay entitled "Myra's Legacy."

"Myra's Legacy"

By Billy Ellis

It is merely a yellowed faded photograph evoking now down the distant corridors of memory a kinder and gentler era in the tiny country town of Lexington, Mississippi. The photograph depicts a frail little fair-haired boy of four and a hauntingly lovely, raven-haired girl of thirteen. Both children stand in deep snow flanking a robust but lop-sided snowman with a wry, crooked grin. In the background is the modest duplex of my parents, Sarah Elizabeth and William Ellis and me and my sister Sarabeth. We shared the duplex with Herman and Elvera Flowers and their daughters Beth and Anne.

It was the Christmas holiday season during World War II. The girl in the photo was our neighbor Myra Flink, an exotic sounding name in our small town predominately WASP community. The Flinks lived across the street from us and Myra was not only my baby sitter but she soon became like a big sister as well. Myra often took me over to her house to play and visit with her wonderful parents, Morris and Mildred Flink, and her sisters Bernice and Inez. The Flinks [Morris and Mildred] were kind, gentle people who talked (it seemed to me) in a strange accent and ate unusual food like purple soup and tough round bread that had a donut-like whole in it [bagels], and spread with cream cheese topped with some kind of pink fish [lox salmon]. Their food was sure different from my mother's peas and corn bread and country fried chicken! Instead of a Christmas tree, the Flinks had a large candlestick holder [candelabra] that Myra explained was a menorah.

Myra and I and my erstwhile playmate, Beth Flowers (Lebow), enjoyed the previous summer with Myra immensely. Our favorite lark was to hide in the bushes until ole Ira came along in his old-fashioned wooden, mule-drawn wagon. When we jumped out in front of him, Ira would always feign surprise, but he was always delighted to help Myra, Beth and me jump into the creaky old wagon where we all rode down to the creek behind our house. Ira was a courtly, good-natured old black gentleman and he was quite an entrepreneur as well. He drove his wagon down to the creek almost every summer day, loaded it up with sand, where he sold it all over town for sand boxes, cat litter boxes, or to loosen up garden soil. How luscious it was back then to wade barefooted in the gin-clear stream and build massive sand castles during the softly fading twilight.

Every single afternoon right before six p.m., Myra would walk uptown to the old square to meet her father whom she adored and walk back home with him when he got off work.

Some afternoons Myra would also take me up to the town square with its towering old brick court house with the Confederate monument standing in front. Across the street was the IGA grocery store where Myra's father worked as the butcher. He actually owned the meat market and leased it from George Patterson, owner of the grocery store. Mr. Flink, (who I called Winky) would always greet us with delight when we walked into the store. Winky would quickly carve off thick slabs of my favorite food, that Winky called "goosh" liver. The taste of that real goose liver is still deliciously fresh in my memory after sixty years. That goose liver is not to be confused with the present type which is soaked in sodium nitrate, maltodextrin, and erythorbate, encased in a plastic cocoon.

In a world gone mad, we children were thoroughly insulated in a small, loving community inhabited with kind, generous folk who practiced the highest Judeo-Christian values.

During that rare and joyous holiday when snow fell that Christmas, Myra, Beth and I romped and played in our new found white wonderland and built that fine snowman. My birthday occurred about then and Mama dolled up Myra in a Santa Claus costume for my birthday party. When Myra walked into the party dressed as Santa with her bag of small toys, all of the little kids shrieked in terror and bolted for the doors and pandemonium ensued. Only when Myra took off the Santa mask to reveal her lovely face did the partygoers settle down, and Myra, not Santa, became the life of the party.

The day after we built the snowman, Beth Flowers and I went over to the Flink's house to get Myra to come out and once again play in the snow. Mrs. Flink came to the door with a gaunt look of distress on her face. "Myra seems to haff a bad cold," she declared. Several days went by but still no Myra. Mama finally told us that Myra was real sick and I heard her crying back in her kitchen. Looking across the street the next day, I saw a large square-looking truck with a flashing light on top parked in front of the Flink's house. I found out much later that Myra's cold had gone into spinal meningitis and that most of the miracle antibiotics that might have affected her cure were right about then on their way to a place called Omaha Beach.

Myra Flink died the next day. Mildred Flink, racked with inconsolable sobs, told my mother, "Myra loffed leetle Billie like he vas her own leetle brudder." And so it was that the great and inexplicable loss of Myra gradually flowered into dreaded reality for the little blonde-headed boy; and he was also to learn of many other deaths at that time including the supreme sacrifice of our brave American service men and women who even then were dying to free the world of the Axis tyranny as well as freeing a host of Myra's kinsmen in death camps all over occupied Europe. Allied victory came too late, however, for yet another hauntingly lovely little girl about Myra's age named Anne Frank who was captured in Holland by the Nazi's and later died in a concentration camp, right after she had reaffirmed the basic goodness of man in her poignant diary.

[Author's note: There was an amazing likeness in the pictures of these two young Jewish girls, Myra Flink and Anne Frank.]

And around the time of Myra's death, the greatest theologian of our time, Dietrich Bonhoeffer, left his secure tenure at Union Theological Seminary in New York City, gave up his beloved progressive jazz haunts on the lower west side, and returned to his native Germany to risk his life for his theology. He shared the plight of his fellow prisoners in Flossenburg death camp and he was executed there while still reaffirming his message of man's reconciliation with God.

Many months after Myra's death, Winky started taking me with him to the local picture show. Right before the movie *Twelve O'clock High* came on, we watched the Movietone News. In one of the news clips I remember viewing a dark, gray-looking land where the sun seldom shined. There were rows of drab, ominous looking buildings surrounded by a high barbed-wire fence. In my child's eyes I perceived what looked like huge bulldozers pushing thousands of pallid, starkly naked dolls into raw, open dirt trenches and I could feel Winky quietly sobbing in the darkness.

And so each Christmas I study that faded photograph of the lovely young Jewish girl named Myra Flink standing beside that little blonde boy and I remember her pure untainted soul and the awful futility of her death transfixed upon the garish panoply of World War II.

And during each Christmas season I also recall the crucifixion of a young Jewish soul who was a rabbi over two thousand years ago. He professed such radical verities as 'God is love,' 'love one another,' and 'do unto others as you would have them do unto you.'

'God is love'! What a world changing concept that was and still is. How wonderful it would be if we could all be wrapped up in that same simple love that characterized the life of Myra Flink, so that we could ultimately find forgiveness and peace in our own lives.

What an intriguing holiday hope for us all.

First Baptist Church, with Star of David

Lexington Methodist Church, with Star of David

Chapter 46

The Jewish Community and the Black Christian Community of Lexington

Several leading members of the African-American community of Lexington were interviewed about their relationships with the members of the Lexington Jewish community, both past and present.

Based upon their own personal experiences and relationships, these are their stories.

Mary R. McGee
Tax Assessor
Holmes County
County Courthouse
Lexington, Mississippi

Mary R. McGee

"Herman Flowers of Flowers Brothers, Nathan Schur of Schur's department store, Ephraim Cohen of Cohen's department store, they always treated me and my family with dignity and respect."

I suggested that Mrs. McGee first tell me about herself. She became tax assessor in 1982. She was born and lived part of her life in the Newport community of Ebenezer, a small community just southeast of Lexington.

When I mentioned that my brother-in-law, Dudley Burwell, now deceased, came from Ebenezer, she recognized the family name.

Mrs. McGee was born in 1947, so she was only twenty years of age when my father, Joe Berman, was killed in that tragic airliner accident. She only recognized him by name, not by face. She said the same about my mother, Fay, who lived until 1988.

She recognized the old antebellum home of my grandparents and parents, and where I grew up; however, she only knew it as Dr. Downer's home. She knew where Temple Beth El was located on Spring Street.

I then prompted her to relate who in the Jewish community she knew and anything she might have recalled about them.

She said she knew Herman Flowers of Flowers Brothers department store. She also remembered Nathan Schur of Schur's department store. Both of these stores were located on the Lexington square. She recalled Ephraim Cohen of Cohen's department store, also located on the square, and the only remaining Jewish department store in Lexington.

She said she knows Phil Cohen and Edward Schur, who continue to live in Lexington. She met Elvera Flowers (Herman's wife) while in the store, and knew Ellen Schur who worked with her husband, Nathan, in their store.

When inquiring if she remembered anything in particular about any of them, she said those three stores were just about all that the town had so she was very familiar with them. She continued, "They were all nice people and if you couldn't find something at one of their stores, nine out of ten times you could always find what you needed at one of those three stores, without ever leaving Lexington. During those days, not many people, especially of the black community, went out of town to buy. You could normally get whatever you wanted here in one of their stores. They were all three very good merchants. We still trade with Cohen's.

"They always treated me fairly. I know of no problems. Herman Flowers of Flowers Brothers, Nathan Schur of Schur's department Store, Ephraim Cohen of Cohen's department store, they always treated me and my family with dignity and respect. Whenever they had time, they would hold a conversation with us, since they knew us because of my family and daddy, Emmett Ruth, who was known as 'Babe' Ruth."

Mrs. McGee had five brothers and two sisters. She added that she also remembered Joe Stern, who had the Sunflower Food Store just off the square. However, they later moved to Durant, Mississippi, and traded over there. "When we lived in Ebenezer, we did shop some at Joe Stern's supermarket."

She lived in Durant for about thirty-eight years and thus she didn't remember many of the Jewish community other than the merchants on the Lexington square.

She said her husband's brother worked in the Lewis Grocer Co. in Indianola and one of her husband's friends used to work in the Lewis Grocer Co. warehouse in Durant.

Her husband's first cousin, Rudolph Jackson, used to work for the Lewis Grocer Co. in Indianola. He was a truck driver. I personally recalled Rudolph from when I worked there after my college and military days.

I asked Mrs. McGee if she knew the famous musician, B.B. King, from Indianola. She knew of him since she had a girlfriend from Indianola who personally knew B.B. when he started off, playing at churches in that delta town. I related that he had found his way from Indianola to Memphis by a ride on a Lewis Grocer Co. truck. B.B. King has always remembered that ride and tells the story frequently.

I then urged her to talk about the days of the civil rights movement in the 1950s and 1960s, not just in the South but all over the country, and what she recalled about the Jewish citizens of Lexington during that period of time.

She replied that during that time, she was still in high school. She graduated in 1966. When the civil rights movement was taking place, she was not directly involved. She went to the Lexington Attendance Center School, which was an all-black school.

"All I remember, coming out of high school in those days of civil rights, is that the Jewish merchants and others always treated everybody fairly. My daddy was involved in the civil rights movement, but I never heard him say anything about mistreatment from any Jewish people."

She also had memories of Herbert and Henrietta Hyman. She recalled Hyman Real Estate. She remembered when Herbert Hyman was killed and how tragic that was. She said she knew Herbert well. When asked how, she said it was due to different pieces of property she would check out for him. When he would buy land, she would have to work with the deeds and other matters, since that was her job. She never had any problem with Herbert. "He was always very respectful."

In summary, Mrs. McGee said the most she remembered about the Jewish community of Lexington were the merchants, who always treated her nicely. "When you went in their stores, they were always polite and showed you respect." She never had any "run-ins" with any of them.

She went on to say that, "Regardless of one's religion, or race, we've all had our hardships, but we all need to work together, and help one another for the betterment of our community and each other." She concluded that, "I knew Jesus was Jewish, and that by respecting one another, it would lead to peace for all. Then everything else would work out. We may not can save the world, but each of us can do our part in making it a better place in which to live." She continued, "We all need to try to make a difference in a Godly world."

Elder James Rodgers
Guiding Light Church of God in Christ

Elder James Rodgers

"There is no place like Lexington where the blacks and the whites, including the Jewish community, have a great relationship and are continuing to try to make it better."

Phil Cohen

"It was Elder James Rodgers, through his 'Sermon on the Square,' that brought the races together and made peace in the community."

Prior to my personal, one-on-one, interview with Elder Rodgers in his church, he, Phil Cohen and I had lunch together in Lexington, at one of the new restaurants in the old Coca-Cola bottling company building. At that lunch, there were so many statements of significance made by both James Rodgers and Phil Cohen which were relative and pertinent, that I felt it important to preface my interview with Elder Rodgers with some of the comments I taped during that lunch.

James Rodgers was born in Lexington in 1938 and lived there all of his life except for the time he left for work in Chicago in 1958 and the Mississippi Gulf Coast. His first church as pastor was the Church of God in Christ in Sallis, Mississippi. Then he went to the Beulah Grove Church, in the country about five and a half miles from Lexington, which needed a pastor and a building. After building a church there, he came to Lexington as pastor and built the present building occupied by his congregation. They have about 150 members and it is a Pentecostal Church.

At this point Phil Cohen joined us for lunch and the interview.

The discussion began in regard to Saints Academy (formerly Saints Industrial), a black private school in Lexington. According to Elder Rodgers, a Bishop Charles Harris Mason founded the religion Church of God in Christ, which owns the Saints school—a Pentecostal school. Bishop Mason was initially a Baptist evangelist. He started the first Pentecostal Church in the area known as St. Pauls Church of God in Christ, located on Highway 17 near the Lexington Country Club. The Church of God in Christ was actually started in a tent house on the banks of Big Black Creek.

Incidentally, Big Black Creek meanders through the town of Lexington. "Black" Creek is actually a misnomer, for there is seldom any blackness in its continually flowing waters. It is a wide, mostly shallow creek, with crystal clear water in its shallowest parts, running over a smooth sandy bottom and having broad, white sandy beaches. It is recalled that my cousin Henry Paris and I, as young boys in the mode of Tom Sawyer and Huckleberry Finn, used to seine for minnows in Black Creek. We had a big wide net with poles on each end. After locating a school of minnows, which could be easily spotted in the clear water while wading barefoot down the middle of the creek, we would corner them into the net. After harvesting several hundred or more, we would fill our buckets and take them to our minnow pond located on the grounds of Faymorcele. Then we would sell them to local fisherman for bait. The only danger in that venture was avoiding the large, deadly water moccasins that would be sunning on the banks and slither into the water in search of the same minnows we were chasing. One day I came upon a large water moccasin, about six feet long and two to three inches wide. We startled one another. He apparently wanted to get away from me as much as I wanted to distance myself from him. However, it happened that in so doing, we each went into the water below, on top of one another. After scrambling for safety, I was glad to be as far away from that deadly reptile as I could get. Contrary to some opinions, they can bite underwater.

Black Creek is also where we learned to smoke, or rather not to smoke. There was a vine that grew along the creek bank which we called "cross vine." It was about one-quarter to one-half-inch thick. We would cut it in sections the size of a half-smoked cigar, light it up and smoke it. The only problem was that it bit the devil out of your tongue. That's why we gave it up and never smoked anything else after that. Perhaps if young people in today's society who think it stylish to smoke could be started out on "cross vine," they would quickly give up their desire to smoke at all, before it ever developed into a terrible habit—and marijuana would likely be out of the question.

Back to the school: it was initially called Saints Industrial School because they grew almost everything they ate, and it was like a vocational school. Started in 1924, Dr. Arenia Mallory came in 1929 to head the school.

I inquired about what actually happened with Arenia Mallory and James Rodgers during the civil rights days. I asked, "Were you all able to get along with the white community?" He replied, "During the era of civil rights, Dr. Mallory was always out front. She got along with the white community, had a strong personality, and had the respect of both races. There was never any conflict between the white community and the Saints Academy." Phil Cohen added, "She was probably as influential as any member of the black community in Holmes County."

Phil said that when he moved back to Lexington after working elsewhere, Elder Rodgers called him and said he would like to meet with him and have a prayer session about the racial discord. That private meeting helped break the stalemate between the blacks and whites during that time. That was in 1978.

Phil continued that when he started thinking of members of the black community he could communicate with, he wished that Arenia had still been living because he felt she could have resolved the conflicts promptly. Phil and James knew that the times were difficult for both races. However, they knew they had to learn to live together in peace. "During that time, people on both sides were so hard and stiff in their opinions and ways," said Elder Rodgers. They agreed that each side had to learn to give and take in order to end the strife.

At that time, for several months the blacks had been demonstrating and boycotting on the square. So Phil Cohen and James Rodgers, a

Jewish member of the white community and a black preacher, met. They felt that particular meeting marked the beginning of the end of the racial strife that had almost paralyzed the business community.

I questioned why the blacks had been boycotting. Elder Rodgers said, "They had an agenda that they demanded, and since they couldn't get it right away, they started boycotting." In 1978, nearly everything had been integrated including all public facilities and businesses, except the schools, churches and club. I asked what had caused the boycott.

Phil Cohen said they actually had boycotts in 1967 and 1971, in addition to the one in 1978 in which Phil Cohen was involved after he returned to Lexington. Phil said one of the persons in the black community who was influential was the Reverend C.L. Clark. He was the head of the black Baptist churches in the area. He and Phil Cohen served together on the bi-racial committee.

I asked when the first bi-racial committee in Lexington had formed. Phil said before he returned to Lexington, in about 1972-73. Elder Rodgers said he was not on that committee because his role was not to get involved on either side so he could stay "straight in the middle of the road." He didn't get involved in any of those bi-racial committees or the boycotts. He felt he could best mediate and help resolve the issues if he remained in the middle.

I wondered if, when the blacks boycotted, did they boycott both the Jewish and the Christian businesses? Elder James Rodgers said, "All the merchants." Phil Cohen replied, "They had a group of Franciscan nuns down here who became very much involved in the racial situation and they demonstrated for one full week. Herman Flower's son-in-law, Harry Lebow of Lebow Clothing, has pictures of this, where the nuns marched across the storefronts of the Jewish merchants with swastikas." They actually brought a suit against Phil Cohen for interfering with their peaceful demonstration when Phil was not even in Lexington at the time, but in Dallas, Texas at his nephew's bar mitzvah.

Speaking of German swastikas, my grandfather, Morris Lewis, Sr., had handsome large white flower pots displayed on the wide front porch of Faymorcele in Lexington. On each side of these were carved swastikas, designed as an ancient symbol, long before the Nazis adopted it as the emblem of their National Socialist German Workers' Party. Once the Nazis made that emblem their symbol, he immediately had those on the flower pots filled in, leaving a flat surface—erasing any symbol of Nazi Germany in his midst.

The people that the demonstrators brought the suit against had to go to federal court. These merchants were Phil Cohen of Cohen's, Herman Flowers of Flower Brothers department store, and Nathan Schur of Schur's department store, along with three other merchants, including Jitney Jr. (a convenience store). The demonstrators had marched around with swastikas, saying that the Jewish merchants in particular should be in sympathy with their causes because of the past persecutions of the Jews. It didn't really go over very well with any of the white community, who were sympathetic to the white merchants, most of whom were Jewish—and they all resented the swastikas! So they had to go to federal court in Jackson. Three of the people who went to Jackson with Phil Cohen and Herman Flowers, to appear in court and testify on behalf of the Jewish merchants of Lexington, were Reverend C.L. Clark, a black minister, Robert Smith, who was president of the Holmes County Chapter of the NAACP at that time, and Lee Jessie Johnson. They had to appear in court because they were being sued by the United League for civil rights violations. The United League was a group behind the boycott, along with the Franciscan nuns, who were very much involved.

I asked what the Franciscan nuns had finally done. Phil Cohen responded that they had come to Lexington originally to work in the hospital, as all were nurses. They worked in the maternity ward until it was closed.

I questioned if these nuns were African-American or white. It was stated that all were white and from Minnesota. When asked who had brought them in, it was stated that initially, it was some kind of federal program to aid the hospitals in smaller communities. The hospital finally eliminated that program. However, Phil Cohen mentioned that the nuns actually did a lot of good in some ways. They helped many people get assistance to which they were entitled.

I asked how Phil and the other merchants (mostly Jewish) had come out in court. Phil said they finally filed for an injunction to keep the boycotters from demonstrating in front of their businesses, mainly because Robert Smith, a schoolteacher and president of the county NAACP, was threatened with being shot for testifying in favor of the merchants. After that threat, Phil Cohen called the FBI. They sent an agent (who, incidentally, was black). After investigating the situation, he commented to Phil that Lexington was unlike many other communities having racial strife. He said Lexington was a much more peaceful community, where the blacks and the whites at least spoke to one another and communicated.

Phil said what started it all (the 1978 boycott) was a black woman who had committed suicide named Shirley Boyd. She had been in and out the state mental institution, Whitfield, numerous times. Once she had to be arrested on Beale Street where she had taken off all of her clothes. James knew her; at one time, she had been a member of his church, but later changed to another church.

As a member of the bi-racial committee, Phil Cohen (and others) questioned the police chief, Ed Ellison. Phil asked him to come into Fred Power's office at the Holmes County Bank and tell them what happened. He swore to them that he had never touched her, which Phil said was true. However, Phil said he found out later that the dispatcher at the police station had slapped the woman after she began cursing him. At that time, she was in jail for disturbing the peace by publicly shouting a lot of obscenities. She later hanged herself in her home. All of that was the excuse or reason used for the 1978 boycott. The blacks were trying to put pressure on the merchants, many of whom were Jewish, to fire the police chief because they erroneously believed he had slapped her.

In relation to this event, Phil Cohen made the front page of the *Wall Street Journal*. Phil had been interviewed because of the boycott. A woman reporter from the *Wall Street Journal* had come into his store and interviewed him about the situation. He clarified to us how a person can be misquoted. She had asked Phil what he thought of the police chief. Phil had said he had known him all of his life and really didn't even know why he wanted the job. What was actually printed was that Phil didn't even know how the police chief had gotten the job—which, of course, changed the entire meaning of what Phil had said. The timing of the article was very poor as Phil was going to a college reunion at Tulane. The article came out on a Wednesday morning and the reunion was on Thursday, and a number of his former classmates from around the country had seen it.

Phil continued that not only the *Wall Street Journal* but the *New York Times*, the *Los Angeles Times,* and others covered the boycott events. I asked how the 1967 and 1971 boycotts had ended. Phil and Elder Rodgers said the boycotts had apparently just run out of steam.

I asked Phil what had happened with him, Herman Flowers, and others in the federal court suit. He responded that the federal courts had continued it. There had never actually been a hearing on it. They had gone down to Jackson, and since the court had continued it, they really didn't do anything about the suit. Phil, Herman and others then went to the circuit court in Yazoo City, seeking an injunction to restrict the demonstrators and require them to move seventy-five feet away from their businesses. Judge Courtwright ruled in their favor. Once the demonstrators were restricted in that manner, that was about the end of the boycott.

Phil Cohen said the next year, by coincidence, he went to a convention in Washington, D.C. They asked if he wanted to see his senators or congressman. As Phil was getting off the plane, Mississippi Congressman Sonny Montgomery, was also getting off the plane. Phil knew Congressman Montgomery, so they had some discussions about other matters. Then Phil asked him about the Rural Legal Services, which was really pursuing all the lawsuits in question. They were being represented by a law firm in Greenwood, who had told Phil that they were being inundated with these lawsuits. At the same time, Tupelo, in northeast Mississippi, was also experiencing demonstrations. They appealed to Mississippi Senator James Eastland to see if he could get the Rural Legal Services to put a stop to the lawsuits. However, he had done nothing to stop them. Phil had also previously gone to Mississippi Congressman Thad Cochran (now Senator Cochran) who also had done nothing. Congressman Sonny Montgomery explained to Phil why the Mississippi senators had done nothing to help. Senator Eastland had been the one to author the bill creating the Rural Legal Services, and at Eastland's request, Thad Cochran had introduced it in the House of Representatives. It was for the purpose of providing legal services to the indigent who couldn't afford to be represented. That was why they had, understandably, ignored Phil's calls for help in the matter.

Then Phil had gone to see Senator John Stennis, but he had not been in at the time. His administrative assistant was Eph Cresswell, whom Phil had never personally met. However, they spoke for an hour about the situation. About two weeks after Phil had returned home from Washington, a federal agent from the Justice Department had come into his store to tell Phil that all the lawsuits had been dropped and that they were closing the Rural Legal Service office in Lexington. Phil felt that Eph Cresswell, with the consent of Senator John Stennis, had a lot to do with that and the relief it had brought to the merchants and town of Lexington.

During the 1978 boycott, when tempers were getting somewhat heated and feelings were strained, Elder James Rodgers called Phil Cohen on the telephone to ask if they could discuss the situation to see how it could be resolved. So Phil went out to James Rodgers' home, sat down in his kitchen, and had a cup of coffee. James was telling Phil about his ideas of having a prayer session on the square — which they did. Phil said that feelings were running so strong at that time and he was so heated over the situation, he didn't know of anyone else with whom he would have been willing to talk.

They talked about it and afterwards Elder James Rodgers conducted a prayer session on the south side of the town square. That was the beginning of the end of the conflict between blacks and whites and the latest and final boycott. The Franciscan nuns and all the other parties to that major conflict were at the prayer service. Both sides were there — the ones perpetrating the boycott and the white merchants being boycotted. It was a mixed group. Even though the injunction to prevent the demonstrators from marching within seventy-five feet of the merchants' stores had been filed before the prayer service, it was put into effect afterwards. However, by then, after the prayer service, the crowds of demonstrators had diminished considerably. After the prayer service, which served to calm everything down, the injunction was mostly moot.

Thus a great deal of credit goes to Phil Cohen and, without question, to such a Godly man as Elder James Rodgers who personally organized the prayer service and effectively got the races to come together for the betterment of the entire community.

After the black woman's suicide which sparked the 1978 boycott, the black community brought up a number of other issues that needed resolving. Nevertheless, Phil Cohen stated Reverend James Rodgers had done a mitzvah (very good deed in Jewish terms), through his "sermon on the square" that brought the races together and made peace in the community.

The first bi-racial committee was formed in about 1972, before Phil Cohen moved back to Lexington in 1975. At that time, Leroy Paris, a leading member of the Jewish community, was serving on the committee. When he had a heart attack, he had to resign, and Phil Cohen was asked by Ed Thurmond, mayor of Lexington, to serve on the committee. Although Lexington's population today is predominately black, there has never been a black mayor. However, Lexington is the county seat of Holmes County, which has a black tax assessor, a black chancery clerk, a black circuit clerk, a black sheriff, and a black state legislator, Bryan Clark—who replaced his father, Robert Clark, the first black member of the state legislature since the days of Reconstruction. My interview with Robert Clark follows my interviews with Sheriff Willie March, O.W. Hodges, and his wife, Mattie, all of whom are members of the black community of Lexington.

Elder James Rodgers

This one-on-one interview took place after our lunch, in the church of which Elder James Rodgers is pastor. The church is of a grand design, personally designed by Elder Rodgers. Including the balcony, the sanctuary can seat 400 to 500 people. The pulpit has a place for a musical ensemble, which is typical of Pentecostal congregations with their grand liturgical gospel music.

I explained to Elder Rodgers that when I was growing up in Lexington in the mid 1930s, the black community was referred to as coloreds. It seems that was somewhat denigrating and implied a subservient status. Therefore, I asked him in what way did the black community want to be referred—black or African-American. He said either was proper.

In our earlier conversation over lunch with Elder Rodgers and Phil Cohen, I learned that Elder Rodgers was a leader not only in the black community but in the community as a whole.

I asked if there was any person or situation in particular, with reference to the association of the black and Jewish communities in Lexington, that he would like to talk about, both past and present. I mentioned the names of several of the past and present Jewish community to stir his memory.

He said all of those names rang a bell. As a child, he recalled his mother having accounts at Flower's department store, Schur's department store and at Cohen's. He got to know all of the owners of these stores and said they were good people. "They would give you a chance to get what you needed and let you pay by the week, or by the month, or otherwise."

Those were and still are, as with Cohen's, good relationships which James Rodgers said he cherishes. He said he has been directly involved with Phil Cohen of Cohen's. Today they work on bi-racial committees together for the benefit of Lexington, and have a very good relationship. The blacks have had some struggles with the white community in the past, but he said they are all putting those things behind them and working together for the betterment of the community—their town.

He continued that, "Both the Jewish and black communities each have a great heritage, people, businessmen and others, that has laid the foundations for a fine community." His uncle, Will Haynes, was a businessman who operated a service station on Yazoo Street. He was one of the early black businessmen who worked with the Jewish community and overall white community of the town. Elder Rogers said he has lived in a lot of places, from Chicago to the Mississippi Gulf Coast and worked at the ship yard. "In my book, there is no place like Lexington, where the blacks and the whites, including the Jewish community, have a great relationship and are continuing to try to make it better."

He said he was proud to be a part of it. Working together, they are making great strides in bringing his Lexington community up to the higher standards of some other outstanding communities. Both races and all religions are working on making Lexington second to none. "It may take some time, but that is our goal." He reiterated that, "The whites and blacks of Lexington, along with the Jewish community have a great relationship."

Of the past, he recalls his grandmother having an account at Nathan Schur's store. He said, "Without Nathan and other merchants of Lexington, Jewish and other's help, we probably would not have survived since money was so short, especially in those days."

He said his church was first out in a small community in the country, but they decided to move and build a bigger church inside the city limits of Lexington. He added that his church backed up to Spring Street, the same Spring Street where Temple Beth El is located, a few blocks west. Ironically the Spring Street rear entrance to his large church is located directly on the same property our Jewish ancestors owned, including the first home of Morris and Julia Lewis, where my mother, Fay Lewis Berman, and her brothers, Morris, Jr., and Celian, were born. I thought it was quite a coincidence to be interviewing Elder Rodgers in his church which sat on the same property formerly owned and lived on by my grandparents, mother and uncles.

Elder James Rodgers stated that he was thankful for my interview and reminded me that when we were both young (he much younger than me) growing up in Lexington, he caddied for me at the Lexington Country Club golf course. Those were the days before golf carts, when bags were carried on one's shoulder. He said I even gave him his first golf bag and four or five clubs. His father, Gadsby Rodgers, was in charge of maintaining the golf course. James said he helped his father maintain the golf course and that's the way he learned about a lot of people in Lexington. He would get on the back nine holes and shoot away and that's how he learned to play golf. He said he would wait for me to arrive as he enjoyed caddying for me. He also caddied for my father and mother, and for Leroy and Irma Paris. He recalled when my father was killed in the airliner crash. He said I had a great father; "he was a good man." He remembered Henry Paris whom he said he had not seen in many years and would like to see again, and John Murrell McRae, a good friend of ours and written about in this book. He recalled that Henry and I were often together as we grew up. James said he and I got along so well together and treated each other with respect. He said he appreciated my kindness as I always treated him as a fellow human being—not just my caddy.

So, he said, "now here we are, some fifty to sixty years later at this interview, which neither of us ever dreamed would have taken place in the church I lead as its elder."

James said he also remembered Herbert Hyman who negotiated the sale of a piece of property he bought and they became friends. He said he was riding in the car with Herbert one day and Herbert told him that when he had been born and as he grew up in Lexington, he didn't have a thing. However, somehow he got with an old plumber who had shown him much of what he knew, including how to farm. That plumber happened to be Will Haynes, an uncle to James Rodgers. That brought Herbert and James closer together.

He also recalled Beale Street where most of the black people congregated, especially on Saturday and Saturday nights, with the many black businesses located there. James said, "That's how they met each other [in the black community]; they worked all week and that would be one of their only outlets. Unfortunately, folks get to drinking on Saturday night and that could easily develop into a problem, especially among the black community—because that was the only relief they had." He said he had a brother named Will and another named Chet, for Chetwyn, who used to run the pro shop at the Lexington Country Club.

He continued that he had gone to Saints Academy (formerly Saints Industrial) for twelve years, and for college there one year, under Dr. Arenia Mallory, "One of the great educators of our time. She was very strict and a character builder," said James.

He further commented that, "We have had racial problems in the past, but with the help of God, the community has overcome most of that hurdle. Everything may not be exactly as you would want it to be, but at least you can tolerate it, and I am proud to be a part of the Lexington community."

I was impressed not only by the openness and spiritual character of Elder Rodgers, but also by the large pylon sign in front of his church, with the following words:

"Seven days without prayer makes one weak"

The O.W. Hodges Family

Mattie Hodges

"There's O.W. Driving Miss Fay"

The following is an interview of O.W. Hodges, eighty-three years old, and his eighty-one year old wife, Mattie. They have been married for sixty-one years. Even though they have aged, they still look about the same as I recall them looking in my youth.

The interview took place at their home in Lexington on August 16, 2005. They had five children, with four living. O.W. Hodges worked for my grandfather, Morris Lewis, Sr., and for my parents, Joe and Fay Berman, for thirty-eight years. His wife, Mattie, also helped out occasionally. During that time, O.W. got to know every living member of the Jewish community in Lexington and also knew most of the history of those who had been.

This is what O.W. and Mattie told me during my interview with them.

O.W. and Mattie Hodges

They reside a couple of miles from Faymorcele. As a matter of fact, after my mother built a new home on the same property as Faymorcele, which she had given to the school system, O.W. and Mattie lived so close that when my mother's security alarm would go off, O.W. could hear it from his home. He would immediately get in his car and drive over to make certain that my mother was okay and not in distress.

O.W. was driving my grandfather, Morris Lewis, home from the Lewis Grocer Company in Indianola when a speeding car near Inverness, Mississippi, blew a tire and ran head-on into their car. My grandfather was sitting in the front passenger's seat and was thrown through the windshield. That was before the days of seat belts or air bag protection. Had they been installed in the car, he likely would have survived the crash, even if he was eighty-four years old at the time. As a result of this, the second major automobile accident in his lifetime, Morris Lewis died a few days later.

O.W. and Mattie have been good friends of our family for many, many years. They have actually been considered a part of our family throughout those years. He started working for my family in 1950 being hired after World War II when my father, Joe, came home from overseas. O.W. worked both at our home and at my father's office, and said that his employment was a good thing for all concerned.

O.W. said, "I was initially hired as a chauffeur. Then they learned I could do most anything: cleaning in the home and the office; maintaining the landscape around the fifteen-acre home; and cooking. I also ran errands whenever it was required." Mattie also worked in the home for special occasions.

O.W. stated, "We got along fine." Mattie replied, "Sure did." O.W. added that he missed them all. He said Phil Cohen kept him informed about the family members that remain.

O.W. said he was in the Holmes County Bank the other day and was asked about our family. He said the banker told him that our family, and Fay Berman in particular, always thought a lot of him [O.W.], and that no one was any better to him than Joe and Fay Berman.

When O.W. would drive my grandfather to the office, I would get a ride to school. However, as a teenager, I would always ask him to let me off a block before arriving at the school grounds, because I did not want any of my schoolmates to think I had a chauffeur. O.W. remembered and got a big laugh out of that. He actually taught me to drive, up and down the long curving driveway that led from the street to our home. As it approached the house, the driveway then encircled a horseshoe-shaped and immaculately trimmed hedge that led to the side door of a screened-in porch.

O.W. said he enjoyed every minute of working for my family, and Mattie concurred. He stated, "They were good to me, and all I had to do was ask for whatever I needed and the family would give it to me."

Mattie said Joe Berman was "crazy about our kids," and that "every time they would make an A in school, he would give them two dollars."

They remembered the day my father was killed in the tragic air crash of Piedmont Airlines. They said they would never get over that incident.

O.W. mentioned that as immaculately as he used to keep the house and grounds, it was a shame that the house has deteriorated as it has done. Today, with some exceptions, it almost resembles Tara in *Gone With The Wind* after the Civil War, compared with its stately appearance during the pre-war years. However, in fairness, repairs have recently been made.

O.W. said he recalled always driving my mother, Fay, to the temple. Then the next morning, he would return and pick up the flowers that were left the evening before. Those flowers were taken to the cemetery and put on the graves of the various former members of the Jewish community.

O.W. said he remembered fondly all those members of the Jewish faith who used to live in Lexington, including in particular Leroy Paris and Eugene Herrman.

He also remembered my grandfather, Morris Lewis, and driving him to Indianola. He said when he got ready to go, "he was ready." If O.W. was driving too slowly, Morris would wave his hand in a forward motion as if to say, "Let's get moving." He would also take Morris riding on Sunday afternoons, as Morris used to say, "just to pass the time away."

When we would go to visit our grandfather Morris, his favorite expression when we departed was, "I'm glad you came and I'm glad you're gone." Even though he loved his family's visits, apparently he had enough. In his later years, Morris had a caretaker named Henreinne. O.W. said each time she had a baby, Morris would send her a case of milk. However, he said she began having so many babies that he finally quit. She had a baby almost every year, and he didn't want to encourage her any further!

O.W. recalled the meals we used to have around the big breakfast and dinner table, and all the different southern vegetables served. When I mentioned Ruth Ammons, the cook we had for many years, Mattie said Ruth was her aunt. I recalled that just after we had returned to Lexington from New York, when I went to escort my mother, Fay, and sister, Brenda, back to Lexington after our father, Joe, was killed, Ruth was coming up the back steps to say hello. I happened to meet her, and she was so shocked by the news when I told her about the tragedy that she almost fell backwards down the stairs. That was the last time I ever saw Ruth.

O.W. recalled that they were working on widening the covered drive at the entrance to Faymorcele when Joe Berman left for his last trip. He commented that he never got to see it completed.

O.W. said, "Joe Berman was a good man. If he ever promised he would do something for you, you could go home and go to bed and never worry about it again, because he was going to do it. He was so nice to everyone and he always had a smile." He recalled that Joe Berman would go by the service station on many mornings to fill up with gas. The attendant at the station was named Foot. He would always tell Joe, who usually dressed in a coat and tie, "Mr. Berman, you sho' look sharp," to which Joe would laugh and reply, "Well, Foot, I'm just trying to live up to my reputation."

He said Joe Berman was a mighty good person to work for. "I never heard him say a bad word during the entire thirty-eight years I was there."

They brought up the name of Daisy who used to do some work for our family in Lexington. I recalled that when we moved to Atlanta, just before the beginning of World War II, where Joe was stationed at army headquarters, we took Daisy with us to do the cooking and house cleaning. We didn't know it at the time, but later found out that Daisy was an alcoholic. The first sign was when my mother, Fay, entertained the colonel's wife for bridge one afternoon, and Daisy brought out the Coke bottles with the tops still on (and no opener). My mother thought that strange, but overlooked it. Actually Daisy had been drinking. The next sign was when Joe and Fay were at an army officer's party at Fort McPherson. That evening, my sister, Joan, and I were outside playing, and when we tried to get back in the house, Daisy had locked us out. All we could see was Daisy sitting in front of a window, using the reflection of the light to comb her hair. I can still picture that scene today. Finally we managed to knock on the door and ring the doorbell enough times that she responded and let us in. After that incident, our parents realized that Daisy had been in the liquor cabinet more than once. Shortly thereafter, Daisy was sent packing back to Lexington.

O.W. added to the story that after Daisy returned home to Lexington, and after the war when our family had returned, she would come up to the house, crying and saying, "Mr. Berman, I'm so down and out and hungry." Joe would go into the pantry and bring out all kinds of foods and supplies for Daisy to take home with her. Then, as she departed, O.W. would hear her say under her breath, "Hell, I ain't hungry." Actually, she was hungry, but not for food— for liquor. He never told Joe Berman what she had muttered. O.W. added that our family never had any problem with him or Mattie about "the drinking part," and that was true.

He also remembers when Joe Stern owned and operated the Sunflower Food Store, just off the square near the Holmes County Bank. He said Miss Fay (pronounced "Miz Fay") would order the groceries and he would go pick them up, sometimes having a grocery list and shopping himself. They said my mother was just like her father, Morris, in that "when she was ready to go, she was really ready to go." She never wanted to be late for anything. While she drove herself on many occasions, on trips out of Lexington to Jackson, Birmingham, Atlanta, Memphis and elsewhere, O.W. drove her, and many times in town during her later years.

When asking if they had ever seen the movie *Driving Miss Daisy*, they laughed and said they had watched it many times. Mattie said that's what many people would say: "There's O.W. driving Miss Fay."

O.W. even had the expression "yesum" (for "yes, ma'am") down pat. It was stated that Miss Daisy's driver became a good friend, just as O.W. had been for my mother. I mentioned to them that The Temple in Atlanta portrayed in the movie was the same temple where Joan and I had attended Sunday school when we lived there during World War II.

After my family returned to Lexington from Atlanta, O.W. continued to drive my grandfather, Morris Lewis, to work each day.

O.W. followed "Crip" and then Albert as all-around chauffeur, housekeeper, cook and gardener. O.W. said he learned to cook from my mother, Fay. Before coming to work for my grandfather and parents, he worked at a service station and at the IGA supermarket. He remembered Morris Flink who leased and owned the meat market.

Mattie said her oldest son, Willie James Pernell, works for a temple in Los Angeles as the shamus [the one that takes care of the synagogue]. Their other children, O.W. Jr., Christine, and Lyndell, all also now live in Los Angeles.

Sheriff Willie March

Willie March

"I said to myself, something is not right with what I saw as I drove past that afternoon; and how I wished I had turned around, but I guess I just didn't follow my instincts."

Willie March is a cousin to Mattie Hodges. He became sheriff of Holmes County in 1986. While he lived in the general vicinity of Lexington and was a police officer in Tchula, he did not go back far enough to remember many members of the Jewish community of the past. However, one he did vividly remember was Herbert Hyman. The sheriff said, as a matter of fact, he saw Herbert the day he was murdered.

He said he was going to a Martin Luther King celebration over in Durant that Sunday. He passed by Herbert Hyman's office building, just west of the prison that is now located on Highway 17. He saw Herbert unlocking the door of his business, and saw a "gentleman" standing behind him who had on a real light green jacket. He had his hands in his pockets, and when he saw the sheriff, the man waved at him until he went out of sight, over a little hill on the road to Durant. He said, "I was kind of concerned why Mr. Hyman was going into his building that time of day on a Sunday afternoon." Nevertheless, the sheriff did not bother to stop and investigate, and he continued on to the Martin Luther King celebration in Durant.

When he returned to his office later that same day, they had received a call that Herbert Hyman was missing from his home. Mrs. Hyman said he had left a roast cooking on the outdoor grill. It was unusual of him not to have come home to check on the roast.

The sheriff said he kept trying to think in his mind who the "guy" with Herbert was. He said, "I know him, I know him. I saw the coat he had on, which was a green Valley State jacket. Then finally I realized. They called him 'Fruit Loop' and he lived down in the old school house bottom in a mobile home." When they picked him up, the sheriff said, "You're the 'gentleman' I saw with Mr. Hyman." The murderer said, "No, not me." The sheriff said, "You're the one with Mr. Hyman; you're the one with the green coat on." He did not admit to it initially, but later on at the trial he pled guilty. But his sister told the sheriff before that, "You got the right one."

I asked what had been the man's motive for killing Herbert. The sheriff replied, "Robbery. He thought he was going to get a bunch of money." The sheriff said, "This 'gentleman' had been in trouble before." He had broken into a board of alderman's house, Otis Stringfellow, and stolen some stuff from him. The sheriff said he really thought he had been on drugs, but he wasn't sure. He said, "His motive was money."

After the man was incarcerated, he broke out of jail, but the sheriff was able to talk with his parents to bring him back in. The man ended up getting a sentence of twenty-five years, [an extra five years due to his escape]. He was initially sentenced to twenty years for manslaughter [even though he murdered Herbert Hyman in cold blood and it was, without a doubt, premeditated to cover up his robbery]. The manslaughter sentence was apparently a plea bargain, since the prosecution did not believe a jury of his peers would have convicted him—and manslaughter was better than no conviction at all.

Now this murderer is free, since the law at that time only required one to serve about five or six years of a twenty-year sentence. He served not much longer than that and only because each time he came up for parole, many of my family vehemently objected to his release. Today, the law in Mississippi says one must serve a minimum of 85 percent of one's sentence before being eligible for parole. But not this killer. He is now on the loose, free to strike again, although the sheriff thought he might still be on probation. The sheriff concurred that his first name was James, the name the couple heard Herbert say on that fateful day. He still lives in the community. The sheriff said, "As a matter of fact, about a month ago he was involved in a shooting where he was shot in West, Mississippi, but he did not bring any charges since it was just a flesh wound."

Sheriff March concluded the conversation by saying, "In hindsight, I wish I had turned around and gone back to investigate the strange situation I saw that Sunday afternoon." In thinking back he said, "My gut feeling was that something was wrong, because of the way the killer waved at me as I drove by." He said normally one waves at a person and takes one's hand down, but the killer kept his hand up in the air until the sheriff had driven past and was out of sight. He said, "I said to myself something is not right with what I saw as I drove past that afternoon; and how I wished I had turned around, but I guess I just didn't follow my instinct." We both concluded that the community and Herbert's family lost a very good and honest man, and an outstanding long-time citizen.

I questioned if the sheriff had known Herbert before. He said he had because Herbert had helped a lot of people in Holmes County. He continued to say that a lot of people borrowed money from Herbert and that was a big help to those who needed it. The sheriff told me Herbert was a very active person in the community, including his real estate business, and was an active Rotarian.

Sheriff March had met Herbert's wife, Henrietta, now deceased, and his two daughters, Barbara and Gina, who continue to operate Hyman Real Estate Company from Dallas, where they reside. At some time in the future, the sheriff said, the county would need to negotiate with the Hyman daughters to purchase the adjacent property in order to expand the county jail next door to the Hyman property. He said the population of Holmes County is now about 85 percent black [approximately 66 percent in Lexington], so the large majority of the prisoners in his jail are African-American, with some whites also incarcerated.

Honorable Robert Clark

Robert Clark

"Now, in days past, there was only so far that a person in the Jewish community could go in openly standing up for blacks. I realized that after I became an adult, but Ephraim Cohen was one of the individuals that came to my rescue when I got fired from the public schools in 1966."

Robert Clark was the first African-American to be elected to the Mississippi State Legislature since Reconstruction after the Civil War.

For this interview on September 13, 2005, I met with him and his wife, Jo Ann, at Nick's for lunch.

Robert lives in the house where he was born, in the Ebenezer community just out of Lexington, three miles southeast of Ebenezer on the Pickens Road—the same general area where Dudley S. Burwell was born. Robert was born on the same place where his great-grandmother and great-grandfather were slaves. This could have been near the Sontheimer place, inherited by my great-great-grandfather, Jacob Sontheimer. After emancipation, Robert's great-grandfather bought the place and some of his family have been there ever since.

Robert went to school in Holmes County. There was no transportation then and he had to walk to school. Being in a black school, his school term was regulated by the need for the students to be on the plantations to pick cotton. He went to grammar school and graduated from high school in the Cypress Flat Community. However, the "white folks" referred to that community as the Hope Well Community, after the name of a church that once was there. In the ninth grade, he went to high school in Lexington for only six weeks and then attended the Mount Olive Vocation High School, north of Lexington almost on the Carroll County line. His uncle and aunt were teaching and living there. He lived in the teacher's home so it was convenient for Robert to go to school there. He attended his last three years of high school in Durant, Mississippi, twelve miles from Lexington. Afterwards he went to Jackson State College for Negro teachers, which is now Jackson State University. Later on, he wanted to pursue an advanced degree, but could not get one in

Mississippi. "Being a colored person, African-American, Negro or whatever you want to call it, I had to go to Michigan State University in East Lansing, Michigan to get my master's degree." He said his master's degree was in educational and administrative services, with a minor in psychology.

Robert was elected to the Mississippi House of Representatives in 1967, and was sworn into the legislature in 1968. He ran as an independent. He said, "Ironically this was the first opportunity I ever had to vote—when I voted for myself in that election. That was because of the poll tax and the hostility in that time of just not allowing blacks to register. There would have been a fictitious 'test' to see if you were qualified to vote, and then they would determine if you passed the test or not. Then another thing was, it was just not safe for black folks to register to vote." We both agreed that, thank God, those days of disenfranchisement are over and past.

Robert served in the state legislature for thirty-six years, retiring in 2004. The last twelve years he served as speaker pro tem of the House of Representatives. "That's a feat I'm proud of, and a lot of folks are proud of, because I think I did a great job for the State of Mississippi. As an example, I met one of the top state officials today when Mrs. Clark and I pulled up on the capitol grounds. He was commending me for my ability to get people to work together. The thing that perhaps I'm most proud of was that I was chairman of the primary and secondary education committee in 1982 when we passed the historic education reform act." [Author's note: That was under Governor William Winter's administration, who is known as the 'Education Governor']. "That had been a fourteen-year battle for me, and this was accomplished during Governor Winter's second year in office." Robert said, "If William Winter had not been governor, I personally would not have been able to accomplish that goal of aiding education reform." He added, "I am confident that if I had not been chairman of that education committee, Governor Winter would not have been able to successfully move that legislation through the legislature."

Robert's youngest son, Bryan, has now succeeded him in the State House of Representatives. When Robert was first elected in 1967, his opponent was J.P. Love of Tchula, who was a former coach of Tchula. Even though Tchula and Durant were each within a few miles of Lexington, the seat of Holmes County, and to some could be considered an extension of Lexington, each of these towns had their own school system. "Therefore, J.P. Love did not have many from the Lexington and Durant communities that 'loved' him, since Tchula was a big rival of each."

Robert said that election was the first time that many individuals had ever voted. He ran as an independent since, "Frankly speaking, I don't know if I could have even been qualified by the Democratic Party at that time, because after I was elected we had to carry the Democratic Party all the way to the [national] convention to get in [the party]."

J.P. Love and Ed Wilburn Hooker, an incumbent, ran against one another in the Democratic primary. "J.P. Love beat Ed Wilburn Hooker, and that's one of the things that contributed to my election. I won by 117 votes. I really think it would have been a whole lot closer if some of the individuals in Lexington who would not have voted for me, but voted against J.P. Love, and that helped tremendously in my election." While Ed Wilburn Hooker did not come out directly and support him, Robert said some of his supporters did. That also gave him some advantage.

"I had a direct relationship with some of the individuals in the Jewish community when I was a young person. I would say the first person in the Jewish community that I can remember that I had a relationship with was Herman Flowers, in the store. As you know, he ran a clothing store. And times were tough, but I could always go to Herman Flowers and so could my father, and we could always go there and get the clothes we needed. We didn't go there for everyday clothes—we could get those at Ebenezer—but for dress clothes. And I never remember Herman Flowers turning us down, no matter how long we were paying him. But we always paid him. When I became an adult, I continued to trade with Herman Flowers. When my boys were born and my wife had passed, and I was raising them myself, I continued to trade with Herman Flowers, to get their clothes there until my boys got large enough to get their own clothes. The last clothes I went to Herman Flowers and purchased for them, they never took them off the hanger in the closet. It was not the clothes, but the style, but what thirteen- and fourteen-year-olds would want. That was my relationship with Herman Flowers, and we continued that relationship until he passed.

"I also knew the Lewis Grocer Company and Mr. Morris Lewis; I didn't know him too well, but I knew who he was. And many African-American individuals worked for him and they praised him to the highest. Frankly speaking, when I boarded in Durant, the man of that house, S. Powell, worked for Lewis Grocer Company. He drove a truck and delivered groceries. S. Powell was the biggest man working there, and sometimes I would go on the grocery truck with him, if I wasn't in school or he left afterwards. He could get a hundred pounds of sweet feed on one hip and a hundred pounds on the other hip, and walked like he had twenty-five pounds on each hip." Robert also mentioned Robert and I.V. Winters, who worked at Lewis, mostly selecting the groceries from the warehouse when the order was called out by the shipping clerk; then bringing it back to put it on the delivery truck. I told Robert that in my teens I worked at the Lewis Grocer Company in Durant, and had worked directly with Robert and I.V. Winters. They, too, were physically strong persons who, remarkably, could remember the entire order, including number of cases called out, sizes and brands. They knew exactly where each was located in the warehouse, and would quickly bring the entire order to the truck, without writing anything down. They had to be intelligent, in addition to their physical strength. They were also friendly and helpful to me when I worked there.

Their brother, D.I. Winters, who was Robert's age, later went on to work at Lewis Grocer Company. "But one of the things they always said was that they got treated, behind everybody else's back, as if they were white. What they meant was that they [Lewis] treated them fair and honest."

Robert told me, "Another individual [of the Jewish community] that I knew growing up, but I didn't have any dealings with him until I came back home in 1961, and that was Ephraim Cohen. Now there was only so far that a person in the Jewish community could go in openly standing up for blacks. I realized that after I became an adult, but Ephraim Cohen was one of the individuals that came to my rescue when I got fired from the public schools in 1966. There was Ephraim Cohen, Hardin Irving and Jewel Knight. Those three people came to my rescue because they knew I had been wrongfully fired. I had been terminated without cause. I was a coach and teacher at the public high school in Lexington. It was the black high school, of course. It was called the colored high school at that time. I can remember those three, and Norman Weathersby, going to the superintendent of education." He said Ephraim Cohen sent for him to come to his store [Cohen's department store]. He went to Ephraim's store and, "He told me, we got your job back and we want you to go on back and take your job. And I can remember well telling Mr. Cohen that I had too much pride to go back to a job where somebody had wrongfully fired me for nothing. I then remember him saying, 'Well, you better eat that damn pride and go on back to that job.' Mr. Cohen knew he could say that because of how well he knew me. We would meet up— my uncles, his family, and most of my family—would meet at Mr. Cohen's store every Christmas Eve to do shopping. It just became a tradition that on Christmas Eve nights we would meet at his store. I guess sometimes there would be some twenty-five to thirty cars on Christmas Eve around Mr. Cohen's store."

Then he said there was Herbert Hyman, who helped many blacks and "went to bat for them. You know there was a time when people got locked up, black folks got locked up, and somebody would have to go to bond [to get them out], and so far as I know, Herbert Hyman was the only white person around Lexington that went on the bond for black folks that were not his servant." He said, "Unless I lived on your plantation and you were my boss, on a Sunday night you would get me out so I could be ready for the fields the next morning [to pick cotton]. I do know there was some resentment in the white community because of that." I injected that Herbert didn't see color; he just loved people. Robert said, "I never did any business with Herbert, but we were close friends and we communicated very often."

He also knew N. Schur of Schur's department store, stating they used to call him "insure." Then he also recalled Joe Stern, who owned and operated the Sunflower Food Store supermarket in Lexington. He said, "We were good friends."

I asked Robert about the 1950s and 1960s, during the peak of the civil rights movement, and whether or not he got involved. I asked if he got any support from the Jewish community during that time period.

He said, "I was involved in it in the mid to latter 1960s. Before then, I was in a classroom [teaching] at that time, and I had to make a decision when it was time for me to be prepared to come out and to give up. But when I came out in 1966, when I was terminated from my [teaching and coaching] job, I imagine that the powers to be thought I would do like a lot of my neighbors, and leave Holmes County and Mississippi, and hide my head and go on to Chicago. But I knew I didn't have anything to hide. But giving you my opinion, from being a native born Mississippian—and I am, and I love Mississippi—if a white person being Jewish or not, if you had come out [in the open] and supported black folk, you would have been run out of the community [ostracized]. In my opinion, you would have first been given a chance to stop; second, you would have been given a chance to leave; and thirdly, you would have been beat up [by certain elements of the community]. That's the opinion that I get from the community. That's just how tough and how hard it was [in those days]."

I asked why he was fired from his teaching and coaching job at a black school. His answer was, "In my opinion, the real reason was that I was going to run for superintendent of education in Holmes County. I had declared my candidacy for superintendent of education. The reason I did that was because I had gone before the superintendent and asked for an adult education program in Holmes County. This was the first time the state of Mississippi had implemented an adult education program. I knew from my education and teaching experience, that in order for students to do better, if their parents could help them with their lessons, then we could do a better job with the students in the school. But the superintendent did not agree, and I asked him if I could come before the board of education. He told me yes, I could come, but don't bring a drove of people. I went before the school board and asked for an adult education [program]. They said they would have an adult education program in Holmes County when the superintendent asked for one."

When questioned if the superintendent was white, he replied "Yes, it was H.M. Thompson. They called him 'Jelly' Thompson, who also used to be a highly successful football coach years before." 'Jelly' Thompson coached the first Lexington High School football team to ever go undefeated. The year was 1932. Several members of the Jewish community were on that team. He was a popular man, and highly respected within the white community because of his success and high position in education. "So, because [of what they said], I declared my candidacy for superintendent of education, and I think that is the real reason for getting fired."

I asked if he ran for that office. He replied, "No, I didn't run for it because they passed a local and private law in Jackson [in the state legislature] that the superintendent would be appointed. I knew that we could have gone to court and eventually beat it, but we had five white males [on the board of education] and I knew even if all five of them wanted to appoint me, that they could not afford to appoint me in Holmes County. Due to the fact that I couldn't run for superintendent of education, I chose to run against those who were responsible for making it impossible for me to run, and that's why I ran for the legislature."

To summarize, in regard to the Jewish community of Lexington, Robert said: "After things lightened up, the Jewish community was friendly and helpful, but there was a caste system where everybody had to go by it; you either did or didn't." We both agreed that we were thankful the racial climate in Mississippi had become far more tolerant and changed for the better for all of its citizens. Now blacks and whites work together to build a greater state.

Robert Clark, the first black person to serve in the Mississippi Legislature since Reconstruction, and successfully work for direly needed education reform, is one person that could have also been included in John F. Kennedy's book *Profiles In Courage*, had it been written at a later date.

Chapter 47

The Jewish Community of Lexington and Rotary

What is the commonality of Rotary International and Temple Beth El in Lexington, Mississippi? Temple Beth El was built and opened in 1905, the same year that Rotary International was founded in Chicago by a young attorney and adventurer named Paul Harris. Most of Lexington's male Jewish community were and are Rotarians and leaders in that great civic organization. Rotary is the oldest international civic organization in the world, having 1,200,000 members in more than 200 countries and geographical areas, with over 32,000 clubs. Its motto is: "Service above self, he profits most who serves best." Rotary was founded in Lexington in 1925. Two members of the Jewish community were among the founders of the Lexington Rotary Club.

Morris Lewis, Sr., and Jesse A. Hyman (half brother to Herbert A. Hyman) were two of the founding charter members of the Lexington Rotary Club. This club has always been a big contributor in effort and money towards the improvement of the overall Lexington community.

Since its founding in 1925, the Lexington Rotary Club has had a majority of the Lexington male Jewish community as its members and leaders. Jewish Lexingtonians that are or have been Rotarians are: Morris Lewis, Sr., Jesse Hyman, Morris Lewis, Jr., Celian H. Lewis, Herbert Hyman, Joe Berman, Leroy Paris, Eugene Herrman, Herman Flowers, Phil Cohen, Edward Schur, Henry Paris, Dudley Burwell and myself. Nearly all of these individuals have also served as president of their respective clubs.

In 1967, Joe Berman, Lexington community leader and past president of the club, was to be nominated as the next district governor of district 6820, with forty-four clubs and 2,500 members. However, the tragic plane crash on which he was a passenger ended that possibility.

Thirty-two years later, that same leadership honor was bestowed upon his son, me. I gave my first governor's talk to the Lexington club, which I've given to all forty-four clubs in the district. It was given there first in honor of my late father, Joe Berman, past president of the Lexington club and my grandfather, Morris Lewis, Sr., a charter member of that club, and to salute the club itself.

At the final banquet of the Rotary district conference, celebrating the 1999-2000 Rotary year when I was the district governor, in addition to my former high school teacher Clara Watson, as mentioned earlier, Rotarians from Lexington were in attendance, including Phil Cohen, Herman Flowers and Charles Carson. Mike Lammons, a member of the Lexington Lions Club, also attended.

Joe Berman would have been especially proud, as are all Rotarians, of Rotary's Polio Plus program to eliminate polio from the entire world. The only other disease ever to be eradicated is smallpox, and Rotary is close, 99 percent, to achieving that goal with polio through their Polio Plus initiative.

Besides contributing well over half a billion dollars to that cause, thousands of Rotarians and their spouses have gone into the hinterlands administering the polio vaccine. Polio Plus is the single largest humanitarian effort ever conducted by any civic organization in history. While the Lions Club, Kiwanis Club, Civitan Club, Exchange Club, and other such civic organizations all have merit, there are two things that most of the Jewish families of Lexington knew about their sons when they were born: they would be circumcised, and they would become Rotarians. Now that women are also members, they, in particular, would only have to meet one of those requirements.

There was an article in the *Los Angeles Times* on Sunday, February 5, 2006, by Daniel Jonah Goldhagen, a member of Harvard's Center of European Studies. It pertains to Hamas, who recently won a majority of votes in the latest Palestinian election. Hamas is currently regarded as a terrorist organization by the United States and the European Union. The article stated that an examination of Hamas' charter reveals that it is not just dedicated to the destruction of Israel. It shows Hamas to be governed by a Nazi-like genocidal orientation to Jews in general. It continued that Israel, by virtue of its being Jewish and of having a Jewish population, defies Islam and the Muslims. It added that Hamas will tolerate Jews and Christians only under the impossible condition that they live under Islamic Fundamentalist Domination (article 31).

Now, how does this doctrine of murder and destruction relate to Rotary per se?

According to the *Los Angeles Times* article, the Hamas charter further states that among the "clandestine" organizations the Jews allegedly use to take over the world, Rotary clubs are highlighted.

Such absurd and hallucinatory rhetoric is, in effect, giving Jews and Rotarians an unintended backhand compliment. It is true that membership in Rotary is an important part of the lives of many Jewish men and women around the world, who even then make up a small percentage of the 1.2 million Rotarians internationally. However, these Jewish men and women are members because it presents them with an outstanding opportunity for "service above self"—to serve their communities, and humanity, and to work for Rotary's ultimate goal of everlasting world peace. That precious goal will only be achieved, not by the domination of any one faith over the others, but by the freedom to live by the faith of one's choice, with tolerance and respect for all the others.

Golda Mier, former prime minister of Israel, expressed it best when she said, "There will be peace in the mid-east, when the Arabs love their children more than they hate the Jews."

An article in the February 2006 *Rotarian* magazine stated: "When Ali Ayad Karim, now 10, and Masuma Hmod, now 1, were born in Iraq, doctors discovered they had a severe congenital heart condition that's routinely corrected with surgery in wealthy countries." It continued to say: "In August (2005), Ali and Masuma flew to Chicago [home of Rotary's first club] to undergo open-heart surgery, arranged and funded through a partnership of Rotarians and Muslim community leaders. They are among more than 4,000 children in 60 developing countries who have received open-heart surgery through Gift of Life International, a nonprofit organization founded and operated by Rotarians."

This Gift of Life program, along with Polio Plus and so many other humanitarian programs of Rotary, are not the work of any "clandestine" organization, but rather that of a worldwide organization filled with good people of all faiths and colors who have love, compassion and goodwill in their hearts.

There are a number of former Lexingtonians who have been—and some still are—members of the Rotary Club of Jackson, including members of the Jewish faith. Among them are past district governor Nick Walker, Morris Williams, Tom Lail, Billy Carter, Julian Watson, Al Povall, Ed Tye Neilson, Jr., Roy Povall, Dudley Burwell, and myself, as past district governor.

As an anecdote about Rotary in Lexington, when this Jackson Rotarian was about to deliver his first club talk as a new district governor to the Lexington Rotary Club, Don Barrett, past club president, stood up and told the following story: He started by saying, "Today is not the first time Bob Berman has spoken to our Lexington club. When he was here in high school, there was an incident when he appeared before this club, first to perform and later to apologize for that performance, so he could graduate from high school. Bob, you may want to expound upon that incident in your talk today."

The incident was as follows: Parham Williams (future dean of law at the University of Mississippi, Samford University and Chapman University), Dudley Burwell and I had been invited, as high school seniors, to a Rotary luncheon to comment about our days in school. The week before, we had attended a Bob Hope show in Jackson. We recalled a number of very funny and innocuous jokes told by that beloved entertainer.

At that Rotary luncheon, rather than say a few words to the club, we decided to act out some of the more hilarious Bob Hope stories we had recently heard. After Dudley, as the straight man, introduced us, Parham and I began our routine. During the performance, the Rotarians roared with laughter—all except the superintendent of education, Bill Kenna. He was a fine gentleman and highly respected educator of great integrity, but also extremely conservative, at least in this instance. He felt the stories we told were off-color and risqué. After the meeting, we three students were summoned to his office, where he threatened to withhold our diplomas unless we reappeared before the club the next week and apologized for what he described as behavior embarrassing to the school. In that apology, we stated that we regretted that some Rotarians were offended by our performance the previous week and we were sorry for it. Afterwards, we were allowed to graduate from high school. I must say that those stories we told, by today's standards, would have been considered quite mild, and rated at the most PG. Also we were speaking to a group of adult males. Of all things, to mimic Bob Hope! He was one of the greatest comedians and patriots this country has ever known. Had he been informed of the incident, I am confident he would have no doubt gotten a big laugh out of it, and said how pleased he was that some of his humor made it all the way to the little town of Lexington, Mississippi. To my good friend Don Barrett, and fellow Rotarians, I say, "Thanks for the memories."

On the bima at Temple Beth El, on the pulpit cover, are words from the Prophet Micah. These words are analogous to the goodness of Rotary, as expressed in the Rotary's "Four-Way Test" of truth, fairness, goodwill, beneficial to all, and Rotary's motto of "service above self."

Micah: "Do justly"

Rotary's Four-Way Test: "Is it the truth?"
                          "Is it fair to all concerned?"

Micah: "Love mercy"

Rotary's Four-Way Test: "Will it build good will and
                          better friendships?"
                          "Will it be beneficial to
                          all concerned?"

Micah: "Walk humbly with thy God"

Rotary's motto: "Service above self"

Had Micah lived in our day and time, I believe he would have made a great Rotarian.

Chapter 48

The Jewish Community of Lexington, as Southerners and Americans

All of the above have a great deal in common. It is a combination of pride, dedication, perseverance, and a can-do attitude.

The Jewish community of Lexington has always taken pride in their Jewish identity. They have been dedicated to their one and eternal God. They have continuously persevered in maintaining their congregation and synagogue. They have felt and proved it can be done.

They have been keenly aware that the last four letters of the word American spell **"I can,"** and they have lived by that example and tradition. Along with their fellow citizens of Lexington, they have proven beyond a shadow of a doubt that people of different faiths, beliefs and races can respect one another and can work together in a peaceful setting for the resolution of whatever problems that may exist.

They have never failed to reflect that same belief in and allegiance to their Southern tradition and American heritage as their land of freedom—freedom of religion, freedom of speech, and freedom of opportunity for all the citizens of this great land. As one of the world's greatest statesmen and leaders, Winston Churchill, once said: "Democracy is the worst form of government in all the world— except for all the others." That aptly applies to America as well. It's not a perfect country, but it's the best there is. The Jews of Lexington have always been thankful and proud to be known as American Jews with a Southern accent. In fact they have forever been consistent.

Consistently Jewish!

Consistently Southern!

Consistently American!

While the Jewish population of Lexington has dwindled, they and the other members of Temple Beth El that reside elsewhere have been determined to keep the synagogue active and alive. Nevertheless, with the continuing outflow of Jews from smaller communities to the larger cities, it is recognized that one day, at some time in the future, there will probably be no Jews living in Lexington. The beautifully landscaped and peaceful Beth El Cemetery on the outskirts of town could be the last vestige of what was once a vital and vibrant part of that community. This book has been written because of the significant history of the Jews of Lexington, both past and present, and their individual and combined impact on and contributions to society—before it is too late to be recorded or remembered.

It is written with a particular poem in mind. Its author is unknown to me and it has no title, other than what I have appropriately given to it, "Too late, too late." It is a poem that was taken from a collection of my father's. It was engraved on parchment paper and framed for me by our daughter, Deborah Berman Silver. It reads:

> Too late, too late,
> Who has not said,
> The mail is closed,
> The time is fled,
> The debt not paid,
> The aid not sought,
> The work not done,
> Neglect makes up
> Life's weary freight,
> And then we cry,
> Too late—too late.

I did not want to wait until it was too late to write about the remarkable story of Temple Beth El and its dedicated and resourceful members, truly *A House Of David In The Land Of Jesus.*

Chapter 49

The Centennial of Temple Beth El

Lexington's Temple Beth El opened its doors for religious services over one hundred years ago. It celebrated its centennial at Sabbath services on Friday evening and Saturday morning, December 2 and December 3, 2005.

On Friday evening, Beth Israel Congregation of Jackson, a sister congregation to Temple Beth El in Lexington, honored Temple Beth El and its members at a Sabbath service at Beth Israel. The following Saturday morning, the centennial ceremony and Sabbath service was held at Temple Beth El in Lexington. Following the service in Jackson, a Shabbat dinner was held for eighty-five current and former members and relatives of the Lexington congregation, at the Jackson University Club. After the next morning's service in Lexington, a delicious "challah and cornbread" southern Jewish luncheon celebration was held at one of Lexington's newest restaurants on the square. This luncheon combining traditional Southern and Jewish cuisine was planned and prepared by congregational members Barbara and Gina Hyman.

At each service, conducted by Beth Israel's rabbi, Valerie Cohen, the featured speaker was Dr. David Ellenson, rabbi and president of the Hebrew Union College—Jewish Institute of Religion. The Hebrew Union College ordains all reform rabbis, while conservative and orthodox rabbis (from other, more traditional branches of Judaism) are ordained by other institutions. Reform Judaism is the more liberal and largest branch of Judaism in the world.

The Hebrew Union College has four campuses. Located in Cincinnati is its original campus, and the others are in New York, Los Angeles, and Jerusalem in Israel.

At each of the two Sabbath services, in Jackson on Friday evening and in Lexington on Saturday morning, the Shirim choir of Beth Israel Congregation sang stirring liturgical music, along with solos by my wife, Sondra "Sondy" Berman. As a lyric soprano, she was the soloist at Temple Beth El in Lexington for many years during the time Joe Berman and I led services. The titles she chose for her solos were "Jerusalem" and "V'ulai." The latter title in English means "Perhaps t'was but a dream"—chosen in remembrance of the dream the founders of Temple Beth El had: a place of their own where they could worship their God of Israel in peace. Both musical selections were sung in Hebrew, with clarity and tones of rare quality.

In the introduction of Rabbi Ellenson at Beth Israel in Jackson, I began with one of my favorite descriptive stories, which I have only used to personify two other legends. The first time was for my introduction of baseball legend Tommy Lasorda, an eagle of the sporting world, when he spoke to the Rotary Club of Jackson at my invitation. The second time was for Dr. Arthur Guyton, a polio victim himself and legend of the medical world, whose medical textbook continues to be used in medical schools worldwide; when he spoke at my request to our Rotary district conference. Dr. Guyton was honorary chairman of the Rotary Club of Jackson's Polio Plus drive, sponsored by Rotary International.

The story, which I felt was most apropos in this instance as well, is that of "The oyster and the eagle." It reflects the quintessential character of each of these three outstanding individuals. It goes like this:

When God made the oyster he built a shell to protect it.
It lies at the bottom of the ocean.
Whenever it is hungry all it has to do is open its shell and food rushes in.
But when God made the eagle, he said go and build yourself a home.
And the eagle built it on the mountain top,
Where storms threaten it every day.
For food it flies through miles of rain, wind, sleet and snow.
It is unafraid of danger or risk.
The eagle, not the oyster, is the emblem of our great country.
And
Rabbi Ellenson is one of the true "eagles" of today's religious world.

At the Sabbath service in Lexington, those attending were greeted by Henry Paris, current lay rabbi. In his opening remarks, he stated that Lexington was such an ecumenical community that on Sunday mornings he could go to Sunday school at Temple Beth El; then that same evening, since there was no Jewish youth group there, he would either attend the Methodist or Baptist youth groups. That demonstrated the ecumenicalism that has always existed in the town of Lexington.

Henry Paris also noted that at the centennial there were attendees from Georgia, California, Texas, Louisiana, Alabama, New York, Arkansas, Tennessee, Illinois, Virginia, Florida, and England. He gave credit to Phil Cohen, "the glue that holds this congregation together," for organizing and arranging the centennial celebration. He also thanked the Hyman sisters, Barbara and Gina, for their contributions in arranging and preparing the luncheon.

Then Phil Cohen, longtime leader of the Lexington Jewish community, gave a descriptive oral history of Temple Beth El and the Jewish community of Lexington, (encompassed in the chapters of this book, in even more detail).

Saturday morning's religious service, conducted by Jackson's and Lexington's Rabbi Valerie Cohen, included a Torah reading by Rabbi Debra Kassoff of the Institute of Southern Jewish Life. When I introduced Rabbi Ellenson, I stated that, "Dr. Ellenson's superlatives clearly speak for themselves."

In Rabbi Ellenson's sermon for the morning Sabbath service at Temple Beth El, he began by extending his greetings to all those in attendance, and thanking Don and Nancy Barrett for hosting a sumptuous southern-style luncheon for him during his first trip to visit Lexington and Temple Beth El. Attending that same luncheon were Henry Paris, Phil Cohen and myself.

In his sermon, he mentioned the Kabalistic (Jewish mystic) conception of the divine sparks scattered all over the world at the time of creation. He said some of those had surely landed on where Lexington would someday be.

During his remarks he referred to the Torah reading that morning by Rabbi Debra Kassoff. He said, "That portion was known as 'toldot', a Hebrew word meaning to 'give birth', generally translated into English as 'history.' The Jewish word 'toldot,' which captures our sense of history in the Jewish sense, is a matter of generations.

But history is not simply about the past and how we arrived at the present. The genealogy in the Bible is incredibly significant. It not only links the present to what has preceded us but reminds us of not only how we arrived at the present, but also of our responsibilities as human beings, which extend beyond ourselves to the generations to come. We have a heritage that we are called upon to preserve; to carry forth what our ancestors began. Remembering what our mothers and fathers and forefathers brought to us and what kind of legacy we will bequeath to our children, and grandchildren, in generations yet to come." Such cogent and wise remarks could only come forth out of wisdom itself. He continued by saying, "There is the obligation to preserve the spirit of this building [Temple Beth El] so that we can pay proper homage to our ancestors that have made us what we are today, and carry it forward to future generations."

That obligation to preserve both the spirit and heritage of Temple Beth El is what the final chapter and Epilogue of this book are about.

Rabbi Irving Bloom, of Fairhope, Alabama, a close and personal friend of Rabbi Ellenson, gave the final benediction at the Temple Beth El service in Lexington on Saturday morning. He was one of four rabbis in attendance at that morning's Sabbath service to commemorate the centennial. That set a record for the number of rabbis in Lexington at the same time.

At Temple Beth El Centennial 2005, L to R
Henry Paris, Phil Cohen, Rabbi Debra Kassoff,
Rabbi David Ellenson, Rabbi Valerie Cohen,
Rabbi Irving Bloom, Bob Berman

At Centennial, L to R Edward Schur, Temple President,
Rabbi David Ellenson, President HUC

At Centennial Luncheon, L to R Sally Stein Cohen, Rabbi Valerie Cohen

At Centennial Luncheon, L to R Stuart Rockoff, Phil Cohen

At Centennial Luncheon, L to R Pat Barrett, Jr., Henry Paris, Don Barrett

At Centennial luncheon, L to R Gina Hyman, Barbara Hyman, Lexington Mayor Robin McCrory, Phil Cohen

Chapter 50

The Future of Temple Beth El
Idealism or Reality
"To be, or not to be: that is the question"[29]
Shakespeare

At the centennial service of Temple Beth El in Lexington, Rabbi David Ellenson, the keynote speaker, made a highly significant analogy pertaining to the great relationship between the Lexington Jewish community and the Christian community. That spirit of love, cooperation and respect has existed since the first Jewish family settled in Lexington in the early 1800s. Recognizing that only twelve Jewish citizens of Lexington remained, he said, "There remain twelve Jewish citizens of Lexington; there were twelve Tribes of Israel; and there were twelve Apostles." That connection was a powerful reminder of the remarkable story of the Jewish people of Lexington, from its very beginning through the present time.

The question today is what will happen to this historic synagogue when there are no longer Jews living in this small community. Reality says that the older families will fade away and the younger ones will no doubt move in search of a more metropolitan lifestyle and better economic opportunities.

The easy approach would be to donate the brilliant antique stained glass windows and the ark with the Torah and other religious symbols to the Museum of Southern Jewish Experience. The building could then be sold to utilize as a church or otherwise.

However, this over one-hundred year old synagogue is currently listed on the Mississippi Historic Preservation Inventory. With its remarkable history of achievement and tolerance, there is a story to be preserved and told. It could be a profound lesson in human relations that would be well worth emulating by people from all over.

Nowhere has there been more respect and friendship between the Jewish people and their Christian and Muslim neighbors than in the congregation of Temple Beth El in the little town of Lexington,

Mississippi, and Holmes County. It is a model for goodwill and understanding among people of all faiths and races, which has actually existed for over one hundred years, in the heart of the "Land of Jesus." What a story to tell and illustrate to the rest of humanity.

After the centennial services on December 2 and 3, 2005, Larry Silver, our son-in-law, made a magnanimous offer to fund the restoration of Temple Beth El to its original grace, and make it even more beautiful than ever, in order to preserve for perpetuity its great heritage. He did this in honor of his wife, Deborah Berman Silver. In so doing, he recognized that if such a restoration took place, there would need to be an endowment fund to be used to maintain the temple over the years to come. He hoped his offer would be an incentive to raise such an endowment, to which he would also contribute.

This temple could be added to the religious tours currently sponsored by the Institute of Southern Jewish Life, along with other religious tours. It could be used for interfaith gatherings and lectures and concerts; even more importantly as a "miniature museum of tolerance," possibly as a small adjunct to the Simon Wiensenthal Center and Museum of Tolerance in Los Angeles, California, which fights anti-Semitism and intolerance wherever it exists around the world. With all the hate and anti-Semitism that currently is rampant throughout western and eastern Europe and the Middle East, there is much need to promote such tolerance and understanding; to follow the Judeo-Christian teachings of love and peace, and the teachings of Jesus, to "Love thy neighbor as thyself," while striving for Rotary International's ultimate goal of world peace.

Lexington, Mississippi, is one of the most ecumenical communities in the entire world, and its story needs to be told over and over again. This could happen through the preservation of Temple Beth El. It is such an important lesson for humanity that perhaps even the city of Lexington, some of its leading citizens, and eventually the state of Mississippi could become involved in attaining that goal.

On Sunday evening, February 12, 2006, the Lexington congregation of Temple Beth El attended an evening service conducted by Rabbi Valerie Cohen. Afterwards they held a congregational meeting which was well attended. The Silver proposal was thoroughly discussed. It was noted that this proposal for a large restoration sum was to be donated based upon the condition that a follow-up endowment fund would be raised to preserve, over the long term, Temple Beth El, once it was restored. At that meeting there were mixed emotions. It was believed that an endowment fund in the minimum amount of $250,000 — and possibly considerably more, according to the interview with Macy Hart, earlier in this book—would need to be raised. While the congregants were most grateful for the Silver offer and would like to see the temple preserved, many were highly skeptical as to whether such a large sum could realistically be raised for that purpose. Macy Hart, a member of Temple Beth El, who has been highly successful in raising funds for the Henry S. Jacobs Camp, the Museum and the Institute, has stated that "preservation dollars are the hardest dollars to raise... people want to know that there is a use for a building, and a reason for the building to continue to exist." There was also the question that, if such funds could be raised, should they not be used for even more important and urgent charitable needs.

With this in mind, the congregation of Temple Beth El responded to the Silver offer. They said they would be grateful to accept the Silver offer and use the funds to restore Temple Beth El. However, they did not believe they could raise the funds needed for an endowment to preserve the temple long term. They said their desire would be to keep the temple going as long as they can, but that longevity does not look bright, based on the few Jewish families remaining. When the time came, they would be pleased to donate the temple and its contents to the Institute of Southern Jewish Life, to utilize and preserve as a museum. I must say that under such terms, long-term preservation for any purpose does not look realistic. In the first place, the restoration offer was made conditioned upon an endowment fund to follow for the long-term maintenance of the temple. Second, Macy Hart, president of the Institute of Southern Jewish Life, has told me that while the Institute would accept the contents, it would not take ownership of any structure unless there was an endowment to fund its perpetuity. He further stated that any funds raised by the Institute needed to understandably be used to support their important goals and organization. Based upon these facts, it would appear that Temple Beth El will not be restored, and it will continue to exist only as long as the few Jewish families in Lexington and the surrounding communities utilize it.

However, there is still another approach to preserving Temple Beth El in a considerably more meaningful manner. This alternative, bold as it may sound, would likely provide far more long-term exposure, visitation and usage to Temple Beth El, as well as accomplish other needed goals.

While I was writing this book, our son-in-law, Larry Silver who offered to restore Temple Beth El, subsequently received a personal letter from Chancellor Robert Khayat of the University of Mississippi. The letter was written as a request for funds to establish a chair for Hebrew [Judaic] studies at the University of Mississippi, in my honor, as a graduate of the University.

The Chancellor's letter and thought were appreciated, and it was felt had considerable merit. However, considering the small number of Jewish students currently attending the University, primarily due to the relatively sparse Jewish population throughout Mississippi, the question would be how many students, Jewish or otherwise, would actually take such a course, in order to make the investment for such a chair feasible. This could hold true even if students of religious studies of all faiths would be attracted to those studies. Would such a professor be kept busy enough or have more than a minimal number of students in the classroom?

Under such circumstances, this suggestion from the highly regarded Chancellor could understandably be respectfully refused. However, there is room for a certain amount of "blue sky" thinking to build upon what the Chancellor suggested in his letter. If, for instance, Temple Beth El, with its one-hundred year history of Jewish achievement, mutual respect and ecumenical acceptance among its Christian neighbors, could actually be preserved and proclaimed as an important "Center and Museum of Tolerance," another small step for humankind could be achieved. But with the almost insurmountable task of locally raising a large sum of endowment funds for the long-term usage and maintenance of Temple Beth El in Lexington, even after it is restored, how could such a Center be attained and become an "idealistic reality"?

There is an answer to such an oxymoron. That answer would be to donate Temple Beth El to the University of Mississippi and physically relocate it to the city of Oxford where the University is located. A new site could be selected, either on the Ole Miss campus or immediately adjacent to it. Besides continuing as a historic synagogue and becoming a "Center and Museum of Tolerance," which could enhance the University's public image in itself, it could also fulfill the Chancellor's wishes for a building to house a chair and classroom for Judaic studies at the University. An addition to the rear of the temple could be constructed to serve as the "Center and Museum of Tolerance," displaying a permanent exhibit of the Lexington Jewish experience, among others, through the Institute of Southern Jewish Life. Such an addition could also serve as a social hall, as a Hillel meeting place for Jewish students, and other students of Judaic studies at Ole Miss, in addition to Jewish residents in Oxford and the surrounding area.

One would enter the Center/Museum/social hall either from a separate outside entrance, or directly from the sanctuary/classroom on the right side of the bima, opposite the choir area.

There should actually be no controversy about locating such a building on the campus, since it would become and house part of the University curriculum. Presently, a non-denominational chapel and a YMCA building are situated on the campus.

Currently there is a Jewish congregation in Oxford known as Beth Shalom (House of Peace), without a house of worship of their own. It was organized in 1979. If Temple Beth El is relocated to Oxford, it would have a ready-made active congregation. The merger of the two synagogues could be known as "Temple Beth El Shalom" (House of God, House of Peace), an appropriate new name for both a synagogue and a "Center and Museum of Tolerance." After meeting for several years in homes, on Friday, February 10, 2006 that congregation held its first Sabbath service in the Paris-Yates chapel, a non-denominational place for religious gatherings on the Ole Miss campus. While the Paris-Yates chapel is a beautiful edifice of spirituality, it is as it should be, non-denominational, displaying a unique Star of David overlaid onto a Cross. However, the Jewish community of Oxford, Ole Miss and the surrounding area deserves a synagogue and house of prayer of their own.

On February 8, 2006, in *The Daily Mississippian*, the University of Mississippi daily newspaper, the following article appeared on Page two:

"A Home of Their Own"

"The Jewish community in Oxford finally has an official place to honor the Sabbath. For 35 years, its members have been meeting in living rooms and other informal gathering places because there is currently no synagogue in Oxford. There are numerous churches of many denominations and even a mosque, but no synagogue. Starting Friday, Feb.10th at 7:30 P.M., the Jewish community will be able to meet at the Paris-Yates chapel—a non-denominational place for religious gathering—to celebrate the Sabbath. Our view is that it's about time. It is almost unbelievable that in a college town, which is supposed to be progressive in thinking or at least up-to-date, a synagogue has never been built. Although there are still no plans for the construction of one, this step is at least one in the right direction. Even though the Jewish population of Oxford is not in the majority, it is a large minority and deserves its own specific place to practice its faith."

That fine article is right on track! Note the words from Exodus 25:8: "Let them build me a sanctuary that I may dwell in their midst."

The Jewish community of Oxford definitely deserves a home of its own, their own place of worship called a synagogue. That's what Temple Beth El Shalom would become, among other things. The founding of Temple Beth El Shalom would be analogous to the days when the Jewish families of Lexington met in the Lexington Opera House. Then came the dream of Morris Lewis, Sr., and Sam Herrman, when they envisioned establishing Temple Beth El in Lexington. However, in all deference to Temple Beth El and its location in the fine community of Lexington, its relocation to Oxford and merger with Temple Beth Shalom would become far more significant. It would serve a multiplicity of uses—as a synagogue, as a part of the University curriculum in Judaic studies, and as a "Center and Museum of Tolerance." All of these would fill important needs within the local and statewide community. Its effects would even be felt throughout a far wider area, including the nearby metropolitan area of Memphis, Tennessee, and the southeastern United States.

Now, where would the rabbi to fill the pulpit and instructors for Judaic studies be found? From the Hebrew Union College—Jewish Institute of Religion, of course! Its president, Dr. David Ellenson, not only was the keynote speaker at Temple Beth El's centennial celebration, but he also spoke at the Gertrude Ford Center for the Performing Arts at the University in 2004, at the invitation of Chancellor Khayat. He is very familiar with and respectful of the University of Mississippi and its Chancellor.

Earlier in this book, it was stated that the largest single bequest ever received at the Hebrew Union College was given by Gus Waterman Herrman, who grew up in Lexington and was confirmed at Temple Beth El. For Gus' $7 million donation, which followed his brother, Cecil's, earlier gift of $3.3 million, the college named its presidential chair in his honor. While Cecil's gift was used by the college to enhance its Cincinnati campus, it never spent any of the millions given by Gus Herrman to further honor him in any material way. Cecil and Gus gave their gifts to the HUC to honor their friendship with Rabbi James Wax, and in gratitude to the HUC for its furnishing student rabbis, such as James Wax, to smaller congregations around the country that have no rabbi. What an appropriate way the HUC could posthumously reciprocate Gus Herrman for his munificence—by materially honoring him, and the temple where he was confirmed—through furnishing those same senior student rabbis to Temple Beth El Shalom in Oxford, to conduct services and teach the Judaic curriculum at Ole Miss. It could be known as the Gus W. Herrman Center for Judaic Studies. Eventually, a full Chair for Judaic Studies and the Center and Museum of Tolerance could be named after those who funded each, respectively.

These senior graduate students from the Hebrew Union College could work directly under the auspices of The University of Mississippi Department of Philosophy and Religion. This department offers BA and MA degrees in philosophy and an undergraduate minor in either philosophy or religion. It is currently chaired by Dr. William F. Lawhead.[30]

Such Judaic studies should also unquestionably include a course in "Holocaust Remembrance," to teach about the most vicious act of man's inhumanity to man ever committed. The Holocaust course in Judaic studies should include as required reading at least three related books. They are *Night* by Elie Wiesel, *All But My Life* by Gerda Weissmann Klein, and *Hitler's Willing Executioners* by Daniel Jonah Goldhagen.

Never before, or since, has there been such an attempt at genocide, where it was the official policy of a major national government, controlling a literate and allegedly civilized population, to eradicate an entire human race and faith of people. This act was done with the complicity of most of the citizens of that country, and even those of surrounding countries. Its goal was to wipe Judaism off the face of this earth, by killing anyone with even a trace of Jewish blood in their background—not for any social or political reasons, but **only because they or their ancestors were born Jewish.** This horrific plan almost succeeded, destroying one-third (six million) of the actual Jewish people on earth at the time, including a million and a half Jewish children. The surest way for such an atrocity to occur again is to forget it ever happened at all.

Since the Holocaust, there have unfortunately been other attempts at genocide in Cambodia, Rwanda, Bosnia and Darfur. However, as horrific as they have been, none had the backing, and meticulous demonic planning, on such a large scale, by a national government of intelligent officials. Nowhere else have so many millions of innocent people been murdered with such efficiency in a "killing factory" environment. Neither have these other horrible events been anywhere near the scope of the Nazi Holocaust, which first, step by step, methodically de-humanized and isolated its victims into crowded ghettos under intolerable conditions, cruelly treating them as sub-human. Then the terrifying roundups, followed by trips to the death camps lasting several days, on stifling, overcrowded cattle cars with standing room only, and no food or water. Upon arrival, there was separating of families and stripping everyone of all personal possessions, including their hair, their clothing and their dignity. There was nothing left but their life, and then the Nazis took that by brutally herding almost everyone into the gas chambers. And finally, the crematoriums. For the relatively few not immediately sent to the gas chambers due to their stronger physical condition, they were used as slaves, never allowed to change clothes or shower, were starved, and either worked to death or died from disease, or gross medical experiments. Regardless, Hitler and Germany's Third Reich wanted to be certain anyone with Jewish blood (whether they claimed to be Jewish or not) would become extinct. Very few survived.

Furthermore, unlike the Holocaust, those other unconscionable genocidal acts of one tribe, sect or ethnicity against another had the attention of the world and the United Nations, who sought to stop them. During the Nazi Holocaust to annihilate the Jews, the world was silent! No one nation, faith or international organization of governments ever spoke out against that atrocity, intervened to stop it, or tried to prevent it from occurring in the first place. It only ran its course because the United States and its allies won the war against Hitler, and the Jewish people and the free world can say "thank God for that!" Nevertheless, that is not to denigrate those later attempts either, as they—or any others—must never be allowed again. Genocide against any people of any race, creed or religion must never be tolerated.

The long list of actions by persecutors against the Jewish people, from Pharaoh in Egypt to Hitler's Germany, is filled with massacres, pogroms, exiles and persecutions. It has required almost superhuman faith to surmount such suffering and continue to preserve our faith in what we believe to be the one and only God of all humanity. Yet that faith remains as strong as it ever has been. When asked how that can be, some turn to the book of Job in the Bible. There is another stirring proclamation of faith written by a Hasidic Jew in times of old. It is one of the most poignant expressions of true faith I have ever read as he talks to God. His words could just as well have been spoken during or after the Holocaust, and even today, where hate and intolerance continue unabated in many parts of the world.

"Yossel Rakover's Appeal to God"

"I believe in you, God of Israel, even though you have done everything to stop me from believing in you. I believe in your laws even if I cannot excuse your actions. My relationship to you is not the relationship of a slave to his master but rather that of a pupil to his teacher. I bow my head before your greatness, but will not kiss the lash with which you strike me.

You say, I know, that we have sinned, O Lord. It must surely be true! And therefore we are punished? I can understand that too! But I should like you to tell me whether there is any sin in the world deserving such a punishment as the punishment we have received!

You assert that you will repay our enemies? I am convinced of it! Repay them without mercy? I have no doubt of that either! I should like you to tell me, however, is there any punishment in the world compensating for the crimes that have been committed against us?

You say, I know, that it is no longer a question of sin and punishment, but rather a situation in which your countenance is veiled, in which humanity is abandoned to its evil instincts. But I should like to ask you O Lord—and this question burns in me like a consuming fire—what more, oh what more, must transpire before you unveil your countenance again to the world?

I want to say to you that now, more than in any previous period of our eternal path of agony, we, we the tortured, the humiliated, the buried alive and burned alive, we the insulted, the mocked, the lonely, the forsaken by God and man—we have the right to know what are the limits of your forbearance?

I should like to say something more. Do not put the rope under too much strain lest, alas, it snap! The test to which you have put us is so severe, so unbearably severe, that you should—you must—forgive those members of your people who, in their misery have turned from you.

I tell you this because I do believe in you, because I believe in you more strongly than ever before, because now I know that you are my Lord, because after all you are not, you cannot possibly be after all the God of those whose deeds are the most horrible expression of ungodliness!

I die peacefully, but not complacently; persecuted but not enslaved; embittered but not cynical; a believer but not a supplicant; a lover of God but no blind amensayer of his.

I have followed him even when he rejected me. I have followed his commandments even when he has castigated me for it; I have loved him and I love him even when he hurls me to the earth, tortures me to death, makes me the object of shame and ridicule.

God of Israel—you have done everything to make me stop believing in you. Now lest it seem to you that you will succeed by these tribulations to drive me from the right path, I notify you, my God, and God of my father, that it will not avail you in the least! You may insult me, you may castigate me, you may take from me all that I cherish and hold dear in the world, you may torture me to death—I shall believe in you, I shall love you no matter what you do to test me!

And these are my last words to you, my wrathful God; nothing will avail you in the least. You have done everything to make me renounce you, and to make me lose faith in you, but I die exactly as I have lived, a believer!

Hear, O Israel, the Lord our God, the Lord is one. Into your hands O Lord, I consign my soul."

Amen.

John F. Kennedy, in his presidential inaugural address on January 20, 1961, most eloquently, with wisdom and keen perception, said the following:

"With a good conscience, our only sure reward, with history the final judge of our deeds, let us go forth to lead the land we love, asking his blessing and help, but knowing that here on earth, God's work must truly be our own."

So in reality, it must be. God gave us this life. Now it's up to us, not God, to do His work here on earth—to make this world a better place in which we all can share and live together peacefully with dignity, justice and compassion.

This proposed Center of Tolerance at the University of Mississippi would be doing God's work right here on earth, in a non-sectarian way. It would be another step toward helping to prevent such evil as genocide from ever reoccurring.

This action should lead to more students of religion and the humanities, including those of both the Jewish faith and other religions, attending the University of Mississippi. It could establish Ole Miss as a true center for tolerance and the humanities. The University of Mississippi, with its relatively new Phi Beta Kappa chapter, prides itself as being a great American public university. With such a dire need for more tolerance and understanding among all faiths and races, this Center of Tolerance would serve to help solidify and enhance that position of greatness for the University of Mississippi. In the lyrics of a song Whitney Houston made popular some years ago, this is "one moment in time" when the University of Mississippi could "be racing with destiny." At what other public university in America is there such a "Center and Museum of Tolerance"? It would be a significant complement to the Center for the Study of Southern Culture and the William Winter Institute for Racial Reconciliation at the University.

Under such judicious conditions, the Silver offer of restoration funds should be enough for the move and basic reassembly. Surely enough additional funds could be raised from the Jewish communities of Oxford and others in Mississippi and the South, including the Institute of Southern Jewish Life, and even elsewhere throughout Mississippi and the nation, for the University to expand and maintain the Center and Museum of Tolerance, and Temple Beth El Shalom year round. These funds are available if the will is there to locate and solicit them.

Now, what about the practicality of moving such a building approximately one hundred miles to north Mississippi? Of course it can be done, unequivocally. It can be moved in sections on flatbed trailers, just as modular homes are routinely transported. Alternatively, it can be dismantled and moved in pieces. A third alternative would be to strip the building of its sacred and symbolic items of beauty, including the stained glass windows, the ark and Torah, the eternal light, the wooden pulpit, the memorial and other plaques, the two golden menorahs, the choir railing and the Star of David. Then reinstall them in a replica of the temple to be built in Oxford.

If Winston Churchill could have artificial harbors (code name "Mulberry Harbours") built and shipped across the English Channel during World War II for the crucial delivery of reinforcements, equipment and supplies on the beaches of Normandy, then Temple Beth El can surely be safely relocated to Oxford, one way or another. Churchill's memo to Lord Mountbatten that launched the Mulberry project was entitled "PIERS FOR USE ON BEACHES." It stated "They must float up and down with the tide. The anchor problem must be mastered. Let me have the best solution worked out. Don't argue the matter. The difficulties will argue for themselves." These artificial harbors were even hauled beneath the surface of the water and raised upon arrival so the Germans would not discover them in advance. Where there is a will, there's a way. "If you will it, it is no dream..." wrote Theodor Herzl, founder of the State of Israel.

In the movie *Field of Dreams*, Kevin Costner's character believed that if the dream of a new baseball stadium was fulfilled and built, people would come and attend games. The film was produced by Larry Gordon and his brother, Charles, Mississippi natives from another small Mississippi town of Belzoni, near Lexington. Larry Gordon was formerly president of 20th Century Fox. The film was sheer fiction, but physically moving Temple Beth El from Lexington to Oxford and Ole Miss is a realistic possibility. It should attract a considerable amount of favorable publicity in both the academic and religious world. Since Oxford has become one of the country's leading retirement communities, the establishment of a "Center and Museum of Tolerance," a synagogue, and a Chair for Judaic Studies at the University could also attract a sizable number of additional retirees and academicians to the area—especially from the large community of Memphis, Tennessee, just sixty miles to the north.

Finally, and importantly, should such a relocation of Temple Beth El become a reality, what would happen to the property in Lexington where it was originally built and currently sits? This historic site could be donated to the Town of Lexington, with the understanding that on part or all of the property would be located a stone monument, displayed within a beautifully landscaped and colorful memorial garden setting. It should be maintained by the city and kept as a permanent memorial to the memory of the Jewish community of Lexington, and its close ecumenical relationship with its Christian neighbors of both races. Such should never be forgotten—as a prime example for humanity to follow. On the monument should be carved a Star of David and a rendering of Temple Beth El, with words of tribute to both the Jewish and Christian communities and the story of its history and relocation to Oxford and the University of Mississippi. Then the town of Lexington would have its own rare historical memorial for all to see and visit.

The decision to restore or not to restore Temple Beth El, to maintain or not to maintain, to relocate or not, "To be or not to be: that is the question."[31] It remains unsettled as of the writing of this book. The relocation to Oxford, as unique and major an undertaking as it would be, makes far more sense in its implications for much broader and more meaningful long-term usage of its facilities. Such a move should attract national publicity in a favorable manner for the University of Mississippi, the Lexington and Oxford communities, the Hebrew Union College, and the Institute of Southern Jewish Life with its Museum exhibits.

However, what is most important is that Temple Beth El be preserved for the future as a tribute and memorial to the Jewish and overall community of Lexington, and as a "Center and Museum of Tolerance" for all to emulate.

The day President Franklin Delano Roosevelt died, he was in the Little White House at Warm Springs, Georgia, preparing an address he was to deliver the next day on "Jefferson Day," April 13, 1945. The final words he wrote before his pen dropped from his hand, were recorded for posterity, and are as follows:

> "The only limits to our realization of tomorrow
> will be our doubts of today. Let us move
> forward with strong and active faith."

"Strong and active faith" is what is needed to fund the restoration, relocation and continued long-term maintenance of Temple Beth El, as a shining example for all to follow.

The need and ideas of how to save Temple Beth El for perpetuity are here in this book. The opportunity is there for this little historic "House of David in the Land of Jesus" to literally make a difference in this world, as so eloquently worded in the final stanza of the benediction in the following Epilogue. However, whatever will be, will surely be.

EPILOGUE

A Prayer for All

The following benediction was given at the conclusion of a Sabbath service at a synagogue in Santa Monica, California, during the summer of 2005. It was later given at the centennial service of Temple Beth El in Lexington on Saturday morning, December 3, 2005, and repeated afterwards at the Rotary Club of Jackson. Ironically, it is a "Franciscan Benediction." I felt such a prayer would be appropriate for any faith, whether Jewish, Christian, Muslim, Hindu, or other believers in a higher being of omnipotent power. It is my firm belief that irrespective of anyone's faith, if the world could live by this benediction, it could bring about one of God's greatest blessings, and that is the blessing of everlasting peace.

A Franciscan Benediction

May God bless you with discomfort,
at easy answers, half-truths, and superficial relationships, so that you may live deep within your heart.
May God bless you with anger,
at injustice, oppression, and exploitation of people,
so that you may work for justice, freedom, and peace.
May God bless you with tears,
to shed for those who suffer from pain, rejection, starvation, and war, so that you may reach out your hand to comfort them and turn their pain to joy.
And may God bless you with enough foolishness,
to believe that "you can make a difference" in this world, so that you can do what others claim cannot be done.
Amen, and amen!

"One man can make a difference,
and every man should try."
John F. Kennedy

The End

Endnotes

1 Eli Evans, *The Provincials;American Jewish Year Book, 2002;* Lee Shai Weissbach, *Jewish Life in Small-Town America, 2005; American Jewish Year Book*

2 Kevin Proffitt, Senior Archivist for Research and Collections, American Jewish Archives

3 Houghton Mifflin Publishers

4 *The Rubaiyat of Omar Khayyam,* 1048-1122

5 Eudora Welty Library, Reference Department; Census.gov

6 "89 Jewish Souls" according to Ephraim Cohen; This approximates 3 percent+ of the Town's population during that time period, as compared to 2.2 percent Jewish population to population of the United States.; American Jewish Year Book 2002; NY, American Jewish Committee 2002

7 Mississippi's Blue Book Registry; 2000 Census: Census.gov; Mississippi Power & Light, Mississippi Statistical Summary of Population 1800 to 1980

8 *Holmes County Herald, Sesquicentennial Edition, August 28, 1986;* and *Lexington, Mississippi, Holmes County, 1833-1976* Compiled by Members of the Magnolia Garden Club, 1976

9 Ibid

10 Ibid

11 Ibid

12 Ibid

13 Note: In 1838, slaves were not considered to be a statistical part of the population

14 *Holmes County Herald* Sesquicentennial Edition, August 28, 1986

15 Ibid

16 Ibid

17 Ibid

18 Ibid

19 Records of Temple Beth El, preserved by Phil Cohen

20 Wikipedia online encyclopedia

21 Google.com; Jewish Virtuallibrary; United States' Jewish population 5,914,682; Israel's Jewish population 5,021,506

[22] Phil Cohen, Lexington's Jewish Historian; Organizer of Holmes County Chamber of Commerce

[23] United States Army-Wikipedia

[24] Orison Swett Marden

[25] *Citizen Soldiers,* Stephen E. Ambrose

[26] Ibid

[27] *The Lexington Advertiser*, Mississippi Archives, Jackson, MS

[28] Michelangelo; explaining the youthful face of Mary, mother of Jesus, which he sculptured holding Jesus across her lap after taken down from the Cross. That sculpture is in the Vatican.

[29] Shakespeare; *Hamlet* soliloquies, part 1 #3 .1.64-98

[30] http://www.olemiss.edu/depts/philosophy/

[31] Shakespeare; *Hamlet* soliloquies, part 1 #3 .1.64-98